SPITFIRE

THE COMBAT HISTORY

SPITFIRE

THE COMBAT HISTORY

Robert Jackson

Airlife
England

First published in the UK in 1995
by Airlife Publishing Ltd

British Library Cataloguing in Publication Data
A catalogue record for this book
is available from the British Library

ISBN 1 85310 514 7

Typeset by Hewer Text Composition Services, Edinburgh
Printed in Great Britain by Butler & Tanner Ltd, Frome and London.

Airlife Publishing Ltd
101 Longden Road, Shrewsbury SY3 9EB

Contents

Introduction

A GREAT MANY books have been written about the Spitfire. In this work, to avoid a lot of duplication, I have concentrated on the aircraft's combat record, and to any readers requiring more technical information, lists of serial numbers, museum pieces, gate guardians and so on, I would recommend two classic works. The first is *Spitfire – The Story of a Famous Fighter* by Bruce Robertson, published by Harleyford Publications in 1960; the second is *Spitfire – the History* by Eric B. Morgan and Edward Shacklady, published by Key Publishing Ltd in 1987. The latter is a masterpiece of compilation, laden with photographs and technical drawings and giving details of the history of every Spitfire that ever was.

Just one point that may annoy the purist. Throughout the book, I have referred to the Messerschmitt 109 and Messerschmitt 110 by their abbreviated designations of 'Me 109' and 'Me 110' rather than the 'Bf 109' and 'Bf 110' much used by present-day aviation historians. The 'Bf', short for *Bayerische Flugzeugwerke*, is of course quite correct; the point is that the abbreviation was never used by the wartime *Luftwaffe*, nor is it used today by the Chief Air Historian of the German Military History Record Office at Freiburg, which seems good enough to me. So 'Me' it is, and I shall await the flood of correspondence.

I have had lots of help in the preparation of this book, but I would like to single out for special mention my old friend Jim Rosser, DFC, who saw a lot of combat in Spitfires and also tested them at Castle Bromwich. I am also indebted to the Royal Air Force Historical Society for permission to quote certain passages from the Society's Proceedings No 10 (Seminar on Photographic Reconnaissance in World War II). For anyone wishing to get to grips with the history of the RAF and the Service's operational record, membership of the Society is essential.

Finally, I should like to thank Phil Jarrett, who supplied most of the photographs used in this book, and Ken Mason, who obligingly came forward to fill in some of the photographic gaps.

Robert Jackson
Darlington, 1995

Chapter 1
Ancestral Lines

LOOKING AT the sleek lines of the Supermarine Spitfire today, it is hard to imagine that such a graceful aircraft was designed as a high speed killing machine – and one, moreover, that made its first flight years before the majority of enthusiasts who thrill to the sight and sound of it at air shows were even born.

If you seek the origins of the Spitfire, you have to go back a long way; almost as far, in fact, as the birth of powered flight in the United Kingdom. Ultimately, the trail leads you to one of the true pioneers of aviation, a man of quite remarkable vision called Noel Pemberton-Billing. His early career in aviation was described in rather charming fashion by his friend C. G. Grey, founder and for many years editor of that respectable journal *The Aeroplane*. The words that follow were written in 1941, as the foreword to a book by Pemberton-Billing called *Defence Against the Night Bomber*.

Noel Pemberton-Billing, the visionary aviation pioneer, with a model of his PB.27 flying boat of 1916.

'Noel Pemberton-Billing – PB to everyone who knows him and to many thousands who do not – had the misfortune to be one of the pioneers of aviation. There is an old jingle which says: "Be not the first by whom the new is tried, nor yet the last to set the old aside". There is a lot of fun in having been one of the first, for there is seldom much money in it, and giving oneself the satisfaction of saying, "I told you so", is the surest way of making an enemy.

PB founded the first aerodrome in this country – The Association of British Aircraft – at a place called Fambridge, in Essex. That was in 1908, long before anybody flew. And although it was an aerodrome, nobody ever really flew there. But he had a big building . . . which used to be an iron works. It had twenty bays, which anybody who aspired to be a builder of aircraft could hire at £1 a week; several early pioneers, including Weiss, Howard Wright, and Robert McFee, were among the tenants.

At Fambridge, PB made what might well be claimed to be the first flight in an all-British aeroplane. The apparatus was a pusher monoplane, and it was driven by the first experimental NEC aero-motor built by Mr Mort of Willesden. Also it had a tricycle undercarriage, so the machine was considerably more than thirty years in front of its time. In it, or on it, PB essayed to fly. That eminently respectable and reliable newspaper *Flight* stated at the time that, after having examined the wheel tracks of the tricycle, its representative could vouch for the fact that there was an interval of sixty feet between the last wheel track and the wreck of the aeroplane. Consequently the assumption was that it had been in the air for twenty yards.

Also in 1908 Mr Pemberton-Billing became the progenitor of the world's first air force. He laid down a scheme for what was officially called the Imperial Flying Squadron. He interviewed a board of distinguished officers at the War Office, and they took the view that if the lad did nothing notable with his quaint ideas, he could not do much harm, and so he was told, only much more politely, what the Admiral told Kipling's friend, Mr Moorshed – namely, "to go and conduct his own manoeuvres in his own damned tinker fashion".

And, after all that, PB's first aeroplane had the distinction of being the first aeroplane in the world to be sold by a sheriff for debt – because the designer-owner pilot was in hospital after the crash and was unable to attend to business. For a remarkable thing about PB's adventures is that he has always paid his debts.

Later on, when flying became quite a serious business, PB acquired a workshop alongside Southampton Water just above the floating bridge, and there started the Supermarine Aviation Works, from which developed the enormous business which was later acquired by Vickers Ltd, and is now turning out that world-famous fighting aeroplane the Spitfire.

Perhaps the most remarkable machine that PB ever built was a little fighting scout that broke all records for its power in 1914. It became known as the "Seven-Day Bus" because it was designed, built, and flown in six days and ten hours. PB chalked-up the outlines on the walls of his works one night as soon after the declaration of war as he could find out what the Admiralty wanted.

Work began next morning, and no-one left that factory until PB.9 was finished. The only engine available was a very old 50 hp Gnome, which developed no more than 18 hp on the bench. With that it did 78 mph and climbed 540 feet in a minute, and it was still in service as a trainer at Hendon up till the time that the RNAS became the RAF.

Two other interesting things that appeared from Supermarine's before PB sold it were the Pusher Projectile fighter and the Night Hawk. The "Push Prodge" was a little single-seater with a perfectly streamlined pusher nacelle and just four triangulated booms to hold the tail instead of the usual birdcage. It was the first fighter in which the gun was fixed and the pilot aimed the aeroplane.'

In fact, the Supermarine Aviation Works Ltd was not known by that title until after Pemberton-Billing had renounced his interests in it, which he did on 10 March 1916 in order to fight the cause of aviation as an MP in the House of Commons. He was outspokenly critical of the failure of either the RFC or RNAS to place an order for his 'Push Prodge', the PB.25, at a time when the Fokker Monoplane was wreaking havoc on the Western Front. In one speech, he said that the pilots of the Royal Flying

The Pemberton-Billing PB.1 flying boat seen on the slipway at Woolston *circa* June 1914.

The Pemberton-Billing PB.9 scout, built and flown in less than a week.

The Pemberton-Billing PB.31E Night Hawk was an attempt to build a night-fighter that could cope with the Zeppelin threat.

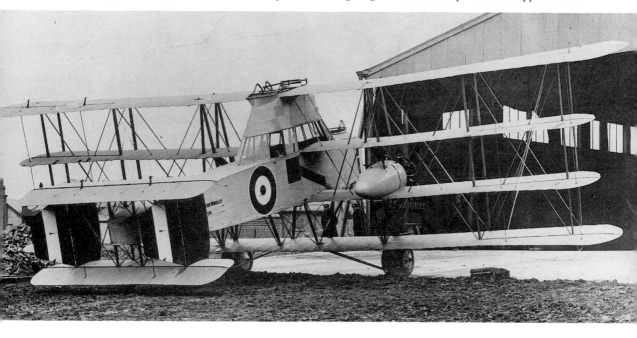

Pemberton-Billing's PB.25, the 'Push Prodge', might have been an answer to the 'Fokker scourge' on the Western Front in 1915.

Corps operating in France had been 'rather murdered than killed'. He attacked the aircraft designed by the Royal Aircraft Factory, and in particular the BE 2c, which was hopelessly outclassed by contemporary German types. It was by no means an unjustified criticism.

Man of extraordinary vision, eccentric, crusader – Noel Pemberton-Billing was all of those things, and he continued to champion the cause of military aviation development throughout his life.

His main legacy, though, was the Supermarine Works, which remained under Government control until the end of the 1914–18 war and which was managed during that period by Hubert Scott-Paine. The factory's main activity during the war was repair and experimental work on behalf of the Admiralty, which predictably led to an interest in seaplanes; the first of these were based on designs submitted by the Air Department of the Admiralty, and were known as the AD designs. One of them, the AD Boat, was already being flight tested when Pemberton-Billing left and the new company was registered. It was followed by two more, the AD Navyplane and the N.1B Baby. Much of the design work was undertaken by a young man who had joined the firm in 1916; his name was Reginald J. Mitchell.

The Supermarine Baby was the first British fighter flying boat. Only one Baby was completed and the type never went into production, but the

concept led directly to the development of two more designs, the Sea King and Sea Lion, both of them important threads in the tapestry of the Spitfire story.

The Supermarine Sea King I – which, like the Baby, began life as a fighter flying boat project – was powered by a 160 hp Beardmore engine and attracted a considerable amount of attention when it appeared at the 1920 Olympia Aero Show. Unfortunately, it failed to attract any customers. Neither did a developed version, the Sea King II, which had a 300 hp Hispano-Suiza. In the meantime, however, Supermarine had produced a design along broadly similar lines and this, powered by a Napier Lion engine, became the Sea Lion. It was one of three British seaplanes entered in the 1919 Schneider Trophy Contest, the others being Fairey and Sopwith floatplanes.

The trophy – or La Coupé d'Aviation Maritime Jacques Schneider, to give it its correct title – had originated in 1912, when Schneider had first offered the 25,000 Franc award, together with a similar sum of money, to be competed for by seaplanes of any nationality over a course of at least 150 nautical miles in length. The contest had been interrupted by the 1914–18 war, but in 1914 it had been won outright by a Sopwith Tabloid at Monaco, and so Britain became the host nation for the 1919 event. This was based at Bournemouth, the focal point of a ten-lap course totalling 200 nautical miles, with

The Supermarine Sea Lion I, which took part in the 1919 Schneider Trophy contest.

Swanage and Hengistbury Head as the other turning points.

The Sea Lion performed well, despite the fact that its hull was holed by an obstacle on take-off and the pilot, Squadron Leader Basil Hobbs, lost his bearings in fog. When he touched down at the first marker point, as required by the rules, the hull filled with water and the aircraft sank, although it was later salvaged. The only pilot to circumnavigate the course was an Italian. Lieutenant Janello, in a Savoia S.13, but he missed the turning point at Swanage on each lap and was disqualified, the race being declared void. The Italians protested, and as a gesture of goodwill the Royal Aero Club, as the organizing body, consented to the following year's contest being held at Venice.

The Italians won the 1920 competition outright in a Savoia S.19, as they did in 1921 with a Macchi M.7. In 1922 the contest was held at Naples, and on this occasion the Italians entered three aircraft, the French two and the British one – the Supermarine Sea Lion II, powered by a 450 hp Napier Lion engine. The British entry was financed entirely independently by Hubert Scott-Paine and Commander James Bird of Supermarine, the British government pleading poverty.

The Sea Lion II, which was Reginald Mitchell's brainchild, was in fact the Sea Lion II of 1921, rebuilt as a racing flying boat. It turned out to represent the only challenge to the Italians, because the French entries were withdrawn at the last minute. On 12 August 1922, the Sea Lion II, piloted by Captain H. C. Biard, won the contest with comparative ease, completing the 200 nm course in 1 hour 34 minutes and 51 seconds at an average speed of 145.7 mph. It was a bitter blow for the Italians, who had gone all-out to win; three wins in a row would have meant that the Schneider Trophy was theirs for good.

Henri Biard's success brought the Schneider Trophy competition to Cowes in 1923. Supermarine's entry was the Sea Lion III, with a 525 hp Napier Lion engine, but the winner was American: a US Navy Curtiss CR-3 floatplane with a 465 hp Curtiss D-12 engine. Its pilot, Lieutenant D. Rittenhouse, took it round the course at an average speed of 177.38 mph, easily outstripping the Sea Lion III, which averaged 157.17 mph. Less than a year later, in July 1924, the Supermarine aircraft was destroyed in a fatal accident at Felixstowe.

Towards the end of 1923 Supermarine embarked on another racing seaplane project, the Sea Urchin, which was to have been powered by a 600 hp Rolls-Royce Condor engine giving it an estimated maximum speed of 200 mph. The project had Air Ministry support but the Sea Urchin was never completed, mainly because of problems with the engine.

At this time, Rolls-Royce Ltd was just beginning to be an up-and-coming force in aero-engine design. Since the early weeks of the First World War, Royal Aircraft Factory and Renault V-8 engines had been produced by Rolls-Royce at Derby for various air-

The Supermarine Sea Lion III was easily outstripped by the American Curtiss CR-3 floatplane in the 1923 Schneider contest.

craft types – albeit with some reluctance, for the surviving partner, Henry Royce, had an extremely poor opinion of them. Royce had already turned his attention to designing and building his own aero-engines, in which he had great encouragement from the Admiralty, and he initially set about designing a 200 hp V-12 engine which was first flown in the new Handley Page 0/100 bomber for the Royal Naval Air Service in 1916. While development of this engine – the Eagle, and its successor the 250 hp Eagle II – was in progress, Royce recognised that there was a market for a lower-powered engine in the 75 hp class, with the emphasis on reliability. Royce approved the development of this engine, which was named the Hawk and which powered the Royal Navy's SS Zero-class patrol airships. As Royce had intended, it was one of the most reliable engines prior to 1918.

It would be some time yet before Rolls-Royce was able to combine reliability with high performance, and in the meantime it was Napier who led the field. The Napier company – having been fully committed to the manufacture of military vehicles during the early part of the 1914–18 War – had not initiated the design and development of its first aero-engine, the Lion, until 1917. This engine, which was progressively uprated from 400 hp to 1,400 hp during its career, was not completed in time for use during the war, but for a period of ten years from 1919 it achieved an enviable success record throughout

the world. In addition to its marriage with the early British entries for the Schneider Trophy contest, it was used in quantity in many types of RAF and civil aircraft, including the record-breaking Fairey III series.

It was a 700 hp version of the Napier Lion twelve-cylinder water-cooled engine that was selected to power Reginald Mitchell's next Schneider Trophy design, the Supermarine S.4. Designed and built in just five months and first flown by Henri Biard on 24 August 1925, the S.4 was a twin-float cantilever monoplane, and as such was a radical departure from anything seen previously; it was highly streamlined and construction was wooden throughout, and its special high speed wing section was developed at the Royal Aircraft Establishment, Farnborough. The Supermarine-Napier S.4, together with the other British contender for the 1925 Schneider contest, the Gloster-Napier III (two of which were entered) was designed to Air Ministry Specification 2/25; in each case the cost was divided between the engine and airframe manufacturer, although the Air Ministry agreed to purchase the winning aircraft.

On 13 September 1925, piloted by Biard, the S.4 set up a new world seaplane speed record of 226.6 mph, and with further engine tuning and a more efficient Fairey-Reed propeller its chances of success seemed good. The aircraft was shipped out to Baltimore, where the 1925 contest was to take place, but on the day before the race it was completely wrecked in a crash believed to have been caused by wing flutter, Biard narrowly escaping with his life. The contest was won by Lieutenant Jimmy Doolittle of the US Army (who in April 1942 was to lead a force of North American B-25 Mitchell bombers from the carrier USS *Hornet* in the famous attack on Japan) flying a Curtiss R3C2 biplane at an average speed of 234.4 mph, Hubert Broad in the Gloster-Napier biplane coming second at an average speed of 199 mph. On 27 October, Doolittle took the world seaplane speed record from the S.4 by achieving 264 mph.

Mitchell's next racing floatplane design, the Supermarine-Napier S.5, was smaller than its predecessor and also differed from it in other respects, such as having low-mounted wings with surface radiators, a repositioned cockpit and all-metal construction. Both the S.5 and its rival, the Gloster-Napier IV, were to be fitted with the new 875 hp Napier Lion engine, but delays in the delivery of these meant that neither aircraft was able to participate in the 1926 Schneider Trophy contest, which was won by an Italian Macchi M.39 monoplane with an average speed of 246.496 mph.

Up to this point, the evolution of British high performance aero-engines had been synonymous with record-breaking and trophy-capturing attempts, and while Napier and Rolls-Royce soon emerged as the principals in this field, it was the Fairey Aviation Company that, at least in the early days, was the quickest to appreciate the advantages of marrying a high performance powerplant to a very clean airframe. In September 1923 Richard

The graceful lines of the Spitfire can already be seen in the Supermarine S.4 twin-float cantilever monoplane, which unfortunately crashed on the day before the 1925 Schneider Trophy race.

Fairey watched David Rittenhouse capture the Schneider Trophy at Bournemouth in his Curtiss CR-3, with a second CR-3 hard on his heels. He thought that the Americans had got it right, and went to the USA to inspect the Curtiss D-12 engine. He was impressed enough to buy a batch, and at once set about designing an aircraft to fit the engine.

The result was the Fairey Fox, which aerodynamically was the cleanest light bomber aircraft of its day. Moreover, it was nearly fifty per cent faster than any bomber then in service, but because of economic restrictions only one RAF squadron (No 12) was equipped with it.

The importance of Fairey's initiative to the central theme of this story is that it spurred other leading British aero-engine manufacturers – and Rolls-Royce in particular – into rethinking their engine design philosophy. While Napier continued to extract as much power as possible from the Lion, which

inevitably became obsolete in due course and left the firm with nothing worthwhile until it came up with the Sabre high performance fighter engine, which eventually powered the Hawker Typhoon and Tempest, Rolls-Royce gradually moved into the lead with new designs. A third aero-engine designer, the Bristol Aeroplane Company, developed an 800 hp supercharged nine-cylinder radial engine for a private entry in the 1927 Schneider Trophy contest, but it crashed on a test flight before the race. The engine later became the Bristol Mercury.

For the first time, the British entry in the 1927 competition, which was held in Venice, was to be an all-RAF affair, and a unit known as the High Speed Flight was formed for the occasion, although this did not achieve official status until April 1928. Three Supermarine-Napier S.5s were built to Air Ministry Specification 6/26 and two were shipped to Venice

Three Supermarine S.5s were built to Air Ministry Specification 6/26, one winning the 1927 Schneider competition.

The Supermarine S.6, designed around the 1,900 hp Rolls-Royce 'R' racing engine, carried off the Schneider Trophy for Britain in 1929.

in the aircraft carrier HMS *Eagle*. The aircraft differed slightly from one another in that one, N219 – which was to be flown by Flight Lieutenant O. E. Worsley – had a direct-drive Lion VIIB engine, while the other, N220 (Flight Lieutenant S. N. Webster) had a geared version of this powerplant. In the event, it was Webster's S.5 that won the race with an average speed of 281.49 mph, with Worsley's aircraft coming second. None of the other competitors completed the course. During the contest, which was held on 26 September, Webster also set up a 100-km closed circuit world seaplane speed record of 283.66 mph.

There was no contest in 1928, but high-speed development work was carried on at Felixstowe by the High Speed Flight under Flight Lieutenant D. d'Arcy Greig, and it was he who, in the course of the year, set up a new British seaplane speed record of 319.57 mph in one of the S.5s. Then, in February 1929, the Air Ministry once again decided to field a team for that year's Schneider Trophy competition.

At the Supermarine Aviation Works (the firm, incidentally, had been acquired by Vickers Aviation Ltd in 1928, Hubert Scott-Paine having resigned to take a directorship with Imperial Airways) Reginald Mitchell's team set about designing a new aircraft, the S.6, which was somewhat larger than the S.5 and powered by a 1,900 hp Rolls-Royce 'R' racing engine, while the Gloster Aircraft Company produced the Gloster-Napier VI, powered by a 1,400 hp Lion VIID engine. For Glosters, the engine choice proved unfortunate. The Napier company had now

pushed the Lion to its limit; the engine had been over-boosted in an effort to obtain sufficient power for a small frontal area, and it was found extremely hard to keep it running without cutting out. On 2 September Flight Lieutenant d'Arcy Greig made two test flights to try to diagnose the problem, but without success, and three days later his fellow pilot, Flight Lieutenant G. H. Stainforth, found it impossible to keep the Lion running at full throttle in the other Gloster. There was no alternative but to withdraw both aircraft from the Schneider Trophy contest.

Although Mitchell, and certain Air Ministry officials connected with high-speed development, had been aware for some time that a new engine would be needed for the 1929 contest, Rolls-Royce – whose output at the time was concerned mainly with the Kestrel – had been reluctant to become involved with the development of a new powerplant specifically for the Supermarine racers. It was not until November 1928 that the firm accepted the Air Ministry invitation, following some changes in top management and the intervention of Henry Royce himself, and by then time was running short. In order to cut a few corners, Rolls-Royce took an engine which was then under development for large flying boats, the 825 hp 'H' type or Buzzard, which was virtually a scaled-up Kestrel, and set about modifying it for the task in hand.

The 'R' type racing engine that emerged was strengthened in certain respects and fitted with a large double-sided centrifugal supercharger to re-

duce diameter, which increased the sea-level power to 1,850 bhp with the engine operating on 100 per cent benzole. During test and endurance running, however, troubles began to manifest themselves at the hot end, with power fall off, exhaust valve distortion and burning and plug sooting on idling that sometimes prevented the engine being opened up to full throttle. Rolls-Royce called in a fuel expert, F. Rodwell Banks (later Air Commodore F. R. Banks) who was then in the Technical Sales Department of the Anglo-American Oil Company and who had helped with the preparations for the 1927 Schneider contest. By the simple expedient of diluting the benzole with a 'light cut' Romanian leaded gasoline, it was possible to get the engine through its tests satisfactorily in time for the race.

Meanwhile, Reginald Mitchell had been tailoring the S.6 design to the new engine. His estimation was that the aircraft would be capable of a speed in the order of 400 mph; his figures included a level speed of 350 mph, a diving speed of 523 mph and a rate of climb of 5,000 feet per minute. In fact, these esti-mates were to reappear as the design characteristics for the Spitfire.

The withdrawal of the Gloster floatplanes meant that there were only two nations in the contest for the 1929 Schneider Trophy, which was held at Spithead on 7 September: Great Britain and Italy, which entered three Macchi seaplanes, one M.52 and two M.67s. All the contestants were monoplanes.

There were hitches during the build-up to the contest. During trials at Calshot, it was found that the S.6 would not 'unstick' from the water because the propeller did not produce sufficient thrust at low speeds; that problem was cured by fitting a new propeller. A more serious problem was discovered on the eve of the race, when a Rolls-Royce engineer, carrying out an engine check on one of the two S.6s, found that a piston had seized and badly scored the cylinder. A spare cylinder block was rushed from Derby, the engineering crew rounded up by the local police, and they worked all night to repair the damage. When the S.6 was lowered into the water from its pontoons on the day of the race, the final

The Supermarine S.6B was the unopposed winner of the Schneider Trophy in 1931.

engine runs having been completed and the pilot – Flight Lieutenant H. R. D. Waghorn – in the cockpit, just two minutes remained before the start.

Waghorn went on to win the contest with a speed of 328.63 mph, and on 12 September, one of the other High Speed Flight pilots, Squadron Leader A. H. Orlebar, flew this aircraft (N247) to a new world seaplane record speed of 357.7 mph.

The Schneider Trophy contest was now held every two years, mainly because of economic considerations, and early in 1931 the British government announced that it was not prepared to subsidize RAF participation on grounds of cost. The news was received bitterly by everyone involved, because Britain had won two consecutive contests and, if she won a third, she would keep the coveted trophy permanently. In the end, it was that great patriot and philanthropist Lady Houston who stepped into the breach with an offer of £100,000. Time was short, so instead of initiating a new design, Mitchell first of all modified the two existing S.6s by fitting them with enlarged floats and re-designating them S.6As, and then built two new machines, based on the existing airframe but incorporating much more powerful

Rolls-Royce 'R' engines developing 2,350 hp. The new aircraft were designated S.6B.

Suddenly, the British found themselves with no competitors; the Italians could not produce an aircraft in time, and the French entry had crashed during trials, killing its pilot. Nevertheless, Britain allowed the 'race' to go ahead, and on 13 September 1931 Flight Lieutenant J. W. Boothman flew S.6B S1595 over the seven laps of the 50-km course at an average speed of 340.08 mph. That same afternoon, Flight Lieutenant G. H. Stainforth set up a new world speed record of 379.05 mph in the other S.6B, S1596. Later, on 29 September, Stainforth pushed up the absolute world speed record to 407.5 mph.

Both S.6Bs are preserved today, one (S1595) in the Science Museum and the other (S1596) at Southampton. They had brought the Schneider Trophy back to Britain for all time; but more important by far, they and their progenitors had made a contribution to the development of high-speed aerodynamics and high-powered engines that, within a decade, would help the nation to survive her hour of greatest peril.

Chapter 2
Fighter Development, 1925–1935

THROUGHOUT THE First World War, the primary role of fighter aircraft – 'fighting scouts' – was to protect their own reconnaissance aircraft while doing their utmost to destroy the enemy's. Indeed, this remained the principal task of France's *Armée de l'Air* right up to May 1940, when circumstances dictated that the emphasis should switch to the destruction of enemy bombers.

The Royal Air Force, an independent Service since April 1918 and the only one to possess its own strategic bombing force, was perhaps more aware than its contemporaries of the importance of destroying bombers, but in the years immediately after the First World War fighter development in Britain suffered serious setbacks, as indeed did the development of other military aircraft. In fact, the RAF itself was brought close to extinction.

Almost before the guns had ceased firing, both the Admiralty and the War Office joined forces in a determined bid to abolish the Royal Air Force, the Service in which technical advance was most apparent, as a separate entity. Both regarded the RAF as little more than a wartime expedient, a viewpoint that was utterly opposed by the Chief of the Air Staff, Air Chief Marshal Sir Hugh Trenchard.

In March 1921, Trenchard laid a proposal before the Committee for Imperial Defence in which he recommended that, in addition to providing the main defence against a possible invasion of Britain, the RAF should also exercise control over naval and military operations in the same way as it already controlled air units attached to the Army and Navy. There followed two months of heated discussion between the three Services until the Committee's conclusions were defined in a report by Harold Balfour, Chairman of the Defence Sub-Committee. The first conclusion was that the RAF must play the leading part in the defence against air attack; secondly, when acting in support of military or naval operations the RAF units involved should come under the control of the senior Army or Navy officer in command; and thirdly, in offensive operations against enemy territory, co-operation rather than subordination should be the keyword.

Shortly afterwards, in August 1921, the Cabinet appointed a 'Committee on National Expenditure' under Sir Eric Geddes to study ways and means of effecting cuts in government expenditure, and in this the armed forces were a primary target. The RAF was to suffer a reduction of £5.5 million, bringing its estimate down to £11 million. It was a serious blow for the RAF, which already had by far the lowest estimate of the three Services. Its strength was now at a very low ebb; apart from training establishments, there were only four army co-operation squadrons and one fighter squadron (No 25, equipped with Sopwith Snipes and based at Hawkinge) in the United Kingdom, with fourteen more squadrons based overseas at various points of the Empire.

The Geddes Committee's recommendations were violently opposed by every Service department, and a new committee under Winston Churchill, who was then Secretary of State for the Colonies, was at once set up to analyse them. As a result of the committee's findings, the Imperial Defence Committee decided to embark on a full review of the requirements involved in the air defence of Great Britain. In April 1922, a defence sub-committee recommended that the strength of the RAF be greatly increased, and the Cabinet gave its approval to the formation of twenty new squadrons totalling some 500 aircraft for home defence. The following October, another committee, under Lord Salisbury, began a further study of the situation; in 1923, this led to a recommendation for a home defence force of 600 aircraft in fifty-two squadrons within a new command, the Air Defence of Great Britain. The final decision to form this, however, was not taken until 1925.

The expansion of the Royal Air Force towards this planned target of 52 squadrons was dictated, apart from economic considerations, by the activities of the French. By the mid-1920s, although an emasculated Germany was not regarded as a serious threat, the idea of France, a mere twenty-one miles away across the English Channel, possessing a larger and more effective air force than Britain's was unthinkable. The speed of formation of new RAF squadrons was therefore dictated by the need to match the French in air matters, and when the expansion of the *Armée de l'Air* slowed down, so did that of the RAF.

Sir Hugh Trenchard had fought to save the RAF from extinction and to forge the embryo Service into a formidable weapon. It now seemed that he was well on the way to achieving his aim, but the task ahead of the Air Staff was daunting. In the spring of 1923 there was still only one fighter squadron in the United Kingdom; No 25 Squadron had gone on detachment to Turkey, but No 56 Squadron, also equipped with Snipes, had returned from Egypt to take its place.

The re-equipment programme had to start from scratch, and to fulfil the air defence role it was decided to standardize on the Sopwith Snipe, the fighter designed during the closing months of the 1914–18 war to replace the Camel. By October 1923 nine fighter squadrons had been re-formed and equipped with the type, two more receiving the Hawker Woodcock. The remaining Snipe squadrons soon re-equipped with the Gloster Grebe and Gloster Gamecock, which from 1926 were mostly replaced by the Armstrong Whitworth Siskin IIIA.

The original target date for the RAF's fifty-two-squadron home defence force was 1930, but in 1927 – French expansion having slowed down again – this was put back to 1936, and two years later it was again postponed to 1938. The somewhat irrational

The Sopwith Snipe – seen here in Macedonia in 1919 – filled the RAF's fighter gap in the early 1920s.

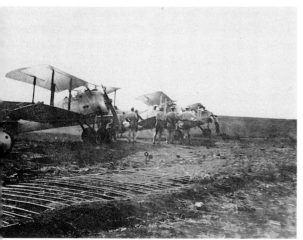

thinking behind these revised target dates was based on a premise called the Ten-Year Rule, the idea being that it would take at least ten years for any power or powers to spark off a major war in Europe. Consequently, in April 1932 the Air Defence of Great Britain comprised forty-two squadrons, of which thirteen were Auxiliary or Special Reserve units.

The primary fighter type during the first three years of the 1930s was the Bristol Bulldog, which equipped ten squadrons and, with a top speed of 180 mph, was much faster than the fighters it replaced. Even so, the Bulldog still conformed to the traditional First World War fighter layout concept of an open-cockpit biplane armed with rifle-calibre machine-guns firing through the propeller disc. That concept was unchanged in the Bulldog's successor, the Gloster Gauntlet, and almost unchanged in the next Gloster design, the Gladiator, although this had an enclosed cockpit and four machine-guns.

The fact that the Gladiator went into first-line RAF service at all was the consequence of the issue, in the autumn of 1930, of Air Ministry Specification F.7/30, which called for a single-seat day and night fighter with a speed of at least 195 mph, exceptional manoeuvrability, long endurance, a low landing speed, high initial rate of climb and excellent all-round view. It was to be armed with four .303 Vickers guns, and R/T equipment was to be fitted.

F.7/30 was the most important specification issued so far, for it represented an attempt to sweep aside the inadequacies shown by the current generation of biplane fighters. Supermarine, Westland, Blackburn, Bristol and Gloster all tendered designs to meet it, Supermarine's submission bearing the Works Type No 224.

The aircraft that emerged was an all-metal monoplane with a thick inverted gull wing and short cantilever undercarriage, the aerodynamic design having been subjected to much wind-tunnel testing. It was powered by a Rolls-Royce Goshawk engine, a not particularly successful derivative of the Kestrel IV. The F.7/30 was Mitchell's first attempt to apply the aerodynamic knowledge gained from the Supermarine Schneider racers to a landplane fighter design, and history records that he was far from happy with the result. Nevertheless, work went ahead, the aircraft was built, and it was flown by Supermarine test pilot J. 'Mutt' Summers on 19 February 1934, after which it went to Martlesham Heath for trials alongside the other contenders. It was not a success, and neither were the

The Supermarine F.7/30 monoplane fighter, which flew in February 1934, was not a success and its performance fell below Reginald Mitchell's estimates.

others; the Air Ministry was left with no alternative but to fill the gap with the Gloster Gladiator, the last of the RAF's biplane fighters.

Despite the failure of the Supermarine entry,

The failure of the F.7/30 meant that the Air Staff had to select the Gloster Gladiator, the last of the RAF's biplane fighters, seen here in the markings of No 72 Squadron.

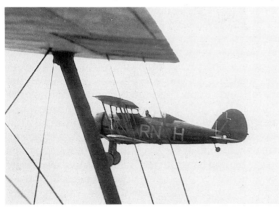

Mitchell continued to work on it, making improvements that included straight, thinner wings and a retractable undercarriage. With these, he calculated that he could raise the F.7/30's maximum speed of 230 mph (achieved during trials at Martlesham Heath) to 265 mph. The developed version was never built, although in concept it was much closer to the aircraft that was to become the Spitfire. As for the original Type 224 F.7/30 (K2890) was concerned, it went to RAE Farnborough in 1935 and from there back to Martlesham in 1937, where it was used as a 'hack' for a time before ending its days ingloriously on the gunnery range at Orfordness.

Meanwhile, the events of 1933, and the rise to power in Germany of the Nazi Party under the leadership of Adolf Hitler, had sent the first shivers of alarm through the British government. Hitler's avowed policy, having broken the shackles of the Versailles Treaty, was one of re-armament and expansion, and as far as the new *Luftwaffe* was concerned that meant a planned strength of 48 squadrons by 1938. Although this was alarming enough, the Air Staff was confident that Germany would be in no position to offer a serious challenge to Britain before the end of 1936, assuming that the rate of German aircraft production did not increase much beyond its 1933 level. However, Air Chief Marshal Sir Edward Ellington, the new CAS, was under no illusion; he knew very well that the Germans, if they so desired, had the capability to build up a combat force of 2,000 aircraft, with reserves, in a relatively short time, and he said so very plainly at a meeting of the Chiefs of Staff in June 1934.

In the following month, the British government adopted Expansion Scheme A, which envisaged, among other things, a force of forty-three bomber and twenty-eight fighter squadrons. The scheme, however, made little provision for reserves. Then, in March 1935, the British government received a profound shock. Two emissaries, Sir John Simon and Anthony Eden, returned from a visit to Berlin with the news that, during a meeting with Hitler, they had been informed that Germany already had a front-line air strength equal to the RAF's home defence force. In numerical terms, that meant about 2,000 aircraft – the figure predicted by Sir Edward Ellington nine months earlier.

In fact, Hitler's claims were false. In March 1935, the *Luftwaffe* had twenty-two squadrons with about 500 aircraft, only about 200 of which were operational first-line types. The British Cabinet, however, was not aware of this, and appointed a special committee under the chairmanship of Sir Philip Cunliffe-Lister to carry out a full investigation into the growth of German air power. Its findings were that the position, though not as alarming as the Cabinet had been led to believe, was nevertheless serious enough.

The Air Staff, for its part, now realised that the provisions of Expansion Scheme A were inadequate. It was not, however, in favour of a crash expansion programme, as the equipment then available was for the most part obsolescent; the most advanced fighter then in RAF service was the beautiful Hawker Fury, much loved by its pilots, but with a top speed of about 200 mph and still endowed with an armament of two .303-in machine-guns. The feeling was that it was better to aim for a gradual expansion based on a new range of combat aircraft then on the drawing board or flying in prototype form, with a strength of about 1,500 first-line machines by 1937 as the target.

Only a handful of men, during those crucial years of the early 1930s, were truly aware of how critically deficient in first-line equipment the RAF really was, and it is to their everlasting credit that they succeeded in making their voices heard in time – but only just in time – to avert the disaster that was only a handful of years away.

One of them was Squadron Leader R. S. Sorley (later Air Marshal Sir Ralph Sorley, KCB, OBE, DSC, DFC) whose far-sightedness and expert opinion are central to the theme of this history. Happily, his very detailed memoirs have been made available by his family. Early in 1933 Sorley, having completed a tour in Aden, returned to a desk job in the Air Ministry and, in his own words, 'began to lead a different sort of life commuting by train to and from London and hating every minute spent in overcrowded trains and buses, and still more the rather dirty and overfilled offices that were then the Air

Ministry in Kingsway. I joined Flying Operations 1 (FO 1) which was responsible for a variety of Air Staff requirements, and occupied one small room with two others, Wing Commander A. T. Williams and Squadron Leader Jock Andrews. AT and Jock devoted most of their efforts to defining the scope and geographical layout of a reorganised system of air defence for the RAF in Britain, which eventually developed into Fighter and Bomber Commands, while I devoted my time to drawing up requirements for new types of aircraft which were badly needed.'

In fact, Sorley joined the Air Ministry at the time when the various aircraft companies were working on their respective entries for F.7/30 (which specification, incidentally, was issued on the instigation of Air Chief Marshal Sir John Salmond, the then Chief of Air Staff. Sorley soon developed some very definite beliefs on how the design of future fighters should progress.

'My earlier experience at Martlesham and also when working in RDA 4 had shown me how our aircraft designers were restricted by having to install old-fashioned equipment left over from the First World War. We still had vast stocks of out-of-date bombs, machine-guns, sights and very many other items which were known as "embodiment loan equipment" and which designers had to use whether they liked it or not. Money for development had been hard to come by and so an attitude of *laissez faire* was to some extent understandable, but by 1933, with Hitler on the warpath, I thought it more than dangerous. Seeing the trend of German aircraft design towards twin-engined monoplane bombers there was plenty of need and scope for some drastic change in our operational requirements, and without doubt the prime necessity was for a monoplane fighter with sufficient speed and hitting power to ensure the destruction of such potential German attackers.

By 1933 the evolution of the monoplane was becoming increasingly clear. Although there were still many controversial features, it seemed that there were many advantages to be gained by adopting the monoplane layout, but certain fundamental features that would be new in its use by the average pilot would have to be accepted. Because of its ability to carry greater loads relative to its size, compared with the biplane, its performance was highly attractive, although to take full advantage a variable pitch propeller would be necessary. In 1933, although a lot of work had been done, no such propeller had yet been developed in the UK.

While the fighting view obtained with a monoplane layout was incomparably better than that possible with the biplane, there was considerable doubt on such features as degree of manoeuvrability, strength for full aerobatics and terminal velocity dives, and in order to carry the loads which seemed necessary a considerable increase in the landing speed compared with the biplane would have to be accepted. Moreover, the all-up weight of a fighter of this type would be considerably greater than that of the biplane, and this was likely to prove unacceptable to, or at least meet with strong objections from, those who held closely to the biplane's exceptional qualities of manoeuvrability.

At the same time, this monoplane formula of design offered to the twin-engined bomber a performance in speed very nearly equal to that of a single-engined fighter. In other words, if the power in the bomber could be increased to a sufficient extent, the comparable fighter was likely to have a relatively small advantage over the bomber for purposes of interception and pursuit . . . It was essential to provide a fighter of the highest possible performance in order that it should have any chance of attacking bombers in the short time available.'

Sydney Camm's Fury monoplane was developed into the prototype Hawker Hurricane, immortalized alongside the Spitfire in the Battle of Britain.

In 1933, with both Hawker Aircraft Ltd and Supermarine working to complete prototypes to the F.7/30 project, Hawker's chief designer, Sydney Camm, was thinking along much the same lines as Sorley. He discussed with Major Buchanan, of the Directorate of Technical Development, the possibility of developing a monoplane fighter from the existing Hawker Fury biplane. By October he had prepared a general design that envisaged an aircraft with a fuselage similar in size and design to that of the High Speed Fury (the prototype of the Fury Mk II), virtually unaltered tail surfaces, a fairly thick cantilever wing structure with slight taper on the leading and trailing edges, a fixed and spatted undercarriage, a Rolls-Royce Goshawk engine and an armament of four machine-guns, two in the fuselage nose and one in each wing.

Detailed three-view drawings of the Fury Monoplane were completed on 5 December 1933 and the whole concept discussed in detail with Captain Liptrot, in charge of the Air Ministry Performance Section. By this time the Air Ministry was showing a good deal of enthusiasm for the Hawker project, and work at the company's Kingston-on-Thames factory began to gather momentum. The first major design change came in January 1934, when Camm abandoned the Goshawk engine in favour of a new Rolls-Royce powerplant, the PV.12. This was a progressive and larger development of the Kestrel engine, and tests with the first completed model on 15 October 1933 left Rolls-Royce optimistic; they told Hawker that the new engine could be expected to provide an increase of forty per cent in take-off power and, with single-stage supercharging, an increase of sixty per cent at altitude over the Kestrel. After further ground running and flight testing in specially-adapted test beds – two Hawker Horsleys, a Hart and the High Speed Fury – the installation of the PV.12 in the Fury monoplane was approved by the Directorate of Technical Development. As events were to prove, this decision was to have enormous significance for both Hawker and Supermarine, and indeed for Britain.

A number of weaknesses were revealed during early running of the PV.12, and it was not until July 1934 that the usual 100-hour type-test could be attempted. This brought out further snags; the cylinder blocks persisted in cracking and the double-helical reduction gear failed, necessitating the substitution of straight spur gears to the same ratio. Nevertheless, all these problems were ironed out in due course, and the PV.12 went on to take its place as the latest in Rolls-Royce's traditional 'birds of prey' series of aero-engines. They called it the Merlin.

Meanwhile, at FO.1, Ralph Sorley and his colleagues had been making progress with the all-important question of armament. As Sorley explained:

'The choice lay between the .303 gun, the .5 gun and a new 20 mm Hispano gun which was attracting the attention of the French, and in fact of other countries in Europe who could obtain knowledge of it from them. During 1934 this gun was experimental and details of its performance and characteristics were hard to establish. On the other hand, designs of better .303 guns than the Vickers had been tested over the preceding years with the result that the American Browning from the Colt Automatic Weapon Corporation appeared to offer the best possibilities from the point of view of rate of fire. Our own development of guns of this calibre had been thorough but slow, since we were in the throes of economising, and considerable stocks of old Vickers guns still remained from the First War. The acceptance of a new gun in the numbers likely to be required was a heavy manufacturing and financial commitment. The .5-inch on the other hand had developed little, and although it possessed a better hitting power the rate of fire was slow and it was a heavy item, together with its ammunition, in respect of installed weight.

The solution to this part of the problem lay in making the best assessment possible of the decisive lethality which could be expected in the very short firing time available. By using eight Browning guns it should be possible to build up a density of 256 rounds in that time. To enable the fighter to obtain the best possible speed in relation to the contemporary bomber it was necessary that it should be kept as slim as possible, thus the size of the fuselage area was of great importance. The mounting of guns traditionally in the fuselage tended to increase the cross-sectional area, so if we were to go for more than four guns it seemed necessary to place them outside the fuselage. The monoplane wing offered a space in which they might well be mounted. This would entail mounting a battery of four guns in each wing, which in turn would demand a rigid mounting and the provision of many new features.'

Sorley, together with several officers of the newly-formed Air Ministry Armament Research Department, made a secret visit to France to watch a demonstration of the 20mm Hispano gun and came away convinced that the Browning was the answer. At that time, the Hispano gun was going through its share of teething troubles, particularly when it came to mounting it in an aircraft.

'The controversy was something of a nightmare during 1933–34 (Sorley later admitted). It was a choice on which the whole concept of the fighter would depend, but a trial staged on the ground with eight .303s was sufficiently convincing and satisfying to enable them to carry the day.

A further complication had to be considered: whether the tactical methods current at the time, of attack by squadrons or flights in formation, would hold good. Squadron or flight formation attacks were necessary in order to produce a concentration of fire by fighters armed with only two or even four guns each. They required a high degree of skill and extensive training of pilots. This factor, in conjunction with the greatly increased speed to be expected, and the very short time for decisive action, pointed to new tactical methods, but too little thought was put into this aspect during 1935–37 and operating fighters in pairs was not adopted by the RAF until 1941.'

On 19 July 1934, a very important conference on the whole question of fighter armament was held at the Air Ministry. A number of senior officers expressed their views, including Air Commodore L. A. Pattinson, the Air Officer Commanding the newly-created Armament Group, and two officers representing the Air Defence of Great Britain, Wing Commanders L. McLean and C. N. Lowe. But it was Ralph Sorley who put forward the strong case for an eight-gun fighter, and his views were backed by Captain F. W. Hill, the Senior Technical Officer (Ballistics), who showed the committee the results of the extensive firing tests that had been carried out at the Aeroplane and Armament Experimental Establishment, Martlesham Heath. Hill produced charts showing fields of fire, firing rations and concentrations, and photographs of results. The committee was left in no doubt that, with the new generation of monoplane fighters expected to be in service before long, nothing less than eight guns with a rate of fire of not less than 1,000 rounds per minute would be necessary if the target was to be destroyed or disabled in the brief firing time available.

Meanwhile, Sorley and his colleagues had been paying close attention to the design work in pro-gress at Hawker and Supermarine (in the latter case, this meant the revamped F.7/30 project at this stage).

'The Supermarine and Hawker aircraft differed essentially in one important feature. The Supermarine was designed for a thin wing whereas the Hawker design used a thick one. As a result the installation of the guns in the Hawker aircraft was a somewhat easier problem, enabling four guns to be grouped together in each wing. In the Supermarine the depth of the wing entailed the guns being installed separately; in fact the outer guns of the four on each side were well out towards the tip of the wing.'

On 16 November 1934, the Air Ministry issued Specification F.5/34 in connection with the proposed monoplane fighter. Its opening paragraph strongly reflected the general awareness that there was now a very narrow margin indeed between the speed of a fighter aircraft and that of the bomber it was intended to destroy.

'The speed excess of a modern fighter over that of a contemporary bomber has so reduced the chance of repeated attacks by the same fighter(s) that it becomes essential to obtain decisive results in the short space of time offered for one attack only. This specification is issued, therefore, to govern the production of a day fighter in which speed in overtaking an enemy at 15,000 feet, combined with rapid climb to this height, is of primary importance. The best speed possible must be aimed at for all heights between 5,000 and 15,000 feet. In conjunction with this performance the maximum hitting power must be aimed at, and eight machine-guns are considered advisable.'

Reginald Mitchell and his design team had already seen a draft of this specification in October, and at that time the Air Ministry suggested that it might be met by the revised F.7/30 with a Napier Dagger engine, a proposal which (fortunately) was rejected. In November, the Board of the Supermarine Aviation Works (Vickers) Ltd, under the chairmanship of Sir Robert McLean, authorised Mitchell to proceed with an entirely new fighter design as a private venture. It was to be powered by the Rolls-Royce PV.12, and in fact Rolls-Royce contributed £7,500 towards the cost of building a prototype.

On 1 December 1934, Supermarine received an Air Ministry contract for the redesigned fighter prototype, which was allocated the Company Type No 300. It was covered by Specification F.37/34, received on 28 December (F.36/34 covered the Hawker fighter monoplane, later to become the Hurricane.)

As the *History of Supermarine Aircraft Since 1914* states, 'Despite the Spitfire's legendary reputation, there was in fact no mystique about Mitchell's design. It was a straightforward merger of all the technical knowledge of the time into one complete piece of machinery, including its powerplant which, with the airframe, had embodied all the experience of high-speed flight gathered from the Schneider Trophy races. Mitchell was in fact much more practical than is commonly supposed and has been described by his closest technical collaborators as more an aeroplane enthusiast than a theoretician. The same could be said about other designers at that time, when so much of their creative thought had to be checked by the time-honoured method of trial and error. In the case of the Merlin Spitfire everything came right at the psychological moment – a rare event in aircraft and engine design.'

The aircraft that took shape on Mitchell's drawing board was a long way removed from the Type 224, even in its much revised version. Whereas the latter had been angular in appearance, with a wing planform resembling that of the Hurricane, the Type 300 could only be described as beautiful, its lines blending into one another in a way that was almost poetic. The wing was elliptical in plan, a shape that Mitchell had selected once before in a 1929 project for a six-engined flying boat. The wing had a high-speed NACA 2200 aerofoil section. It is not clear why Mitchell chose the elliptical shape, because it was difficult to engineer and calculations showed that it offered an aerodynamic performance at high speed less than one per cent better than a wing with a straight taper; but there is no doubt that it was successful. In the original design the wing was perfectly elliptical – in other words, formed from two half ellipses with a swept main spar – but was redesigned to produce the familiar Spitfire wing shape, the main spar being straight along the main axis.

Interestingly enough, one aircraft was already flying with elliptical wing and tail surfaces. This was the Heinkel He 70, a single-engined low-wing monoplane which had first flown in December 1932. Designed for high-speed communication and mail transport, the He 70 could outstrip most contemporary fighter aircraft. What is even more interesting is that one He 70, D-UBOF, modified in 1935 to take a Rolls-Royce Kestrel engine and, re-registered G-ADZF, was used as a flying test-bed by Rolls-Royce at Hucknall up to 1944. One cannot help wondering whether Mitchell was in some way influenced by the Heinkel He 70's aerodynamics in finalising the Spitfire's design; if so, it would have been a splendid historical irony. (What is also ironic is that the prototype Messerschmitt Me 109 fighter was powered by an imported Rolls-Royce Kestrel V engine in 1935, due to delays in the delivery of its designated Daimler-Benz motor.)

Although referred to above as the Spitfire, the prototype Supermarine 300, which gradually took shape in the Woolston factory during 1935, had not yet been officially named. Sir Robert McLean, chairman of Vickers-Supermarine, suggested that it should begin with 'S' and sound venomous; Shrew and Shrike had been suggested for the F.7/30, and according to some sources so had Spitfire. McLean particularly liked the latter name, although neither Mitchell nor the Air Ministry did. Mitchell, in fact, is reported to have called it 'bloody silly'. But it stuck, and it was formally adopted after the Type 300's maiden flight.

While construction of the prototype Supermarine 300 continued under conditions of great secrecy at Woolston, the prototype Hawker Hurricane (K5083) flew for the first time on 6 November 1935, and went into its initial test flight phase before being handed over to the A&AEE at Martlesham Heath in February 1936.

Early in January 1936 the airframe of the Supermarine Type 300, which had now been allocated the serial K5054, was at last complete, having undergone a considerable number of modifications as it developed. The engine had already been fitted in the previous November, so all was now set for the first flight.

This took place on the morning of 5 March 1936, and 'Mutt' Summers was the pilot. The flight was made from Eastleigh Airport and the Type 300 took off thirty-five degrees across wind; experience with the racing seaplanes had revealed a strong tendency to swing to port because of the high torque. There was indeed a tendency to swing, but it was easily checked by the application of opposite rudder. The aircraft seemed to drift into the air and the maiden flight, which was made with the undercarriage locked down, was effortless – so much so that when Summers landed, he told the Supermarine engineers and designers not to touch anything.

Mitchell's choice of an elliptical wing for the Spitfire was not an innovation; Heinkel had already used it in the design of the He 70 fast mail aircraft.

The only thing that was touched, in fact, was the propeller. For the maiden flight K5054 had been fitted with a fine-pitch propeller to give the pilot more rpm and therefore more power on take-off; this was replaced by a normal-pitch one for the second and subsequent flights, Supermarine test pilots George Pickering and Jeffrey Quill now joining Summers in the test programme. Quill's name was to become synonymous with that of the Spitfire, as he became responsible for most of the flight test work.

After some minor modifications, including the fitting of the undercarriage fairings and the sealing of some oil leaks, K5054 was flown to Martlesham Heath by George Pickering on 26 March, and in the following month embarked on a series of high-speed trials. During these, it reached a speed of 430 mph IAS in a dive, which was indicative of its potential.

On 10 June the Air Ministry wrote to Supermarine approving the name Spitfire, and on the 18th the aircraft went back to Eastleigh to be unveiled before an invited audience of 300 people from the aircraft industry. During the demonstration flight an oil connection broke, but Jeffrey Quill brought the aircraft down for a perfect landing.

On 27 June K5054 appeared with the prototype Hawker Hurricane at the Hendon Air Pageant, where it was flown by Flight Lieutenant J. H. Edwardes-Jones, RAF, and three days later 'Mutt' Summers flew it at the Society of British Aircraft Constructors' display at Hatfield. After this the prototype went to Farnborough for spinning trials, then returned to Eastleigh for further flight testing and more minor modifications before going back to Martlesham Heath for full handling trials on 23 February 1937. Performance figures logged during these included a true air speed ranging from 330 mph at 10,000 feet to 349 mph at 16,800 feet, the TAS falling to 324 mph at 30,000 feet. Time to 20,000 feet was 8 minutes 12 seconds at 1,770 feet per minute, while rate of climb at sea level was 2,400 feet per minute. All these values far exceeded those demanded by the Air Ministry specification.

More modifications were carried out. The original Rolls-Royce Merlin C engine was replaced by a Merlin F, giving 1,045 hp; a reflector sight was installed and a tailwheel fitted, replacing the simple skid that had been used so far.

On 22 March 1937, with Flight Lieutenant J. F. McKenna at the controls, K5054 was making a flight to test the effectiveness of modified aileron controls when the oil pressure dropped sharply and the engine began to run rough. McKenna switched everything off and made a belly landing on a heath beside the Woodbridge-Bawdsey road. The aircraft sustained only minor damage, and was soon flying again.

On 11 July Reginald Mitchell died of cancer, the disease having been diagnosed four years earlier. He was forty-two years old. His place as Vickers-Supermarine's Chief Designer was taken by Joseph Smith, who had been his assistant. Smith was to be responsible for all future Spitfire design developments.

By September 1937, K5054 had been fitted with its eight-gun armament and had been brought up to Spitfire Mk I production standard. On 23 October it was taken on RAF charge at Martlesham Heath, and after returning to Eastleigh for more modifications – including the installation of gun heating ducts, a new Barr and Stroud Type GD 5 reflector sight and a G22 camera gun – it returned to Martlesham on 12 May 1938 for full armament trials. Prior to this it had suffered damage in two accidents in March, the first when it went over on its nose after the pilot overshot the runway and ran into soft ground, and the second when it bounced after a heavy touch-down and ground-looped, forcing the port undercarriage leg up into the wing.

By this time the Spitfire was in full production. On 3 June 1936, Supermarine had received an initial order for 310 aircraft under Expansion Scheme F, which had supplanted Scheme C earlier in the year. The new Scheme called for a front-line force of 1,736 aircraft by 1939, the force to include thirty home-based fighter squadrons. For the first time, Scheme F laid emphasis on the provision of reserves; first-line squadrons were to have a minimum of seventy-five per cent reserves available for immediate use, and there was to be a further reserve of 150 per cent available to maintain the RAF at full combat strength in the event of war. Just how important these provisions were would be apparent within four years.

Quantity production presented many problems for both Supermarine and Hawker, the latter having received an order for 600 Hurricanes. The solution lay in sub-contracting, and the Air Ministry adopted a breakdown system whereby major components – wings, tail, fuselage, undercarriage – were made separately, often by different constructors, and then assembled into a complete aircraft at a central erecting establishment. With three-quarters of Spitfire components sub-contracted in this way there were bound to be snags; there were delays, for

The prototype Spitfire K5054 flew for the first time on 5 March 1936, with test pilot 'Mutt' Summers at the controls.

K5054, brought up to Mk I production standard, pictured in its warpaint.

example, in the supply of wings, which were built by General Aircraft Ltd. As a result, six production Spitfires had been completed by the end of 1937, but none of them had wings. In the end, Supermarine undertook to manufacture wings, in addition to fuselages and other components, and put plans in hand to extend the facility at Woolston.

Meanwhile, early in 1937, the Air Ministry had realised that, if the *Luftwaffe* continued to expand at its present rate, the provisions of Scheme F would not be sufficient to maintain first-line parity in 1939, as had been planned. Accordingly, a revised plan – Scheme H – was submitted to the Cabinet, calling for an increase in the RAF's metropolitan first-line force to nearly 2,500 aircraft at the earliest possible date after April 1939. The increase was to be made possible by drastically cutting down the number

feared – and this at a time when, in Spain, German and Italian air units were already training for the next war!

It was nevertheless clear to the Cabinet during the spring of 1937 that, with the threat to European peace posed by the activities of Germany and Italy, and the potential threat to peace in the Far East posed by the expansionist aims of Japan, the whole question of Britain's defence policy was in need of review. Defence thinking so far had been dictated by the prospect that Britain would have to cope with a single enemy – first France, then Germany – and now it looked as though she might find herself faced with three at the same time.

Two more expansion schemes, J and K, were proposed by the Air Ministry in 1937; Scheme K was accepted, but with the proviso that planned

K9787, one of the first batch of production Mk I Spitfires used for trials.

of machines in reserve and allocating them to first-line units.

The revised scheme was rejected for two main reasons: first, it would have meant that obsolescent aircraft would have to be committed to battle in unacceptable numbers in the event of war, and second, the Government had received assurances from Germany that the limit of the *Luftwaffe*'s expansion would be much lower than the British

fighter strength would be retained at the expense of first-line bomber squadrons and reserves.

The overall picture was a gloomy one. At an Air Staff meeting held in January 1938, the Chief of the Air Staff pointed out that the changes recommended in Scheme K meant that the RAF would have only nine weeks' reserves, and if war came the full potential of the aircraft industry would not have time to develop. He advocated a possible solution by making cuts in non-operational areas, such as training establishments.

However, it was the Germans themselves who provided the ultimate solution to the dilemma by marching into Austria in March 1938. The Cabinet, hitherto slow to react and still unable to agree on Britain's air defence needs, was at last galvanized into action. Scheme K was quietly forgotten and replaced by Scheme L, which was drawn-up in conditions of near panic in that same month. This envisaged the rapid expansion of the RAF's air strength to 12,000 aircraft over a period of two years, should war make it necessary, but the emphasis was still on fighter production and there was no provision to increase the strength and efficiency of Bomber Command to the point where it could launch an effective counter-attack on Germany.

For Supermarine, the immediate result of Scheme L was an order for 200 more Spitfires. At this time (March 1938) only four sets of wings had been delivered, although thirty-five fuselages had been completed at Woolston and twenty-five transferred to Eastleigh for final assembly. Once Supermarine began building Spitfire wings at Woolston, however, the flow rapidly increased, and forty-nine Spitfires were delivered by the end of the year.

The two new British monoplane fighters, and in particular the Spitfire, represented such a major advance in fighter technology that they quickly attracted the attention of foreign air forces. Between 1936 and 1939 the governments of thirteen foreign nations approached the Air Ministry for quotes, with France heading the list. (The others were Belgium, Estonia, Turkey, Romania, Portugal, Switzerland, Yugoslavia, Holland, Greece, Bulgaria, Iran and Lithuania.) The French, who were pursuing enquiries in the United States with a view to purchasing 100 Curtiss Hawk 75A fighters, were the biggest potential customers, and asked if Supermarine could deliver 100 Spitfires by the middle of 1939, and were interested in obtaining a manufacturing licence, as were Switzerland, Yugolavia, Belgium and Holland. Two *Armée de l'Air* pilots came to England to fly the Spitfire in September 1938 and one aircraft (the 251st production machine) was supplied to France for evaluation in July 1939. But Supermarine was unable to provide the Spitfires the French so badly wanted, their entire production being allocated to the RAF. Had the type been in service alongside the Curtiss Hawk instead of inferior types such as the Morane 406 when the Battle of France began in May 1940, the *Luftwaffe* might have had a much harder task in achieving the air superiority that was so essential to the successful outcome of the land battle.

The French were particularly interested in acquiring a military version of the High Speed Spitfire, which was a one-off digression from the main stream of Spitfire production. Between 23 July and 1 August 1937, Germany entered five Messerschmitt Me 109 fighters – first seen in public at the 1936 Olympic Games in Berlin – in the international flying meeting held at Zürich. Two of them, the Me 109V-10 and V-13, were fitted with early examples of the Daimler-Benz DB 600 engine of 950 hp and had exceptional performance. Predictably, the Messerschmitts swept the board; the international Circuit of the Alps race was won by an Me 109B-2, the climb and dive competition was won by the Me 109V-13, the speed event was also taken by a Me 109B-2 and the team race was won by a pair of Me 109B-1s.

The Germans boasted that they possessed the world's fastest fighter; Supermarine, on the instigation of the Director of Technical Development, Air Commodore R. H. Verney, set out to prove them wrong. The Company received a contract to prepare a Spitfire for an attempt on the World Air Speed Record, and took an aircraft off the Mk I production line to be suitably adapted. A Rolls-Royce team set about developing a racing version of the Merlin II engine, capable of producing 1,995 hp to give a level speed of 375 mph and fitted with a de Havilland four-blade metal propeller. The wing was shortened and given a new tip, and the cockpit area was streamlined. The aircraft was duly modified and flown, and in July 1938 it was exhibited at the Brussels Air Show. By this time, however, serious doubts were being expressed about its performance, and the project was abandoned. It reverted to RAF charge and was later used by the Photographic Reconnaissance Unit. In any case, the Germans had already established their domination of the speed record field on 26 April 1939, when a Messerschmitt Me 209V-1, specially designed for the purpose, set up a new absolute speed record of 469.22 mph. It was not bettered by another piston-engined aircraft for thirty years.

Returning to the main theme, the first production Spitfire Mk I, K9787, flew at Eastleigh on 14 May 1938, and on 27 July it went to A&AEE Martlesham Heath for official handling trials. Two days later it was delivered to No 19 Squadron at Duxford, Cambridgeshire – the first Spitfire to be taken on Fighter Command's inventory.

The high-speed Spitfire, looking somewhat the worse for wear, at Eastleigh. It was later allocated to the Photographic Development Unit.

Chapter 3
The Road to War

T HE INITIAL delivery of Spitfires to No 19 Squadron was slow, averaging one aircraft per week. The Squadron suffered its first training accident on 30 September, when Pilot Officer G. L. Sinclair, making his first flight in the new type, flared-out a little too high and stalled, the aircraft (K9792) bouncing and turning over. The pilot escaped with nothing more than a severe shaking.

No 66 Squadron, the other fighter unit at Duxford, received its first Spitfire, K9802, on 31 October 1938; it was damaged beyond repair in a wheels-up landing at Duxford in April the following year. With pilots who had been used to fixed undercarriages, forgetting to lower the wheels was a persistent danger; a warning horn was fitted and was designed to sound off when the pilot reduced speed on the approach, but it was affected by vibration and often sounded at much higher speeds. One 19 Squadron pilot, who inadvertently belly-landed K9798 on 18 April 1939, told the subsequent Court of Inquiry that the horn sounded so frequently that he had forgotten what it was for.

By the end of 1938, forty-five Spitfires had been delivered to the RAF, permitting the full re-equipment of Nos 19 and 66 Squadrons with almost 100 per cent reserves. However, the production schedule for the initial batch of 300 aircraft, due for completion in March 1939, had slipped badly, and it was not until mid-August 1939 that it was fulfilled. In the meantime, an order for a further 200 aircraft had been placed with Supermarine as a result of the Munich crisis of 1938, when it appeared that Britain and her allies had averted war by a hair's breadth as the result of some shrewd political bargaining; it would be some time before the sham of Munich was fully exposed, although there were some in authority who recognised it for what it was.

Supermarine's inability to cope with Spitfire production requirements had been causing serious concern in the Air Ministry for some time, and at one point consideration was even given to halting

A combination of high engine power, long nose and narrow-track under-carriage made life difficult for some pilots converting to the type from more stately biplane fighters, as these photographs of a No 72 Squadron Mk I show.

production and switching to other types such as the twin-engined Westland Whirlwind (the prototype of which flew on 11 October 1938). That this did not happen was due mainly to one man: William Morris, Lord Nuffield, the pioneer of the inexpensive, mass-produced car for the British market.

In May 1938, Nuffield was invited by the Air Ministry to bring his expertise in mass production techniques in the motor industry to aircraft production. There were plans to build a so-called 'shadow factory' for this specific purpose, and the government wanted it to be sited in Liverpool in order to alleviate the high unemployment rate there. Nuffield, however, pointed out that the need to train a skilled workforce in Liverpool would result in more unacceptable production delays. Such a skilled workforce already existed in the Birmingham area, the hub of the motor industry, and ultimately it was agreed to establish the 'shadow factory' at Castle Bromwich. The Air Ministry purchased a projected housing area of 1,414 acres from the Birmingham Corporation at

£1,000 per acre and work on the factory began on 12 July 1938. The first contract, dated 12 April 1939, called for the production of 1,000 Mk IIA Spitfires, but initial production was slow and the first aircraft (P7280) was not delivered to A&AEE Boscombe Down until 27 June 1940, the first squadron delivery taking place on 17 July. Between June 1940 and December 1945, when the factory closed, 11,939 Spitfires were built there, with production reaching thirty aircraft per week, and 33,918 test flights were carried out from the adjacent airfield.

Apart from the order for 1,000 Spitfires placed with the Nuffield Organisation, Vickers-Armstrongs (Supermarine) was responsible for all the Mk I Spitfire orders up to August 1940, when to relieve the pressure an order for 300 aircraft was placed with Westland Aircraft Ltd. In fact, these were completed as fifty Mk Is and 250 Mk Vs. To summarize, the orders placed with Supermarine up to the outbreak of the Second World War were as follows:

Fuel management caused some problems, too. The pilot of this No 41 Squadron aircraft, from Catterick, made a forced landing in a North Yorkshire cornfield after running out of petrol. Willing helpers are seen towing it along the Scarborough–Pickering road to another field, from which it took-off after topping up.

THE ROAD TO WAR 31

3 June 1936: 310 initial production aircraft in the serial range K9787–L1096. Deliveries from July 1938 as Mk I. The first 74 aircraft were fitted with Merlin II engines, the remainder with the Merlin III. The first 77 aircraft had a mahogany, two-blade, fixed pitch propeller; all were retrofitted with the constant speed, three-blade de Havilland propeller, which was also replaced from June 1940 by the constant speed propeller unit.

September 1938: 200 aircraft in the serial range N3032–N3299. Deliveries from 9 August 1939.

29 April 1939; 200 aircraft in the serial range P9305–P9584. Deliveries to the RAF (181 aircraft) began on 20 January 1940; two exported to Turkey, May 1940; seventeen cancelled. Some were modified for the PR role.

9 August 1939: 450 aircraft in the serial range R6595–R7350. 354 delivered from 29 April 1940 as Mk Is; 78 as Mk V; twelve as PR.IDs.

Luckily, production of the all-important Rolls-Royce Merlin engine was much swifter and more efficient than production of the Spitfire airframes, a second aero-engine plant having been opened at Crewe in May 1939; it would be followed, in October 1940, by another facility near Glasgow, and in the following year the Ford Company's Manchester plant also began to manufacture Merlins.

In the spring and summer of 1939, with the virtual certainty now that war with Germany was a matter of months, perhaps even weeks away, the Spitfire-equipped squadrons trained intensively, concentrating on air-to-air gunnery, dog-fighting, formation flying and formation attacks. Experienced pilots usually converted to type on the squadron, while new men from advanced training depots, where they flew the Miles Magister and Master I, spent a few weeks at an Operational Training Unit before being posted to a fighter squadron. In 1939, most squadrons converting to Spitfires were allocated a Fairey Battle light bomber to give pilots experience with a Merlin-engined monoplane.

Spitfires participated in Anglo-French air exercises in August 1939. On the 17th, following an 'attack' in daylight on Paris by Wellingtons of Bomber Command, a small force of French Bloch 200 bombers made a simulated raid on Birmingham under cover of darkness, and Spitfires of No 19 Squadron were sent up to intercept them. The

Mk I Spitfires, fitted with constant-speed, three-blade de Havilland propellers, lined up for inspection, probably at Duxford.

RAF pilots made a couple of sightings, but the exercise proved only one thing: that single-engined day fighters like the Spitfire and Hurricane were totally unsuited to night operations. Night flying in a Spitfire was very difficult at the best of times, because blue flames and sparks emitted from the exhaust – invisible during daylight – were prone to dazzle the pilot. The problem was partially solved later on by fitting exhaust baffles.

Air exercises apart, the real value of the 1938–39 'breathing space' to RAF Fighter Command was that it enabled the Spitfire and Hurricane squadrons to become fully integrated with the Air Defence Control and Reporting System. It was sometimes called the Dowding System, because from 1936 Air Chief Marshal Sir Hugh Dowding, the AOC-in-C Fighter Command, was responsible for bringing it to operational status, but the real architect was Major-General E. B. Ashmore, who had perfected the London Air Defence Area layout in 1918. Ashmore also founded the Observer

Corps, an invaluable asset that Dowding inherited, although in 1936 it was greatly in need of expansion. He also inherited quite a lot of Army sound locators, which were almost completely useless.

The advent of radar – or radio direction finding, as it was then known – changed the picture completely. Following early experiments at Daventry in 1935, the Bawdsey Research Station was very rapidly set up to pursue the concept, and from then on the pace of development was quite remarkable. Scientists and engineers were brought in at a very early stage, and they worked in harmony as part of the total enterprise. In a decade characterized by muddle and confusion in defence matters, the British government for once acted quickly, very efficiently, and got it right.

By September 1939 the planned chain of twenty radar stations at home – the Chain Home (CH) stations – had been completed, stretching from Southampton to Newcastle-upon-Tyne. Each had twin masts, the taller – 350 feet – for transmitting,

Mk I Spitfires of No 19 Squadron at Duxford. No 19 Sqn was to pioneer in-service developments on the Spitfire, including the use of 20mm cannon.

and the shorter, 240 feet, for receiving. The CH stations, known for security reasons as Air Ministry Experimental Stations – AMES – could detect aircraft up to 100 miles away, and could give the bearing and approximate indication of the height and number of an approaching formation. The main stations were being supplemented by another series, Chain Home Low (CHL) which were designed to detect aircraft flying below 3,000 feet. On the face of it, the radar stations, with their huge towers and associated maze of electrical cables, seemed very vulnerable; in fact they were to prove very difficult to bomb, although some did suffer substantial damage in the Battle of Britain.

These electronic eyes of Britain's defences were backed up by the human ones of the Observer Corps. While the radar stations were responsible for tracking hostile aircraft before they reached the British coast, the volunteers of the Observer Corps were responsible for tracking and reporting on them once they had crossed it. The link between the two phases was the Sea Plotter, whose task it was to accept incoming tracks picked up by radar and alert coastal posts in the path of the raid to watch out for it. The raid would then be continuously tracked by other Observer Corps posts inland. By mid-1940 there were thirty-one Observer Corps Groups in Britain, each incorporating between thirty and fifty posts that were manned around the clock and totalling some 30,000 personnel.

Information from these reporting agencies, and later from signals intelligence gathered by the RAF's 'Y' Service, was passed by landline to HQ Fighter Command at Bentley Priory, where it was rapidly filtered and processed for re-transmission to the sector airfield operations rooms at key locations such as Biggin Hill and Hornchurch, which in turn passed it on to the fighter squadrons at readiness on their forward airfields.

In the end, it all came down to the ability of the fighter squadrons to react quickly in response to the information they received, and to that of the Sector Controller to vector them to the right location and altitude in order to make a successful interception. Once the responsible unit commander had sighted the enemy, the controller transferred executive responsibility to him and only recovered it when the fighters had completed their attack and were heading for home. The whole system was highly flexible, and in an emergency one Sector could control another Sector's aircraft to a limited extent; the maximum number of squadrons one Sector could cope with was six.

One of the drawbacks in the system, in 1939–40, was that it relied on the use of HF radio, which could be indistinct and suffered from range problems; the transmissions could become so faint as to be inaudible. There was a pressing requirement for VHF radio equipment, but this did not become available until the late summer of 1940. The first recorded Spitfire fitment was in R6833 of No 19 Squadron on 20 August that year.

By July 1940, just in time for the onset of the great air battle over Britain, and after many trials and tribulations, the Dowding System had been practised and re-practised until virtually every snag had been eliminated. Speaking after the war, General Adolf Galland, the renowned German fighter leader, paid this tribute to it.

> 'From the first the British had an extraordinary advantage, never to be balanced out at any time during the whole war, which was their radar and fighter control network and organization. It was for us a very bitter surprise. We had nothing like it. We could do no other than knock frontally against the outstandingly well organized and resolute direct defence of the British Isles.'

At the outbreak of war on 3 September 1939, nine RAF squadrons had fully equipped with Spitfires and a tenth, No 609 Squadron, had just begun to equip. During September No 603 Squadron at Turnhouse also began to receive Spitfires, and it was the two Scottish Auxiliary Air Force squadrons, Nos 602 and 603, that were the first to make contact with the *Luftwaffe* over the United Kingdom.

RAF Spitfire Squadrons: Order of Battle at 3 September 1939

Squadron	Mark	Location	Remarks
19	I	Duxford	Equipped August 1938
41	I	Catterick	Equipped January 1939
54	I	Hornchurch	Equipped March 1939
65	I	Hornchurch	Equipped March 1939
66	I	Duxford	Equipped November 1938
72	I	Church Fenton	Equipped April 1939
74	I	Hornchurch	Equipped February 1939
602	I	Abbotsinch	Equipped May 1939
609	I	Catterick	Equipped August 1939
611	I	Duxford	Equipped May 1939

Chapter 4
First Contact: The North Sea Approaches, September 1939–April 1940

O N THE OUTBREAK of war, the German formation responsible for operations in the North Sea area was *Luftlotte 2 (Nord)* under *General der Flieger* Hellmuth Felmy. Under his command was the recently-formed *Fliegerdivision 10* under *Generalleutnant* Hans Ferdinand Geisler, whose specific task was to conduct a campaign against British shipping in northern waters.

For both commanders, the first weeks of the war were frustrating. Already, on the second day of hostilities, Blenheims and Wellingtons of RAF Bomber Command had attacked German warships at Wilhelmshaven, and there had been other incursions during September. Admittedly, the RAF raids had achieved no result and the attackers had suffered severe losses, but Felmy and Geisler had been

A Spitfire Mk I of No 72 Squadron, Church Fenton, over the Yorkshire coast.

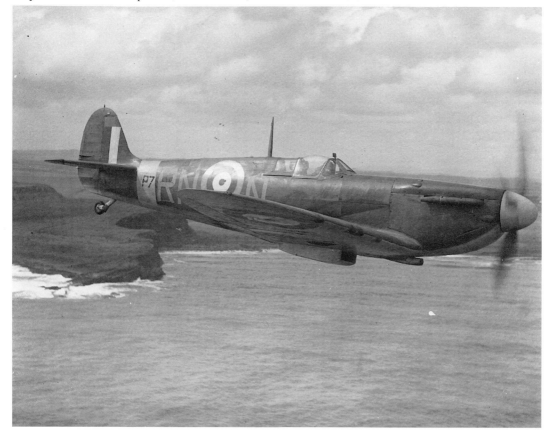

powerless to retaliate because their bomber forces had been tied up in the Polish campaign. It was not until the first week of October 1939 that the Heinkel He 111s of *Fliegerdivision 10*'s principal bomber unit, *Kampfgeschwader 26*, returned from the east in full strength to their usual bases in the Heligoland Bight area, within striking distance of the British Isles.

The *Fliegerdivision*'s other bomber asset, I/KG 30, was based at Westerland on the island of Sylt and was equipped with Junkers Ju 88s under the command of *Hauptmann* Helmuth Pohle. I/KG 30, the first unit to receive the Ju 88 dive-bomber, had only recently reached operational status; on 26 September some of its aircraft had made an abortive attack on warships of the British Home Fleet in the North Sea (an event that led the Germans to claim, erroneously, that the aircraft carrier *Ark Royal* had been sunk), and on 9 October it had joined forces with KG 26 in further fruitless attacks on the British warships.

So far, the *Luftwaffe* had not ventured into British airspace. That situation changed on 16 October, when I/KG 30 took-off from Westerland with orders to attack British warships – primarily the battle cruiser HMS *Hood* – in the Firth of Forth. The Germans knew of the *Hood*'s presence, because the warship had been sighted heading for the Firth by a reconnaissance aircraft; what they did not know was whether she was in open water or berthed in Rosyth dockyard. In the latter event, Pohle had specific orders not to attack her for fear of causing civilian casualties.

The Ju 88s flew in loose formation as they approached the target area some seventy-five minutes after take-off, their crews expecting little opposition. *Luftwaffe* intelligence had indicated that Scotland was defended only by a handful of obsolescent Gloster Gladiator biplane fighters; the Germans were completely unaware of the presence of Nos 602 and 603 Squadrons at Drem and Turnhouse respectively. It was not the last time that the *Luft-*

No 72 Squadron later moved to Acklington in Northumberland. Its Spitfires are seen here climbing out over the Farne Islands.

waffe's bomber crews would suffer from inadequate intelligence during their operations over the British Isles.

No 602 Squadron had in fact flown into Drem on 13 October, after spending a week at Grangemouth. On the 16th it was minus its Green Section, whose three Spitfires had landed at Leuchars to refuel after chasing an unidentified plot over Fife. Similarly, a section of No 603 Squadron was refuelling at Turnhouse after pursuing a suspect aircraft (which was in fact a Heinkel 111 of KG 26 on reconnaissance) over the Lothians.

At 13.00, Red Section of No 603 Squadron was scrambled from Drem to investigate another plot, which turned out to be two Fleet Air Arm Skuas. At 14.22, after they had landed to refuel, Flight Lieutenant George Pinkerton led Blue Section out on patrol, and ten minutes later Yellow Section was ordered to patrol Turnhouse at 10,000 feet in response to an unconfirmed report that a formation of

What German bomber crews hoped never to see: a Spitfire curving in for a stern attack.

unidentified aircraft was heading in towards the Forth Bridge. Shortly afterwards, Yellow Section of No 603 Squadron under Flight Lieutenant George Denholm was ordered up from Turnhouse.

Climbing to 10,000 feet, Pinkerton and his pilots sighted nine Junkers 88s dive-bombing warships off Rosyth and gave chase, latching on to the leading bomber as it pulled out of its dive and raced away over May Island. The Junkers – it was Pohle's aircraft – was attacked by each of the three Spitfires in turn. The burst of gunfire killed Pohle's flight engineer and rear gunner and mortally wounded the navigator. First one engine failed as bullets tore into it, then the other. Pohle spotted a trawler and turned towards it, using all his skill to keep the Junkers airborne. Then the bomber ploughed into the sea and he lost consciousness. A few minutes later the trawler crew fished him out of the sinking aircraft, severely concussed; he woke up five days later in Port Edwards hospital.

Meanwhile, Red Section of No 603 Squadron led by Squadron Leader E. H. Stevens, had pursued a twin-engined bomber north of Dalkeith. The aircraft was a Heinkel of KG 26, sent to cause a diversion and also to observe the results of the Junkers' attack. Another section of No 603 Squadron, lead by Flight Lieutenant Pat Gifford, also joined in the chase, and between them they sent the Heinkel down into the sea off Port Seton. Three crew members were picked up shocked but unhurt; the fourth was dead.

The CO of No 602 Squadron, Squadron Leader Douglas Farquhar, and the two other pilots of Green Section, Flight Lieutenant A. V. R. Johnstone and Flying Officer Ferguson, got away from Leuchars in time to catch the tail-end of the raid. They found a Ju 88 heading east at 2,000 feet off Aberdour, and, joined by two Spitfires of No 603 Squadron, made repeated attacks on it until it went down into the sea. None of the crew got out.

In addition to its losses, I/KG 30 had four Ju 88s damaged, and the day's action was not yet over. About an hour after the attack, pilots of No 603 Squadron damaged a Heinkel 111 over Rosyth and shot a second down into the sea. One of the pilots in George Pinkerton's section on this first day of action for Fighter Command was Flying Officer Archie McKellar. A diminutive man, only five feet four inches tall, McKellar was born in Paisley in 1912 and had two childhood ambitions: to become a plasterer and to learn to fly. Overcoming all manner of family objections, he achieved both. In 1936 he joined No 602 (City of Glasgow) Squadron, Auxiliary Air Force – having already gained his pilot's licence at the Scottish Flying Club – and was called-up for active service at the outbreak of war.

On 29 November 1939, Red Section of No 602 Squadron, including McKellar, was scrambled to intercept two Heinkels, one circling on reconnaissance over Rosyth, the other over Dalkeith. McKellar, guided by anti-aircraft fire, was the first to sight the second Heinkel, and drew ahead of the rest of his section. Diving to the attack, he opened fire at 200 yards, giving the bomber two bursts. The first struck the Heinkel's wing root and killed its dorsal gunner; the second riddled its tail surfaces. McKellar drew away to make another firing pass, but was beaten to it by three Spitfires of No 603 Squadron, whose fire hit the bomber's starboard wing and cockpit area. The Heinkel crash-landed in a field at Kidlaw, near Haddington, with both gunners dead and the pilot wounded. Only the navigator was unhurt. It was the first enemy aircraft to fall on the British mainland in the 1939–45 war, and as such it attracted a great deal of publicity. More importantly, it was dismantled and taken to Farnborough, where a lengthy technical report was compiled on it. Unfortunately, the report did not appear until August 1940, long after the Heinkel 111's heyday on operations over the British Isles.

Four days before Christmas, McKellar was one of several pilots who were scrambled to intercept a formation of suspect aircraft approaching the Scottish coast. Over the Firth of Forth they sighted six twin-engined bombers with twin tail fins slipping in and out of cloud. Identifying them as Dornier 17s, the Spitfire pilots attacked them and shot two of them down. But the bombers were not Dorniers: they were Handley Page Hampdens of No 44 Squadron, returning from an armed reconnaissance over the North Sea and, because of a serious naviga-

P9450, a Mk I Spitfire serving with No 613 Squadron and, later, with No 64 Squadron. This aircraft was damaged in combat with an Me 109 near Rouen in June 1940.

tional error, making landfall much too far to the south. They had been heading for RAF Lossiemouth, and had mistaken the Firth of Forth for the Moray Firth. One crew member was drowned; the rest were saved. This 'friendly fire' incident was particularly tragic, for the Hampden squadrons had already taken a severe beating on operations over the North Sea; on 29 September, No 144 Squadron had lost five out of eleven aircraft, surprised by Messerschmitt 110 fighters over the Heligoland Bight.

Although the two Auxiliary squadrons in Scotland had several skirmishes with the enemy in the winter months of 1939–40, results were mostly inconclusive, but on 13 January 1940, No 602 Squadron teamed up with Hurricanes of No 111 Squadron from Acklington, in Northumberland, to destroy a Heinkel off Carnoustie.

The majority of 'kills' so far had been shared between several pilots, although Squadron Leader Farquhar had been given the credit for the Junkers destroyed on 16 October. Farquhar's next chance came on 9 February, 1940, when, accompanied by Flying Officer A. M. Grant on a patrol over the mouth of the Firth of Forth, he was vectored by ground control to intercept an enemy aircraft some twenty miles out to sea. The enemy turned out to be a Heinkel 111, which dived into cloud as Farquhar attacked. The Spitfire pilot followed into the murk while Grant circled, waiting to catch the Heinkel in case it feinted back, but Farquhar caught up with it in a clear patch and opened fire, hitting it in one engine. The Heinkel turned in towards the coast and made a wheels-up landing near North Berwick. Three of its crew escaped unhurt, but Farquhar's machine-gun fire had seriously wounded the dorsal gunner, who died later in hospital.

Farquhar was in action again on 22 February. Together with Flying Officer George Proudman, he attacked a Heinkel 111 at 11.50, his fire wounding the German dorsal gunner in both legs and putting the bomber's engines out of action. The enemy pilot turned in over the coast and made a skilful crash-landing at Coldingham, near St Abbs Head in Berwickshire. Farquhar, circling overhead, saw the crew scramble clear, assisting the injured gunner, and realised that they were about to set fire to their more or less intact aircraft, so he decided to land alongside and stop them. Unfortunately, the Spitfire hit a patch of mud as it rolled down the field and turned over on its back.

Farquhar was unhurt, but hung helplessly upside down in his straps until the Heinkel's crew, seeing his predicament, ran across and helped him out of it – having first set light to the nose section of their bomber. Farquhar, seeing some armed Local Defence Volunteers approaching, advised the German crew to surrender to him, which they did. Farquhar collected their Luger pistols, and was promptly arrested by the LDV, who took him for one of the enemy. He extricated himself from this fresh embarrassment by delving into his pocket and producing an Inland Revenue tax return form, which he had received that morning!

One interesting point about this action is that Proudman's Spitfire (serial L1007) was the only Spitfire in the RAF to be armed with cannon. The aircraft, fitted with two 20mm Hispano guns, had undergone trials at Martlesham Heath in July 1939, and after attachment to other units for a while, it had been assigned to Drem, where there was a prospect of some action. Proudman had actually opened fire on the Heinkel as the bomber made for North Berwick, but after forty rounds – all of which missed – the cannon jammed, an occurrence which at that time was quite normal. It had happened on 13 January, in the action that resulted in the destruction of the Heinkel 111 off Carnoustie. It has sometimes been stated since, quite erroneously, that the cannon-armed Spitfire destroyed the enemy bomber; in fact, its guns jammed after only a few rounds had been fired.

While the Scottish fighter squadrons sparred with the *Luftwaffe* during the first winter of the war, those based south of the border – at Acklington in Northumberland and Catterick in North Yorkshire – had also seen some action. On 17 October 1939, three Spitfires of No 41 Squadron from Catterick caught a reconnaissance Heinkel 111 twenty-five miles off Whitby and shot it down into the sea; the pilot and navigator survived and were rescued from their dinghy at dawn the next day, becoming the first German prisoners to be landed on English soil in World War Two. Although most of the enemy aircraft destroyed off north-east England during this phase fell to the Hurricanes of Nos 43 and 111 Squadrons, the Spitfires had their share; on 3 February 1940, for example, three Spitfire pilots of No 152 Squadron, Acklington, destroyed a Heinkel off the coast.

The punishment was not all one-sided; several Spitfires were damaged by return fire, and some pilots had lucky escapes. The luckiest of all, perhaps, was Flight Lieutenant Norman Ryder of No 41 Squadron, Catterick, who intercepted and shot

Although of poor quality, this photograph is interesting in that it is probably the only one in existence showing a Spitfire of No 41 Squadron deployed at the Squadron's satellite airfield at Greatham, near Hartlepool, during the 'Phoney War' period.

down a Heinkel 111 between Redcar and Whitby on 3 April 1940. His Spitfire was hit in the engine and he was forced to ditch in a very rough sea about half-a-mile from a trawler. The impact knocked him unconscious, and he was some distance below the surface in the sinking aircraft when he came to. He recalls:

'I remember sitting in the cockpit and everything was a bright green. I was very fascinated by the stillness of it all – it was amazing, and I recall watching a lot of bubbles running up the wind-screen before my nose and parting as they got to the front. I sat there fascinated by the sight and not a bit afraid. The calm was so restful after the noise. The green colour around me was lovely, but it turned to blackness before I got out. I started to get out by undoing my straps. I stood on my seat and just when I thought I was clear I found my parachute had caught under the sliding hood, and I could not move. I got partially into the cockpit again and at this point noticed that it was getting very much darker as the aircraft sank. I was again nearly hooked up by my parachute, but I wriggled and got clear. By now it was very black and I just saw the silhouette of the tail-plane pass my face. I still had on my parachute which hampered my movement, but I managed to dog paddle my way upwards.'

After considerable difficulty, Ryder freed himself from his parachute harness and, completely exhausted by his efforts, was picked up by the trawler crew. He had the dubious distinction of being the first Spitfire pilot to be shot down by the *Luftwaffe*, a fact compensated for to some extent by the award of the Distinguished Flying Cross.

Spitfire squadrons based in the south of England also had an occasional chance to come to grips with the enemy. It seemed, in fact, that their opportunity had come in the first week of the war, when Spitfires of No 74 Squadron from Hornchurch and Hurricanes of No 56 Squadron from North Weald were scrambled in response to an air-raid alert. An air battle developed over the Thames Estuary and two Hurricanes were shot down – by the Spitfires. The squadrons had been fighting one another, and the unhappy incident, which cost the life of one of the Hurricane pilots, passed into legend as the 'Battle of Barking Creek'.

The alert was real enough, though, when in January 1940 a section of 54 Squadron Spitfires went up from Rochford to investigate a 'bogey' off the Thames Estuary; it was a Heinkel 111, and the Spitfire pilots damaged it. Further north, in the same month, Spitfires of No 66 Squadron from Horsham St Faith shot down a He 111 attacking a trawler off Cromer.

In March, the Heinkels of KG 26 began a series of attacks on British shipping in the southern area of the English Channel; in the first, on 2 March, the 8,441-ton passenger vessel *Domala* was set on fire off the Isle of Wight, and on 20 March the 5,439-ton freighter *Barn Hill* was sunk in the same area. In both instances, the attackers got clean away. In the meantime, on 16 March, eighteen Ju 88s of KG 30 and sixteen He 111s of KG 26 made the first major raid on the north since the previous year, attacking units of the Home Fleet at Scapa Flow, AA positions and airfields on the Orkneys. The heavy cruiser HMS *Norfolk* was damaged in the attack, and all the raiders escaped interception, although Hurricanes of Nos 43 and 605 Squadrons were scrambled from Wick. Some Fleet Air Arm Skuas also went up, but their rate of climb was insufficient to get them to height before the attackers had turned for home. The situation was redressed somewhat when, during a second attack on the Orkneys on 10 April defending fighters and AA fire claimed seven enemy bombers.

The day before this, German forces had invaded Denmark and Norway. The Spitfire's war was about to begin in earnest.

Spitfire Mk Is of No 65 Squadron, 1939. The nearest aircraft is flown by Flying Officer (later Wing Commander) R.R.S. Tuck.

Chapter 5
Initiation: Dunkirk, May–June 1940

O N 10 MAY 1940, with the Norwegian campaign still in progress, the Germans invaded France and the Low Countries. Within a week the Allied armies had been cut in two and the British Expeditionary Force was making a fighting retreat towards the port of Dunkirk.

The Spitfire played no part in the campaign in France and Belgium. The air fighting there fell to the Hawker Hurricane squadrons attached to the BEF Air Component and the Advanced Air Striking Force, and to a couple of squadrons of out-dated Gloster Gladiators. The Hurricanes, in fact, had been in action virtually throughout the period of the so-called Phoney War, the AASF units (Nos 1 and 73 Squadrons) skirmishing with the *Luftwaffe* over the Maginot Line.

By 21 May, the battle situation had deteriorated to such an extent that the seven Hurricane squa-

HM King George VI being shown a Spitfire cockpit during a visit to an unidentified RAF station, early 1940.

drons now assigned to the Air Component and the AASF were ordered to evacuate to bases in England. In their depleted state, their arrival did little to bolster Fighter Command's resources. As Sir Hugh Dowding commented to the Air Ministry on 24 May, 'The withdrawal of seven squadrons from France has converted a desperate into a serious situation'.

Dowding was determined that air cover over the evacuation areas should be provided only by Air Vice-Marshal Keith Park's No 11 Group, based in south-east England, and that other groups should not be stripped of their fighters. Nor would he commit tired or incompletely trained pilots to the battle. This meant that the brunt was inevitably borne by the Hurricane squadrons. The number of Spitfire squadrons on Fighter Command's inventory had now risen to nineteen, but several of these were still working up to operational standard and were newcomers to single-engined fighters; No 222 Squa-

dron, for example, had exchanged Blenheim IFs for Spitfire Is in March 1940.

From 10 May, the Spitfire squadrons of Nos 11 and 12 Groups were authorised to carry out offensive patrols across the Channel. The Duxford Wing was particularly active, being well placed to cover the Dutch coast from the East Anglian airfields of Coltishall and Horsham St Faith, to which No 66 Squadron deployed in May from its main base at Duxford while its sister squadron, No 19, deployed south to Hornchurch in No 11 Group's area. By the end of the first week of operations, mainly in The Hague area, No 66 Squadron had claimed the destruction of four enemy aircraft, with three more damaged. On 13 May, Spitfires of No 74 Squadron, deploying forward to Rochford from Hornchurch, provided an escort for the British destroyer HMS *Hereward*, bringing Queen Wilhelmina of the Netherlands and members of the Dutch Royal Family to exile in England, and for the destroyer HMS *Wind-*

Spitfire Mk I R6923 of No 92 Squadron. This aircraft was shot down over the English Channel by an Me 109 in June 1941.

sor, evacuating members of the Dutch government later in the day.

On 18 May, Air Vice-Marshal Trafford Leigh-Mallory, AOC No 12 Group, visited Duxford prior to No 19 Squadron's departure for Hornchurch and told personnel that the Squadron would shortly deploy to France; in the event, the situation on the continent deteriorated so rapidly that no such deployment was made.

The first major contact between No 11 Group's Spitfires and the *Luftwaffe* did not come until 23 May, when the Group provided fighter cover for units of 30 Brigade, crossing the Channel to reinforce the garrison at Calais. This was the first occasion on which Spitfires encountered Me 109s and Me 110s, and in the heat of battle the RAF pilots made some quite outrageous claims, as doubtless did their opponents. No 92 Squadron, for example, claimed to have destroyed seventeen Me 110s and six Me 109s during a series of patrols between Calais and Dunkirk; the Germans admitted to losing two of each type, while No 92 Squadron lost three Spitfires, N3194, P9370 and P9373. One of these was flown by Squadron Leader R. J. Bushell, who was taken prisoner and who later in the war was shot by the Germans for his part in the famous *Stalag Luft III* tunnel escape.

No 74 Squadron also lost a Spitfire that day, when K9867, flown by the squadron commander, suffered an engine failure and had to make a forced-landing on Calais-Marck airfield, which was expected to fall into enemy hands at any moment. The pilot was picked up by a Miles Magister escorted by two Spitfires, which had to beat off an attack by Me 109s. The Spitfires, flown by Flight Lieutenant (later Group Captain) Al Deere and Pilot Officer J. Allen, were from No 54 Squadron.

The next day, 24 May, was a bad day for No 74 Squadron, which lost three aircraft – K9952, N3243 and P9321. No 54 Squadron also lost P9455, while P9374 of No 92 Squadron failed to return. All of these losses were sustained during covering actions in the Calais-Boulogne areas.

On 25 May small numbers of medium bombers drawn from *Fliegerkorps I* and *IV* made sporadic attacks on Dunkirk, where the evacuation of the BEF was getting under way. The German air onslaught against Dunkirk was slow in developing; the plan was for the port to be heavily attacked by the Junkers Ju 87 *Stukas* of *VIII Fliegerkorps*, but most of their aircraft were heavily committed elsewhere on the front. The Ju 87s of *Stukageschwader 2* furnished air support for German Army units fighting in the streets of Boulogne and Calais, and it was during these operations that this unit had its first taste of Spitfires. The Messerschmitt escort managed to hold

Spitfire P7618 of No 41 Squadron, purchased by the Observer Corps' Spitfire Fund. The pilot is Sqn Ldr D.O. Findlay, DFC. The aircraft, a Mk II, failed to return from operations in February 1941 while serving with No 74 Sqn.

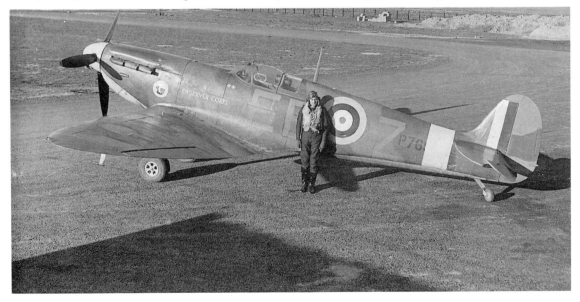

most of the British fighters at bay, but nevertheless four *Stukas* failed to return.

Boulogne fell on the morning of 25 May, and the *Stukas* were now free to turn the full weight of their attacks on Calais, where the 10th *Panzer* Division was suffering badly from the gunfire of British warships lying just off the coast. At noon a call for assistance reached *VIII Fliegerkorps*, and forty Ju 87s set out to attack the vessels. For most of the pilots, it was their first mission against this type of target; the result was that all their bombs missed the warships, which were destroyers and able to manoeuvre rapidly. As the *Stukas* formed up and left the target area they were attacked by Spitfires and three of the dive-bombers were shot down. No 54 Squadron was in the thick of the fighting and lost three Spitfires, N3096, N3103 and P9388.

The fighters of No 11 Group were highly active throughout the 26th, when Dunkirk was subjected to a series of heavy air attacks, with some sixteen squadrons patrolling the Dunkirk-Calais area in relays. Between 04.30 and 19.30, twenty-two patrols were carried out at squadron strength, the RAF claiming twenty victories for the loss of five Hurricanes and one Spitfire (P9437 of No 65 Squadron). The fighters accounted for six Dornier Do 17s of III/KG 3, and several more sustained severe battle damage; at one blow, half of III/KG 3's effective strength had been wiped out. III/KG 2 fared little better, as its commanding officer, *Major* Werner Kreipe, reported: 'The enemy fighters pounced on our tightly knit formation with the fury of maniacs'. According to German records, *Fliegerkorps II* lost twenty-three bombers on 26 May 1940, with sixty-four aircrew killed and seven wounded.

Under the Dowding System, the standing cover of sixteen fighter squadrons assigned to cover the evacuation was frequently rotated, those which suffered a high rate of attrition being sent north for a rest and replaced by fresh units drawn from Nos 12 and 13 Groups, so that in fact thirty-two RAF fighter squadrons participated at one time or another in Operation *Dynamo*, as the Dunkirk evacuation was code-named.

On 27 May – the day in which the *Luftwaffe* carried out twelve major attacks on Dunkirk – AVM Park's sixteen fighter squadrons, with 287 serviceable aircraft at their disposal, carried out twenty-three patrols over Dunkirk between 05.00 and nightfall; these patrols varied in strength from nine to twenty aircraft. In the course of the day six Spitfires and eight Hurricanes were lost, the RAF claiming the destruction of thirty-eight enemy aircraft (a claim which, once again, was greatly exaggerated). The Spitfires that failed to return on this day were N3200 and N3237 of No 19 Squadron, N3030 of No 54 Squadron, K9875 and L1084 of No 74 Squadron, and L1003 of No 610 Squadron, the latter having moved up to Gravesend from Biggin Hill on the previous day to take part in the operation. The RAF Biggin Hill war diary tells the story of No 610 Squadron's encounter:

'On their first sortie the pilots of 610 Squadron, flying in their Spitfires at 18,000 feet, sighted a twin-engined Heinkel 111 bomber some 3,000 feet below. Anxious, in this his first combat, to make certain it was a Hun, Squadron Leader Franks dived down and calmly flew alongside taking a good look: the swastika on the tail, the black crosses on the wings were plain to see. Franks ordered Red Two and Red Three to attack. Flying Officer Smith poured all his ammunition into the Heinkel, only breaking off when the starboard engine was enveloped in flames. Sergeant Medway followed him up with a five-second burst, then the three Spitfires of Yellow Section joined in. Blue Section lined up to speed the Heinkel to its doom, but were called off by Franks. Plunging down out of control, the German pilot managed to fire Very signals which brought forty Messerschmitt 109s to avenge him. Undismayed by odds of more than three to one, the Spitfire pilots went straight in to attack and sent three Messerschmitts spinning down in flames, with another three probables.

The following day, 28 May, was overcast and the weather grew steadily worse as the day wore on. Although German bomber formations attacked Ostend and Nieuport, very few got through to Dunkirk itself. No 11 Group flew eleven squadron patrols in the Dunkirk sector during the day, with 321 individual fighter sorties. Three Spitfires failed to return from operations on this day: N3180 of No 54 Squadron, P9435 of No 65 Squadron, and K9804 of No 66 Squadron.

The following morning was even worse from the weather point of view, with pouring rain and a cloud base down to 300 feet. Around noon, however, the clouds began to break up, and *Luftwaffe* attacks were able to resume. The RAF carried out nine patrols during the day, with formations of between twenty-five and forty-four fighters providing cover over the Dunkirk sector. They succeeded

It was during the Battle of France that the shortcomings of the Dornier Do 17 were revealed, particularly its weak defensive armament. RAF personnel examine one brought down on a reconnaissance sortie over France about the time of the German invasion.

in intercepting three out of five major attacks launched by the *Luftwaffe*, but all the German raids were heavily escorted by fighters and the RAF could not succeed in breaking them up. The score at the end of the day was marginally in the *Luftwaffe's* favour, with sixteen British fighters shot down against fourteen German aircraft. The six Spitfires that failed to return on 29 May came from two squadrons, Nos 64 and 610. The latter suffered particularly badly, losing L1006, L1062, N3177 and N3289. No 64 Squadron's losses were L1052 and N3272.

Fog curtailed air operations on 30 May and persisted right through into the following morning. It began to clear towards midday, permitting the *Luftwaffe* to carry out several attacks, but these were restricted to relatively small formations and never reached the intensity of the raids of the 29th. The RAF fighters claimed seventeen enemy aircraft and again six Spitfires failed to return: K9813 of No 64 Squadron, K9992 of No 74 Squadron, N3295 of No 222 Squadron, L1081 and N3202 of No 609 Squadron, and N3274 of No 610 Squadron. No 609 Squadron had been operating from Northolt since 19 May, having come down from Drem.

The morning of 1 June was bright and clear, and the Germans took the opportunity to throw every available aircraft against Dunkirk. Fighter Command carried out eight squadron-strength patrols during the course of the day, claiming the destruction of seventy-eight enemy aircraft – a figure that was officially reduced later on to forty-three. However, *Luftwaffe* records admit the loss of nineteen bombers and ten fighters only for 1 June, with a further thirteen damaged in air combat; and since the Royal Navy claimed ten aircraft destroyed and French fighters another ten, the actual score must remain in doubt. What is certain is that Fighter Command lost thirty-nine aircraft in the air battles of 1 June 1940, nine of them Spitfires. The losses were K9836, No 19 Squadron; N3107, No 41 Squadron; L1053, No 64 Squadron; P9372, P9317 and N3232, No 222 Squadron; L1058, No 603 Squadron; N3222, No 609 Squadron; and K9948, No 616 Squadron.

For the Spitfire squadrons, it was the worst day so far, and six more aircraft failed to return on 2 June. No 66 Squadron lost N3028, N3033 and N3047, No 266 Squadron N3092, and No 611 Squadron N3055 and N3064. *Luftwaffe* activity over Dunkirk was very much reduced on this day, the reason being that the German combat squadrons were being held in readiness for a major operation which was to take place on 3 June: a massive air attack on factories and airfields in the Paris area, code-named Operation *Paula*.

During the nine days of Dunkirk, between 26 May and 3 June 1940, the RAF fighter squadrons committed to the battle over the beaches and beyond had flown 2,739 sorties. Spitfire losses during the period of 18 May–3 June were fifty-two aircraft, the last one being N3290 of No 92 Squadron on 3 June. (No 222 Squadron's N3197 also failed to return from operations on 5 June, although this is marginally outside the period in question.) Total Fighter Command losses, 26 May–3 June, amounted to ninety-nine aircraft of the home-based fighter squadrons, to which must be added a further forty-six aircraft of Coastal and Bomber Commands. This figure excludes Fleet Air Arm losses.

On the other side of the coin, the pilots of Fighter Command claimed the destruction of 377 enemy aircraft, a figure that was later reduced officially to 262; the gunners of the Royal Navy and the French Navy claimed thirty-five more. German records for this period, however, admit a loss of 240 aircraft of all types along the whole Franco-Belgian front, of which 132 were lost in the Dunkirk sector. The same kind of ratio between the losses of RAF Fighter Command and the *Luftwaffe* was to apply later, in the Battle of Britain.

It should not be forgotten though, that the ratio of daily RAF losses over Dunkirk was generally higher than that experienced during the Battle of Britain a few weeks later – or that for the majority of the British fighter pilots who took part this was their first taste of action, whereas many of their opponents were already veterans. The RAF pilots were also operating at a disadvantage in that they were separated from their bases by the Channel – a short stretch of water that seemed never-ending when struggling to keep a combat-damaged aircraft airborne, as the Germans were also to find at a later date.

The Dunkirk experience, and the campaign in France that preceded it, produced a number of lessons for RAF Fighter Command; one was that armour plating behind the pilot's seat, far from reducing an aircraft's performance, saved valuable lives. Another was that German fighter tactics, based on the 'finger four' combat element of two pairs, were far superior to the British penchant for tight formations; and still another was that when the guns of a Spitfire or Hurricane were harmonized so that the shot converged at 250 yards, instead of 400, enemy aircraft that were attacked were shot down.

All these lessons, and the experience of the fighter pilots who had fought in France, would be assimilated throughout Fighter Command in time; but as the British Army strove to reorganize itself after Dunkirk, and as France collapsed in defeat late in June, it was apparent that time was something the RAF's fighter squadrons might not have.

Chapter 6
Spitfires in the Battle of Britain

BY 4 JUNE 1940, RAF Fighter Command had suffered such attrition that its first-line strength was reduced to 331 Spitfires and Hurricanes, with only thirty-six fighters in reserve. Within a month, however, the number of fighters available for operations had risen to 644, although the total included Boulton-Paul Defiants (which were to prove an utter disaster in the coming battle) and the fighter version of the Bristol Blenheim. Nineteen squadrons were equipped with Spitfires.

No attempt will be made in this chapter to repeat the often-told story of the Battle of Britain, except to summarize its events and highlight the part played by the Spitfire. Historians like to have neat start and finish dates for campaigns, and it is now generally accepted that the Battle of Britain began on 10 July 1940, when the *Luftwaffe* began attacking convoys in the English Channel, and ended on 31 October, when the Germans abandoned their daylight offensive. RAF Fighter Command, however, had been in action against the *Luftwaffe* over British territory almost since the beginning of the war, when the Auxiliary Air Force Spitfire squadrons made first contact with enemy bombers over Scotland; and in May 1940 the fighters were in action against enemy bombers making penetrations into eastern England. On the night of 18/19 May, for example, Spitfire pilots of No 19 Squadron shot down two Heinkel He 111 bombers over East Anglia; one of the Spitfires was hit by return fire and burst into flames, the pilot baling out.

There were further skirmishes over the English Channel and the North Sea in June 1940, with losses on both sides, and some authorities maintain that the so-called 'contact phase' of the Battle of Britain began as soon as the Battle of France ended. More realistically, perhaps, it may be said to have begun at the beginning of July, but in the first six days of the month only one Spitfire (P9449 of No 64 Squadron) was lost to enemy action, failing to return from a cross-Channel sortie. The other two Spitfires lost were K9928 of No 74 Squadron and N3294 of No 222 Squadron, both as a result of accidents. (K9928,

in fact, crashed with fatal consequences near Margate after being struck by lightning.)

On 7 July, following a night of sporadic air attacks on towns in southern England (Godalming, Aldershot, Haslemere and Farnborough) in which sixty-two people were killed, No 11 Group scrambled its fighters to intercept reconnaissance Dornier 17s (three of which were shot down by Hurricanes) and fighter sweeps over the south coast by Me 109s. In the morning the Messerschmitts bounced 'B' Flight of No 54 Squadron, damaging three Spitfires, and in the evening No 65 Squadron experienced a smiliar bounce, losing three Spitfires (N3129, R6609 and Err15). The Spitfires had taken off to intercept a formation of forty-five Dornier 17s attacking a convoy off Folkestone; two of the enemy bombers were damaged. It was hardly a promising start for the fighter defences.

On 8 July Fighter Command shot down seven enemy aircraft, including four Me 109s, for the loss of four, two of which were Spitfires. K9907 of No 65 Squadron was shot down and the pilot, Squadron Leader Cooke, killed. The pilot of R6634 of No 609 Squadron was more fortunate, baling out as his aircraft went down into the Channel. Four Spitfires were lost on 9 July, all the victims of Me 109s in skirmishes over the Channel: L1075 of No 603 Squadron, N3183 and R6705 of No 54 Squadron (Pilot Officer Evershed and Pilot Officer Garton) and R6637 of No 609 Squadron (Flying Officer Drummond-Hay). All the pilots were killed.

The first official day of the battle, 10 July, began with an attack by twenty-six Do 17s, escorted by six fighter *Staffeln* on a large convoy off Dover. Eight enemy aircraft were shot down for the loss of one Hurricane. Three Spitfires were compelled to make forced landings after suffering combat damage: they were K9863 and P9399 of No 74 Squadron (Plt Off Freeborn and Plt Off Cobden) and P9446 of No 54 Squadron (Sgt Mould). All the pilots were safe.

On 11 July, a day of very heavy air fighting over the Channel, the RAF shot down fifteen enemy aircraft for the loss of six, two of which were Spitfires. These were L1069 and L1095 of No 609

Squadron, shot down in combat with Me 109s of III/ JG 27 off Portland. Flt Lt P. H. Barran baled out of L1069, badly burned, and was picked up, but died later; the other pilot, Plt Off G. T. M. Mitchell, was posted missing. His body was washed ashore later.

During the next five days it was the Hurricane squadrons that bore the brunt of the fighting over the Channel convoys. Four Spitfires were lost in accidents, although several were damaged in combat. The only loss of 17 July was K9916 of No 603 Squadron, which took off from Turnhouse on an operational patrol; neither it nor its pilot, Flying Officer C. D. Peel, was seen again.

Two Spitfires were lost in the air combats of 18 July, which cost the RAF and the *Luftwaffe* five aircraft apiece. Flt Lt F. J. Howell of No 609 Squadron, Warmwell, was engaging a Junkers Ju 88 off Swanage when his aircraft was hit by return fire. He baled out and was rescued by a Royal Navy craft.

His Spitfire was R6634. Earlier in the day, Plt Off P. Litchfield of No 610 Squadron was shot down over the Channel by *Hauptmann* Tietzen of II/JG 51, the pilot being posted missing.

Fighter Command lost ten fighters against four German aircraft destroyed on 19 July. Six of the British aircraft were Boulton Paul Defiants, the others Hurricanes. On the following day Spitfire K9880 of No 152 Squadron from Warmwell went down into the Channel before the guns of *Oberleutnant* Homuth of III/JG 27; the pilot, Plt Off F. H. Posener, was posted missing. The other Spitfire was N3201 of No 610 Squadron, Biggin Hill, which had its tail shot off in a combat over Hawkinge by *Oberfeldwebel* Schmidt of I/JG 51. The pilot, Plt Off G. Keighley, baled out with minor injuries.

The Spitfire squadrons suffered no further combat losses before 24 July, when P9549 of No 54 Squadron was shot down by Me 109s of III/JG 26 near

Spitfires of No 616 Squadron landing after a sortie during the Battle of Britain.

The repair and overhaul of damaged Spitfires and Hurricanes was one of the major feats of the Battle of Britain. The aircraft is P9516 of No 222 Squadron.

Margate. The pilot, Flying Officer J. L. Allen, was killed. Another Spitfire, N3192, made a forced landing on the beach at Dunwich after it ran out of fuel and was written off, although the pilot was unhurt. Three more of No 54 Squadron's aircraft suffered combat damage, though all were repairable. No 66 Squadron, operating from Coltishall, lost Spitfire N3041, which came down in the sea during a patrol; the pilot, Sgt A. D. Smith, was picked up.

On 25 July the *Luftwaffe* adopted a change of tactics, sending out strong fighter sweeps to bring the RAF fighters to battle before launching its bomber attacks. As a result, sixty Ju 87 *Stukas* were able to bomb a convoy with impunity while the fighters of No 11 Group were on the ground refuelling. Later in the day, the convoy was attacked by thirty Ju 88s, escorted by Me 109s. The attacks continued until 18.30, and fifteen RAF fighter squadrons were engaged, losing nine aircraft. Seven of these were Spitfires, and once again No 54 Squadron from Rochford suffered badly, losing three aircraft. Flt Lt B. H. Way was shot down and killed in R6707

after a battle in the afternoon over the convoy between Dover and Deal in which he destroyed an Me 109, and in the same battle P9387 was written off in a forced landing near Dover after sustaining damage, Pilot Officer D. R. Turley-George escaping unhurt. In the later battle off Dover, Plt Off A. Finnie was killed when R6816 fell victim to the Me 109s.

No 64 Squadron from Kenley lost two aircraft: P9421 crashed into the sea off Dover in the middle of the afternoon and its pilot, Fg Off A. J. O. Jeffrey, lost his life. Later, L1035 also went down into the Channel, Sub-Lieutenant F. D. Paul being picked up badly wounded by the German air-sea rescue service. He died later in the month. Fg Off E. C. Deansley of No 152 Squadron, Warmwell, was also wounded in the course of a battle with Ju 87s and went down into the sea with K9901, but was rescued by the SS *Empire Henchman*. Squadron Leader A. T. Smith of No 610 Squadron, Biggin Hill, was killed while attempting to land at Hawkinge in R6693 after being hit by Me 109s, but on the credit side No 610 Squadron destroyed four Me

Typical of their time: pilots of No 41 Squadron, with mascots, at their dispersal, August 1940.

109s. The *Luftwaffe*'s total combat loss for 25 July was thirteen aircraft.

Operations were severely hampered by poor weather on 26 and 27 July, one Spitfire being lost during this 48-hour period: this was N3023 of No 609 Squadron, Warmwell, which was shot down by *Oberleutnant* Framm of I/JG 27 in a combat over a convoy off Weymouth. Plt Off J. R. Buchanan was posted missing. The weather again restricted operations on 28 July, a day in which Fighter Command lost four aircraft in combat – two of them Spitfires – against the *Luftwaffe*'s nine. The two Spitfire squadrons principally engaged on 28 July were No 41 from Manston and No 74 from Hornchurch, the former accounting for at least three Me 109s. No 74 Squadron lost P9336, shot down by Me 109s of 9/

JG 26; the pilot, Sgt E. A. Mould, baled out wounded. P9547 of No 74 Squadron also failed to return, being shot down into the Channel by *Oberleutnant* Müncheberg of III/JG 26. Plt Off J. H. R. Young was killed.

Monday, 29 July, was a bad day for No 41 Squadron, which lost three Spitfires together with two more badly damaged, but repairable. All the casualties occurred in an early morning combat with a strongly-escorted force of Ju 87s attacking a convoy off Dover. The first Spitfire to be lost, at 07.45, was N3038, Fg Off D. R. Gamblen being posted missing. Five minutes later, N3100 was also badly hit; Fg Off W. J. Scott escaped from a crash-landing that destroyed the aircraft at Manston. A quarter-of-an-hour later, Plt Off G. H. Bennions also wrote off his battle-damaged N3264 in an emergency landing at Manston. The other Spitfire loss of the day occurred in the afternoon, when Plt Off L. W. Collingridge crashed on the beach at Orfordness after attacking a Heinkel He 111; he escaped with injuries, but N3042 of No 66 Squadron was a write-off. The RAF lost six fighters in combat on this day; the *Luftwaffe*'s loss was thirteen, including eleven bombers.

There were no Spitfire combat losses on 30 July, but on the last day of the month No 74 Squadron lost P9398 and P9379, together with their pilots, Sgt F. W. Eley and Plt Off H. R. Gunn. Both were shot down off Folkestone by Me 109s of 4/JG 51.

Spitfire Deliveries and Losses (All Causes) July 1940

	Into Service	Damaged (Repairable)	Destroyed	Hurricane Losses	
				Damaged	Destroyed
1	2	2	–	–	1
2	2	4	–	–	–
3	–	–	1	1	–
4	–	1	1	1	–
5	1	5	1	–	–
6	–	2	–	–	–
7	5	2	4	–	2
8	–	4	2	–	–
9	3	2	4	2	–
10	5	6	–	3	2
11	5	2	3	3	4
12	12	1	1	5	3
13	14	2	2	4	4
14	11	–	–	1	1
15	–	3	–	2	2
16	5	1	–	2	1
17	2	2	1	2	–
18	3	7	2	1	–
19	2	4	–	3	4
20	7	1	2	3	6
21	8	–	1	6	1
22	10	3	–	–	2
23	3	3	–	1	2
24	6	5	3	1	2
25	3	7	7	3	1
26	7	4	–	1	1
27	6	–	1	1	1
28	8	5	3	1	3
29	4	4	4	6	1
30	7	2	–	–	–
31	2	3	3	–	2
Totals:	83	51	27	31	27

The first week of August 1940 was notable for its lack of activity; there had been no really heavy attacks on Channel convoys since 25 July. Almost all the losses on both sides in the first few days of August were attributable to accidents, although on Monday, 5 August Nos 64 and 65 Squadrons lost a Spitfire each (L1029 and P9436) in a morning battle with Me 109s of JG 54 off Dover. Then, on 8 August, the Germans launched a very heavy attack on a convoy between Dover and Wight, and the battle was on once more.

Nos 64, 65, 152, 609 and 610 Squadrons were in the thick of the fighting, the first three losing five aircraft between them. No 64 Squadron, hotly en-gaged by Me 109s of III/JG 51 north of Dover, lost P9369 and L1039; the first was bounced by *Hauptmann* Johannes Trautloft and its injured pilot, Sergeant J. W. C. Squier, survived the subsequent forced landing, but Plt Off P. F. Kennard-Davis baled out of the other aircraft with serious wounds and died two days later. Spitfire K9911 of No 65 Squadron was shot down in flames over Manston by a Me 109 of 9/JG 26 and its pilot, Sgt D. I. Kirton was killed, as was his colleague Flt Sgt N. T. Phillips in K9905, shot down in the same place during the same action five minutes later. In the afternoon, the Spitfires of No 145 Squadron tangled with Me 109s of II/JG 53, losing R6811; Sgt D. N. Robinson baled out

Spitfire X417? (the last digit of the serial appears to be missing) runs up at its dispersal. Note the patches over the gun ports to prevent icing at altitude.

unhurt. The RAF suffered heavily that day, losing eighteen fighters (thirteen of which were Hurricanes), but the *Luftwaffe*'s combat losses were higher: ten Me 109s, three Me 110s and nine Ju 87s.

Friday, 9 August was relatively quiet, although No 64 Squadron had three Spitfires damaged in combat with Me 109s during a patrol. The only *Luftwaffe* losses of the day were two Heinkel He 111s, shot down while making reconnaissance sorties over the north-east coast. The next day was even quieter, operations being confined to a few sorties by aircraft of Bomber Command against enemy airfields at Cherbourg and Schipol.

However, the fighting on Sunday, 11 August, proved to be the heaviest so far. In the morning, 165 German bombers escorted by Me 109s and Me 110s made heavy attacks on Portland and Weymouth; eight RAF fighter squadrons intercepting in mid-Channel were heavily engaged by the fighter escort, allowing the bombers to slip through. The *Luftwaffe* also made separate attacks on a Channel convoy. The heaviest Spitfire losses of the day were sustained by No 74 Squadron, whose first casualty was P9393, shot down into the Channel off Dover while attempting a lone attack on twelve Me 109s. Its pilot, Plt Off P. C. F. Stevenson, baled out and was rescued from the Channel by an MTB. Later in

The Junkers Ju 87 *Stuka* suffered badly in combat with RAF fighters; this gun-camera sequence shows one going down over the south coast on 15 August 1940.

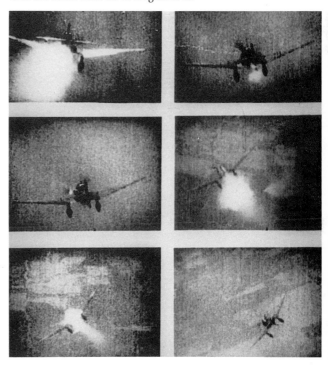

the day, R6757 and R6962 were shot down in combat with Me 110s east of Harwich; both pilots, Pilot Officers D. G. Cobden and D. N. E. Smith, were killed. Pilot Officer J. S. B. Jones, flying R6614 of No 152 Squadron, also lost his life in a mid-Channel fight against Me 109s. No 610 Squadron sent two Spitfires, R6918 and R6630, to patrol off Calais late in the morning, and both failed to return. The pilot of the former, Flt Sgt J. H. Tanner, was confirmed killed, and the other pilot, Sgt W. J. Neville, was posted missing. In addition to the six Spitfires lost, four more were damaged; but it was the Hurricane squadrons that suffered the most severely, with twenty-two aircraft shot down and thirteen damaged. The *Luftwaffe* lost thirty-five aircraft.

On 12 August, as a preliminary to their main air offensive, the Germans sent bomb-carrying Me 109s and 110s of *Erprobungsgruppe 210*, together with Ju 88s of KG 51 and KG 54, to attack radar stations on the south coast, putting the one at Ventnor on the Isle of Wight out of action and damaging three others. While these attacks were in progress, Dornier 17s of KG 2 raided the airfield at Lympne, causing some damage; a convoy in the Thames Estuary was also bombed by *Stukas*. In the afternoon, Manston was attacked and temporarily put out of action by *Erprobungsgruppe 210*, while enemy bombers struck at Hawkinge and again at Lympne, causing heavy damage to both airfields. By nightfall on 12 August, *Luftflotten* 2 and 3 had sent 300 bombers against British targets.

During the day's fighting the Hurricane and Spitfire squadrons lost eleven and seven aircraft respectively, with eleven of each type damaged. Of the seven Spitfires, one, X4018 of No 64 Squadron, was shot down by Me 109s over the south coast in the afternoon; its pilot, Plt Off A. G. Donahue, baled out, although he had suffered extensive burns. No 152 Squadron lost two aircraft, P9456 and K9999, both of which went down in an engagement with Ju 88s off the Isle of Wight shortly after noon. Their pilots, Flt. Lt L. C. Withall and Plt Off D. C. Shepley, were both listed as missing. No 266 Squadron from Tangmere also lost two Spitfires, N3175 and P9333, in action against Ju 88s in the Portsmouth-Isle of Wight area; Plt Off W. S. Williams made a forced landing in the former aircraft and escaped from the burning wreck, but Plt Off D. G. Ashton was lost with his aircraft. His body was later recovered and buried at sea. No 610 Squadron from Biggin Hill, in action against Me 109s over New Romney early in the morning, lost

Spitfire Mk I R6923 of No 92 Squadron first flew in July 1940 and was later converted to Mk V configuration.

L1044 and P9495; both pilots escaped, although one (Plt Off E. B. B. Smith) was burned. The *Luftwaffe's* loss in the day's action was twenty-seven aircraft.

Tuesday, 13 August 1940, is the day that has gone down in history as the start of Operation *Adler Angriff* (Eagle Attack), the air offensive against England. Its initial objective was to neutralize RAF Fighter Command by striking at its airfields, and by drawing the fighter squadrons into combat. H-Hour at 07.30 was postponed because of bad weather, but the Dorniers of KG 2 failed to receive the order and set out over the Channel without fighter escort. They were attacked over the Thames Estuary and five bombers were shot down, although the remainder caused heavy damage to Sheerness and Eastchurch. In the afternoon, Ju 87s of *Stukageschwader 2*, escorted by Me 109s of JG 53, set out to attack RAF airfields in the Portland area. They were engaged by Spitfires of No 609 Squadron and four *Stukas* were shot down. Soon afterwards, Ju 88s bombed Southampton harbour and the airfields of Middle Wallop and Andover.

Over Kent, fighters of No 11 Group were heavily engaged against *Stukas* of *VIII Fliegerkorps*, which had carried out heavy attacks on several airfields. The hardest hit was Detling, which was bombed by 86 Ju 87s. At the close of the day the *Luftwaffe* had flown 485 sorties, mostly against RAF airfields; three had been badly damaged, but none was a fighter base.

The brunt of the air fighting was borne by the Hurricane squadrons, which lost twelve aircraft, with thirteen more damaged. Only one Spitfire was lost in combat; this was N3091 of No 74 Squadron, shot down by return fire from a Dornier 17 of KG 2 over the Thames Estuary. Its pilot, Flt Lt S. Brzezina, baled out unhurt. The *Luftwaffe* lost thirty-four aircraft.

On the next day operations were frustrated by bad weather. Only one major raid was carried out by Me 110s of *Erprobungsgruppe 210*, which attacked Manston and lost two aircraft. The RAF lost one Spitfire – N3024 of No 609 Squadron – along with its pilot, Fg Off H. McD. Goodwin. Six other Spitfires were damaged. The Hurricane squadrons lost five aircraft, with five damaged, and the *Luftwaffe* lost nineteen, mostly in sporadic actions involving aircraft operating along the south coast in ones and twos.

It was to be a far different story on Thursday, 15 August, which turned out to be the heaviest day's fighting of the whole battle.

In the morning, 40 *Stukas* of *II Fliegerkorps*, escorted by a similar number of Me 109s, attacked Lympne and Hawkinge airfields, causing severe damage to the former. At the same time, aircraft of *Luftflotte 5* from Norway and Denmark launched a major attack on north-east England. Flying from Stavanger, sixty-three Heinkel 111s of KG 26, escorted by twenty-one Me 110s of ZG 76, made landfall on the Northumbrian coast and were intercepted by Spitfires of Nos 41 and 72 Squadrons and

Next to the RAF, it was the Polish fighter squadrons that made the biggest contribution to victory in the Battle of Britain. Later in the war, Fighter Command's Spitfire squadrons became truly cosmopolitan. Here, pilots of No 340 *Ile-de-France* Free French squadron carry out a practice scramble.

Hurricanes of Nos 79, 605 and 607 Squadrons, which destroyed eight Heinkels and six Me 110s for the loss of one No 79 Squadron Hurricane which was written off in a forced landing after sustaining combat damage. Forty Junkers Ju 88s, attempting to attack airfields in Yorkshire, were engaged by Hurricanes of No 73 and Spitfires of No 616 Squadrons and six were shot down, although the attack badly damaged RAF Driffield and destroyed several Whitley bombers on the ground. No RAF fighters were lost.

In the afternoon, the airfields of Eastchurch and Rochester were heavily bombed by the Dornier Do 17s of KG 3 and severe damage was inflicted on the Shorts aircraft factory at the latter, setting back production of the Stirling bomber by several months. Eleven RAF fighter squadrons were scrambled to intercept the incoming raids, but these became involved with the massive enemy fighter escort. In addition, the airfield of Martlesham Heath was severely damaged by the bomb-carrying Messerschmitts of *Erprobungsgruppe 210* and put out of action for thirty-six hours. At 17.00, a mixed formation of Ju 87s and Ju 88s, again under heavy escort – about 200 aircraft in all – attempted to attack airfields on the south coast. They were engaged by fourteen fighter squadrons and suffered very heavy losses. In the evening, twenty-three Messerschmitts of *Erprobungsgruppe 210* bombed Croydon, south London, in mistake for Kenley. Six Me 110s and an Me 109 were shot down by Hurricanes of Nos 31 and 111 Squadrons and by Spitfires of No 66 Squadron. This brought the day's combat losses for the *Luftwaffe* to seventy-one aircraft, mostly bombers and Me 110s. Fighter Command's loss was thirty. This total included twelve Spitfires; seven more were damaged. No 54 Squadron, Hornchurch, lost N3097, R7015 and R6981; the pilot of the former, Sgt N. A. Lawrence, had just shot down a Ju 87 off Dover when he fell victim to an Me 109. He baled out and was picked up from the Channel, severely shocked. The other two pilots, Sgt W. Klozinsky and Flt Lt A. C. Deere, also had lucky escapes, taking to their parachutes with relatively minor injuries – a sprained wrist, in Al Deere's case.

No 64 Squadron at Kenley lost R6990 and its pilot, Fg Off C. J. D. Andreae, and also K9964, which chased an Me 109 across the Channel and got itself shot down at Calais-Marck. The pilot, Plt Off R. Roberts, survived to face a long war in PoW camp. No 152 Squadron at Warmwell lost K9954, badly damaged in combat off Portland; Flt Lt P. B. A.

Boitel-Gill brought it back to base, but it was written off in a crash landing from which he emerged unhurt. No 234 Squadron, engaging enemy fighters off Swanage, lost four aircraft: R6998 (Plt Off C. H. Hight, killed), P9363 (unnamed pilot safe), N3277 and R6985. The pilots of the last two, Pilot Officers R. Hardy and V. Parker, had allowed the fight to take them across the Channel as far as Cherbourg, where they were shot down and taken prisoner. No 266 Squadron, Hornchurch, lost N3189 and N3168, together with both pilots.

The day's fighting had proved a point; that it was the Me 109 which was causing the Spitfire and Hurricane squadrons their biggest problems. In the northern air battle, the RAF had easily mastered the Me 110. As the weeks went by, the Me 110 units would continue to suffer appalling losses. On 16 August the *Luftwaffe* attacked eight RAF airfields in the south, but only three of them were fighter airfields. Forty-six training aircraft were destroyed in an attack on Harwell, and the radar station at Ventnor was attacked again. In the afternoon, poor weather frustrated further attempts by the *Luftwaffe* to mount airfield attacks; nevertheless, air combats during the day cost the *Luftwaffe* forty-four aircraft and Fighter Command twenty-six, some of which were destroyed on the ground.

Of this number eleven were Spitfires, nine more being damaged. No 64 Squadron, Kenley, lost P9554, shot down by an Me 109, but Sqn Ldr A. R. D. MacDonnell baled out unhurt. No 65 Squadron had K6618 destroyed in a strafing attack on Manston, while K9915 was shot down off Deal and its pilot, Plt Off L. L. Pyman, killed. No 234 Squadron, in No 10 Group's area at Middle Wallop, lost R6967 and X4016 in combat with Me 109s over Southampton, but both pilots (Flying Officers K. S. Dewhurst and F. H. P. Conner) baled out and were saved.

No 266 Squadron, Hornchurch, took the worst casualties of any Spitfire unit on this day, losing R6768, N3240, N3095, P9312 and K9864 in combat with Me 109s over Canterbury. Three of the pilots, Sqn Ldr R. L. Wilkinson, Sub-Lieut H. L. Greenshields and Plt Off N. G. Bowen, were killed; the other two, Flt Lt S. H. Bazley and Plt Off S. F. Soden, baled out. No 610 Squadron, Biggin Hill, lost R6802 and its pilot, Flt Lt W. H. C. Warner.

Bad weather brought a merciful, if brief respite for the hard-pressed squadrons of Fighter Command on 17 August, and there were no combat losses. On 18 August, however, the *Luftwaffe* launched a series of heavy attacks on the important sector stations of Kenley and Biggin Hill. Kenley was badly hit, and its operations room put out of action. In the afternoon, a strong force of bombers attacked the airfields at Ford, Gosport and Thorney Island. The aircraft involved were the *Stukas* of *VIII Fliegerkorps*, and they ventured over the coast with inadequate fighter escort. They were engaged by the Hurricanes of No 43 and the Spitfires of Nos 152 and 602 Squadrons and eighteen aircraft of the Caen-based StG 77 were destroyed.

The *Luftwaffe* lost sixty aircraft in the day's fighting, the RAF thirty-four. The Hurricane squadrons took a terrible mauling, losing twenty-nine fighters, some in airfield attacks, with a further thirteen damaged. The Spitfire squadrons, on the other hand, escaped relatively lightly, with five aircraft destroyed and fourteen damaged. Six of the latter were hit in a surprise attack by Me 109s on No 266 Squadron's base at Hornchurch; two more, X4061 and X4066, were destroyed in the same attack just after they had landed to refuel. The other Spitfires lost that day were R6713 of No 65 Squadron (Fg Off F. Gruszka killed); N3040 of No 92 Squadron (Flt Lt R. R. S. Tuck baled out slightly injured); and L1019 of No 602 Squadron, which ditched after being hit by return fire from a Ju 87. Its pilot, Sgt B. E. P. Whall, escaped unhurt.

Meanwhile, behind the scenes, events were unfolding which would help to change the course of the battle. The devastation of another sector station

on 18 August added to Dowding's and Park's already crushing anxieties, and the next day Park ordered his pilots to pay more attention to the enemy's bomber formations and less to tangling with the Me 109s. The 'Tally Ho' procedure was introduced, formation leaders having to give the 'Tally Ho' call as soon as the enemy was sighted, stating height, course, number of enemy aircraft and approximate position. It was stressed that the enemy bombers must be intercepted before they reached their targets.

By coincidence, *Reichsmarschall* Hermann Göring, already nervous over the fact that his squadrons were failing to achieve their objectives despite the casualties they were taking, also called a conference of his senior commanders on 19 August. He stressed the importance of wearing down the British defences by day and night; he gave the fighters more freedom, although still tying them to their escort duties, and fighter leaders who did not show enough fighting spirit were soon replaced by younger and more daring ones. Göring also mentioned switching part of the offensive to industrial targets whose destruction had little to do with the primary objective of defeating Fighter Command. Time was passing; unfavourable weather prevented large German attacks between 19 and 23 August, and the German Propaganda Minister, Josef Goebbels, began to prepare the German people for the possibility that the war might drag on well into the coming winter.

K9912 served with No 65 Squadron, and then as a Rolls-Royce test-bed after being damaged on operations in 1940.

During the period 19–23 August the emphasis was on precision attacks by enemy bombers operating singly or in small numbers and flown by experienced crews used to poor weather conditions. Three Spitfires were lost while intercepting this type of raid on 19 August. N3182 of No 66 Squadron, in No 12 Group's area at Coltishall, was hit by return fire from a He 111 and crashed in the sea off Orfordness; its pilot, Plt Off J. A. P. Studd, was picked up by a lifeboat but died without regaining consciousness. No 92 Squadron lost R6703 to return fire from a Ju 88 over the Solent; Plt Off T. S. Wade got out unhurt. The third loss was P9423 of No 602 Squadron, shot down in flames off Bognor by a Ju 88; Plt Off H. W. Moody escaped with slight burns.

A skirmish over the Thames Estuary on 20 August cost No 65 Squadron R6818, damaged and forced down by an Me 109. The aircraft was a write-off, but Plt Off G. K. Hart escaped unscathed. On the next day the scene once again shifted to No 12 Group's area, No 611 Squadron being scrambled from Digby in Lincolnshire to intercept a raiding force of Dornier 17s off Skegness. Six Dorniers were destroyed and four Spitfires damaged, but all were repairable.

The Me 109s were once again out over the Channel on 22 August and got the best of their encounter with the Spitfires, which lost four aircraft for nothing in return. Sgt G. R. Collett was killed when R6708 of No 54 Squadron was shot down off Deal, and Sgt M. Keymer suffered a similar fate when K9909 of No 65 Squadron went down off Dover. Sgt D. F. Corfe was luckier, parachuting to safety when R6695 of No 610 Squadron was shot down in flames over Folkestone in the afternoon; Fg Off H. S. L. Dundas of No 616 Squadron, Kenley, also had a lucky escape when cannon shells from Me 109s set his R6296 ablaze over Dover; he managed to bale out despite wounds in his arms and legs.

There were no Spitfire losses on 23 August, but on the following day the *Luftwaffe*, taking advantage of clearing weather, renewed its intensive attacks on Fighter Command. They were to last for two weeks, and marked a crucial phase in the battle. Both sides had used the break to reinforce; the fighters of *Luftflotte 3* in Normandy were moved to reinforce those of *Luftflotte 2* in the Pas de Calais, while the RAF took deliveries of replacement fighters – receiving, for example, a much-needed injection of sixty Spitfires from 19–24 August. The provision of adequate aircraft reserves was not yet causing serious concern, but the supply of trained pilots was, especially to the battered Hurricane squadrons.

On 24 August several airfields were heavily bombed, including Manston – which ceased to function by mid-day – Hornchurch and North Weald, as well as Portsmouth naval base. The RAF destroyed thirty enemy aircraft and lost twenty, although this figure included four Boulton-Paul Defiants of No 264 Squadron and a Blenheim, shot down by friendly fire. The losses included six Spitfires, with five more damaged but repairable. No 54 Squadron lost P9389 (Plt Off C. Stewart baled out injured); No 65 Squadron's R6884 went down with its pilot off Margate; No 234 Squadron lost N3239 to an Me 109 of I/JG 53 over the Isle of Wight, Plt Off Jan Zurakowski baling out; and No 610 Squadron lost R6686, X4102 and a third aircraft whose serial number is unrecorded, all three pilots (Sgt S. J. Arnfield, Plt Off D. McI. Gray and Plt Off C. Merrick) escaping with slight injuries.

On Sunday, 25 August, heavily-escorted formations of bombers attacked Portland, Weymouth and Warmwell airfield, although the Warmwell attack was broken up by Hurricanes of No 17 Squadron and the base suffered only minor damage. Dover was heavily attacked in the early evening. The *Luftwaffe* lost twenty aircraft and the RAF eighteen, of which eight were Spitfires: N3268 of No 92 Squadron (Flt Lt R. R. S. Tuck, crash-landed after engagement with Do 215); R6810 and R6994 of No 152 Squadron (Plt Off R. M. Hogg and Plt Off T. S. Wildblood) missing over Channel after fight with Me 109s; N3226 and P9381 of No 602 Squadron, shot down in combat with enemy fighters (Sgt M. H. Sprague and Fg Off W. H. Coverley baled out); K9931 of No 610 Squadron, shot down over Dover (Fg Off F. T. Gardiner baled out with slight wounds); and R6966 and K9819 of No 616 Squadron, shot down in the Channel (Sgt T. E. Westmoreland missing, Sgt P. T. Wareing PoW.)

From 11.00 on 26 August, No 11 Group fought a running battle between Canterbury and Maidstone against fifty German bombers escorted by eighty fighters. In this action No 616 Squadron lost no fewer than seven Spitfires, although five of the pilots were saved. The aircraft were R6701 (Plt Off W. L. B. Wood, baled out wounded); R6632 (Fg Off J. S. Bell uninjured); R7018 (crash-landed, Fg Off E. F. St Aubin burned); R6633 (Sgt M. Ridley killed); N3275 (Fg Off G. E. Moberley killed); K9827 (Sgt P. Copeland wounded); and R6758 (Plt Off R. Marples wounded). All these aircraft were the victims of Me 109s; Göring's policy of reinforcing *Luftflotte 2* seemed to be paying dividends.

Four other Spitfires were lost that day. X4188 of No 602 Squadron was shot down by an Me 109 over Selsey Bill, Sgt C. F. Babbage parachuting clear, while No 610 Squadron lost R6595, R6970 and P9496, all to Me 109s. Plt Off F. K. Webster was killed in the first aircraft, R6970's unnamed pilot escaped, and Sgt P. Else baled out with serious injuries.

All available fighter squadrons were committed to intercept a further attack by forty Dornier 17s, escorted by 120 fighters, on Debden and Hornchurch airfields; the latter was compelled to withdraw through lack of fuel and the poorly-armed bombers suffered heavily. A third major attack, by fifty He 111s escorted by 107 fighters, was intercepted by three RAF squadrons and eight bombers were destroyed for the loss of four British aircraft. This marked the last major daylight operation by KG 3 for three weeks. Total losses for the day were thirty-four German, twenty-seven British; Fighter Command was now coming under immense strain.

Tuesday, 27 August was again a day of poor weather, the *Luftwaffe* confining its activities to a few individual night bombing and day reconnaissance sorties. While attempting to intercept a Ju 88 on one of the latter missions, Pilot Officer W. Beaumont of No 152 Squadron was hit by return fire and forced to abandon R6831 off Portland. Two more Spitfires, K9922 of No 72 Squadron at Acklington and P9548 of No 92 Squadron, Pembrey, were lost in accidents, both pilots being unhurt.

The action resumed on 28 August, with Eastchurch and Rochford airfields the main targets. In the air battles that day the *Luftwaffe* lost twenty-six aircraft, the RAF seventeen – four of them the luckless Boulton Paul Defiants of No 264 Squadron, which had lost twelve aircraft and fourteen aircrew in three operational sorties. The Defiant was at last withdrawn from the daylight battle.

Almost all the Spitfire casualties sustained on 28 August were incurred by the Hornchurch Wing, where No 54 Squadron was now joined by No 603 – replacing No 65 Squadron, sent north to Turnhouse for a rest. No 54 Squadron's first casualty of the day was Flt Lt Al Deere, forced to take to his parachute yet again when R6832 was shot down by another Spitfire during an attack on a Me 109; the second was X4053, shot down in combat with Me 109s over Ramsgate in the afternoon. Sqn Ldr D. O. Finlay baled out wounded.

No 603 Squadron, going straight into action on its arrival at Hornchurch, lost three Spitfires almost immediately during the afternoon's fighting. R6751 and L1046 were shot down into the Channel, Flt Lt J. L. G. Cunningham and Plt Off D. K. MacDonald being posted missing, while N3105 crashed in flames after a fight with an Me 109, crashing at Tenterden with the loss of its pilot, Plt Off N. J. V. Benson. The other Spitfire loss of the day was P9511 of No 610 Squadron, shot down over Dover. Plt Off K. H. Cox was killed.

That night, *Luftflotte 3* switched to night bombing, and on the next three nights attacked Liverpool four times. This marked the beginning of a major switch in the *Luftwaffe*'s policy and would ultimately lead to a relief of the pressure on Fighter Command, although this was not yet apparent to Dowding. One of his greatest anxieties during this period of immense strain was the loss of experienced pilots, and so he decided to form three categories of squadrons in order to make the best use of the experience available to him. The squadrons of No 11 Group and those on the immediate flanks, bearing the brunt of the fighting, would be in the 'A' Category. A few outside squadrons were to be in the 'B' Category and maintained at operational strength to relieve 'A' Category squadrons as required. The remaining squadrons were to be placed in the 'C' Category and stripped of their operational pilots for the benefit of the 'A' Category squadrons, and would devote their energies in the main to training new pilots.

Fighter Command's policy of avoiding combat with the Messerschmitts whenever possible was apparent on 29 August. On this day the *Luftwaffe* launched 700 fighter sorties over southern England in an attempt to draw the RAF into battle, but Dowding's squadrons did not respond. This led the Germans, lacking as they were in adequate intelligence, to conclude that they were on the verge of achieving air supremacy. They were wrong.

There were some fighter-versus-fighter combats on 29 August, however, and the RAF lost ten aircraft, four of them Spitfires. No 603 Squadron lost R6753 (Plt Off D. J. C. Pinckney baled out slightly burned) and L1021, the latter crash-landing. Its pilot, Plt Off R. H. Hillary, escaped unhurt. Sgt A. C. Baker also walked away unharmed from the wreck of 610 Squadron's X4011 at Gatwick after a fight with Me 110s, but Sgt E. Manton was killed when R6629 was shot down in combat over Mayfield. The *Luftwaffe* lost twelve aircraft during the day, mostly Me 109s.

Friday, 30 August, began with a fighter sweep across Kent by fifty Me 109s; again, the RAF did not respond. Later, a major attack by 150 bombers, escorted by Me 110s, was broken up by fighters of No 11 Group. From 13.00 onwards, successive waves of bombers and their fighter escorts crossed the coast at twenty-minute intervals. A hit on the electricity grid temporarily disabled seven radar stations. Biggin Hill was severely damaged, and control of its Sector operations transferred to Hornchurch. The Vauxhall works at Luton were attacked and fifty-three people killed. In the day's air combats the RAF lost twenty-five fighters, but the *Luftwaffe* lost thirty-eight aircraft; thirteen of these were Me 109s and six Me 110s. For the Germans, it was a sharp lesson that Dowding's squadrons had a lot of fight left in them.

Eleven Spitfires failed to return or were destroyed in accidents. In No 12 Group's area, No 66 Squadron at Coltishall lost R6715, shot down into the sea during an attack on a Do 17. The pilot, Plt Off J. H. T. Pickering, was rescued unhurt by a light vessel. Up the road at Kirton-in-Lindsey, Sgt W. M. Skinner of 74 Squadron also baled out unhurt from X4022 after a mid-air collision with X4027 (which landed with repairable damage).

In the thick of the fighting in No 11 Group's area, No 222 Squadron, operating alongside No 54 Squadron at Hornchurch, lost six Spitfires and had three more damaged. The losses, which were all sustained in combat with Me 109s, were P9325 (Sgt S. Baxter unhurt after forced landing); P9375 (Plt Off Carpenter baled out unhurt); K9826 (Plt Off H. P. M. Eldridge baled out with burns); R6628 (Sgt J. I. Johnson killed); P9443 (Flt Lt G. C. Matheson seriously injured); and P9323 (Sgt A. W. P. Spears unhurt). The other Hornchurch squadron, No 603, lost L1067, shot down in combat with Me 110s over Deal; Sqn Ldr G. L. Denholm baled out unhurt, as did Sgt A. R. Sarre of the same squadron when an Me 109 shot off the tail of his R7021. At Kenley, No 616 Squadron lost L1012 together with its pilot, Fg Off J. S. Bell.

On the last day of August the *Luftwaffe* once again attempted to draw Fighter Command into battle by sending over high-flying fighter sweeps. Later, thirteen fighter squadrons were scrambled to intercept 200 raiders approaching the Thames Estuary. Fighters of No 12 Group broke up an attack on RAF Duxford, and intercepted another on Debden in time to avert severe damage. Croydon, Biggin Hill and Hornchurch were all badly hit. Casualties during the day's fighting were very heavy, the *Luftwaffe* losing thirty-two aircraft and Fighter Command forty-two.

Some of the RAF fighters were caught on the ground; even so, combat losses were bad enough, amounting to twenty-eight Hurricanes and eight Spitfires. The majority of the Hurricane losses in combat were attributable to Me 110s, which gave the Germans a false impression that the twin-engined Messerschmitt could hold its own in action with single-engined fighters, but they were to be sorely disillusioned before long.

At Duxford, No 19 Squadron, which had been carrying out trials with 20-mm cannon during August with little success, lost three Spitfires on the 31st. X4231 was shot down in flames during an attack on Dornier 17s ten miles east of the airfield, its pilot, Fg. Off J. B. Coward, baling out badly wounded in the leg, which he subsequently lost. Fg Off F. N. Brinsden baled out of R6958 unhurt after being hit in a combat over the Thames Estuary, but Plt Off R. A. C. Aeberhardt lost his life while attempting to land R6912 at Fowlmere after suffering combat damage.

At Hornchurch, No 54 Squadron had three Spitfires destroyed in a bombing attack on the airfield. Flt Lt Al Deere's charmed life continued, the pilot crawling from the wreck of an inverted R6895 with only slight injuries, while Plt Off E. F. Edsall escaped completely unhurt from X4236 when it crashed on the runway after losing a wing. The other loss was N3110, which was unoccupied. Sgt J. Davis had a very lucky escape when X4235, damaged by bomb blast, crashed in the River Ingrebourne just outside the airfield perimeter; the aircraft was later repaired. No 54 Squadron's other loss of the day was X4054, which was thought to have been shot down by a Hurricane after its pilot, Sgt D. G. Gibbins, had disposed of an Me 109. He baled out unharmed.

No 72 Squadron, Biggin Hill, lost Spitfires P9438 (Flt Lt F. M. Smith baled out wounded and badly burned) and P9457 (Fg Off E. J. Wilcox killed), both aircraft destroyed in combat with Me 109s over Dungeness. Plt Off C. G. A. Davies of No 222 Squadron, Hornchurch, also suffered burns after falling victim in P9337 to an Me 109 over Ashford. In addition, No 222 Squadron lost P9360 and P9505 in the raid on Hornchurch. The other Hornchurch squadron, No 603, lost X4273 and its pilot, Fg Off R. M. Waterston, in combat with Me 109s of I/JG 53 over London, and X4271, whose pilot had a bad experience. Baling out of his blazing aircraft over east London, Plt Off G. K. Gilroy landed safely, only to be attacked by an outraged crowd who mistook him for a German. Luckily, he was rescued and taken to hospital, where he recovered.

As August ended, Fighter Command's situation was becoming critical, particularly in the area of replacement pilots, some of whom were reaching the front-line squadrons with as little as twenty hours' experience on Spitfires and Hurricanes. As yet, the squadrons of No 12 Group north of the Thames had not yet been committed in strength to the battle; but before long, necessity would alter that.

Spitfire Deliveries and Losses, August 1940 (All Causes)

	Into Service	Damaged (Repairable)	Destroyed	Hurricane Losses Damaged	Destroyed
1	4	2	1	1	1
2	–	–	3	1	–
3	3	1	–	–	–
4	2	–	1	–	–
5	–	2	2	–	–
6	2	3	2	–	3
7	4	1	2	2	1
8	4	3	6	6	13
9	7	4	–	–	2
10	6	1	–	–	–
11	8	4	6	13	22
12	3	7	11	11	11
13	18	6	2	13	12
14	18	6	1	5	5
15	8	7	12	20	18
16	19	9	11	9	15
17	18	–	–	1	1
18	9	14	5	13	29
19	29	1	3	–	1
20	3	–	1	–	1
21	17	6	–	2	1
22	1	4	3	3	–
23	4	2	–	3	1
24	6	5	6	7	9
25	5	3	8	3	8
26	10	4	11	13	14
27	12	–	3	2	2
28	4	1	6	4	6
29	2	2	4	2	6
30	12	8	11	9	14
31	7	4	14	11	28
Totals:	245	110	136	154	227

From these figures, it will be seen that Spitfire deliveries were able to keep pace with losses throughout the month, although a great deal depended on the repair and maintenance organization. Deliveries up to the end of this period included sixty-six Spitfire Mk IIs produced by the Nuffield factory at Castle Bromwich. The differences between the Mk I and Mk II were minor, the principal one being that the Mk II had a Merlin XII engine that ran on 100 octane fuel and used a Coffman cartridge starter instead of the trolley-accumulator. The Mk II also had 73 lb of armour plate fitted on the production line, whereas the Mk I's armour was fitted in service. A total of 920 Mk IIs were built, 750 as Mk IIA and 170 as Mk IIB, all in the 'P' serial range.

Many of the fighter pilots joining their squadrons early in September 1940 did not survive their first sortie, such was their lack of experience. Others managed to hang on and found themselves being catapulted from the lowly status of new boys to section and even flight commanders in record time. The onslaught against the airfields continued; on 1 September 120 bombers attacked Biggin Hill, Eastchurch and Detling, and in the afternoon the *Luftwaffe* sent two major fighter sweeps over southern England. Under cover of this diversion, a small number of Do 17s made a low-level attack on Biggin Hill, wrecking the Sector Operations Room and all communications. Bristol, south Wales, the Midlands and Merseyside were attacked during the night. The RAF lost fourteen fighters during the day, with nine more damaged. No 72 Squadron at Croydon was badly hit, losing three Spitfires with four more badly damaged in combat with Me 109s in the Hythe area. The losses were P9448 (Fg Off R. A. Thompson baled out wounded); P9458 (Fg Off O. St J. Pigg killed); and X4109 (Fg Off D. F. B. Sheen baled out unhurt). Elsewhere, No 603 Squadron lost L1020 in a forced landing (Plt Off P. M. Cardell unhurt) and No 616 Squadron lost R6778, shot down by return fire from a Do 17 over Kenley. Plt Off L. H. Casson baled out unscathed.

On 2 September several airfields, including Biggin Hill, Lympne, Detling, Eastchurch (three times), Hornchurch (twice) and Gravesend were heavily attacked, together with the Shorts aircraft factory at Rochester and Brooklands aerodrome, adjacent to the vital Hawker and Vickers factories. The Midlands, Manchester and Sheffield were attacked after dark. Fighter Command lost fourteen aircraft, with eighteen more damaged; the *Luftwaffe* lost twenty-six. No 72 Squadron again lost three aircraft: K9938 (Sgt N. R. Norfolk unhurt), X4241 (Flt Lt E. Graham unhurt) and R6806 (Sqn Ldr A. R. Collins wounded). The other Spitfire losses were N3056 of No 603 Squadron (Sgt J. Stokoe baled out wounded) and

X4181 of No 616 Squadron (Flt Lt D. E. Gillam unhurt).

The airfield attacks continued on 3 September, North Weald being very severely damaged. Fighter Command lost fourteen aircraft, the *Luftwaffe* sixteen. Adolf Hitler moved the target date for the invasion of England from 15 to 21 September, following discord among his air commanders. *Generalfeldmarschall* Albert Kesselring, commanding *Luftflotte 2*, expressed his belief that the RAF was down to its last few fighters; on the other hand, Hugo Sperrle of *Luftflotte 3* believed that Fighter Command might have as many as 1,000 aircraft left.

Once again, it was the Hurricane squadrons that suffered the heaviest losses on 3 September, with ten aircraft destroyed and as many damaged. The Spitfire squadrons escaped lightly, losing only four aircraft. These were X4262 of No 72 Squadron (pilot unhurt); X4277 of No 603 Squadron, whose pilot, Plt Off Richard Hillary, baled out with terrible burns and later recounted his experiences in his book *The Last Enemy*; and X4185, also of No 603 Squadron, shot down by an Me 109 of I/JG 26. Pilot Officer D. Stewart-Clark baled out wounded.

RAF Spitfire Squadrons: Order of Battle at 3 September 1940

Squadron	Mark	Location	Remarks
19	I/IIA	Fowlmere	From Duxford, 24.7.40
41	I/IIA	Hornchurch	From Catterick, same day
54	I	Catterick	From Hornchurch, same day
64	I	Leconfield	Equipped April 1940
65	I	Turnhouse	From Hornchurch, 28.8.40
66	I	Kenley	From Coltishall, same day
72	I	Croydon	From Biggin Hill, 1.9.40
74	I/IIA	Kirton-in-Lindsey	From Wittering, 21.8.40
92	I	Pembrey	Equipped March 1940
152	I	Warmwell	Equipped January 1940
222	I	Hornchurch	Equipped March 1940
234	I	Middle Wallop	Equipped March 1940
266	I/IIA	Wittering	Equipped January 1940
602	I	Westhampnett	From Drem, 13.8.40
603	I	Hornchurch	From Turnhouse, 27.8.40
609	I	Middle Wallop	From Northolt, 5.7.40
610	I	Biggin Hill	Equipped October 1939
611	I, IIA	Digby	To Rochford, 14.12.40
616	I	Coltishall	From Kenley, same day

Such, then, was the disposition of Fighter Command's Spitfire assets on the first anniversary of the outbreak of war. On the following day, in addition to his continued pounding of Fighter Command's airfields, the enemy launched heavy attacks on British aircraft factories. Twenty Me 110s attempting to attack the Hawker factory at Brooklands were severely mauled by Hurricanes

of No 253 Squadron, losing six aircraft; the remaining Me 110s attacked the Vickers factory in error, killing eighty-eight people, injuring over 600 and halting production of the Wellington bomber for four days. The *Luftwaffe* lost twenty-one aircraft, the RAF eight Hurricanes and eight Spitfires. Hardest hit among the Spitfire units was No 66 Squadron, which had rotated from Coltishall to Kenley on 3

September. It lost P9316 (Plt Off A. N. R. Appleyard baled out with slight wounds); N3048 (Sgt A. D. Smith died of wounds on 6 September): and R6689 (Plt Off C. A. Cooke baled out slightly wounded.) In addition, three more of the Squadron's Spitfires were damaged.

No 72 Squadron lost two aircraft, R6971 and P9460, but Pilot Officers E. E. Males and R. D. Elliott both escaped by parachute without injury. No 152 Squadron, however, lost Sgt J. K. Barker in R6909, hit by return fire from a Dornier 17 over the Channel, while No 222 Squadron had two pilots killed: Fg Off J. W. Cutts in X4278 and Sgt J. W. Ramshaw in K9962. A third 152 Squadron pilot, Plt Off J. M. V. Carpenter, was blown out of his Spitfire (P9378) by British AA fire in the act of attacking an Me 109 and landed by parachute, slightly wounded.

On 5 September, twenty-two German formations attacked RAF airfields and the oil storage tanks at Thameshaven, the *Luftwaffe* losing twenty-three aircraft and Fighter Command twenty. For once, Spitfire losses exceeded those of the Hurricane: thirteen aircraft against seven. About one third of these were accounted for by No 41 Squadron, which had just moved forward to Manston after spending a day at Hornchurch. It is noteworthy that the heaviest combat losses during this period were being sustained by squadrons newly rotated back to No 11 Group after being rested elsewhere – an indication of the inexperience of their replacement pilots, most of whom were seeing combat for the first time.

Admittedly, two of No 41 Squadron's losses on 5 September were the result of an unfortunate accident, Spitfires R6635 and P9428 colliding and breaking up during an attack on a Dornier 17 over the Thames Estuary. Their pilots, Squadron Leader H. R. L. Hood and Flt Lt J. T. Webster, were killed. The Squadron also lost X4021 (Plt Off R. W. Wallens baled out badly wounded), and R6885 (Fg Off A. D. J. Lovell baled out unhurt), both in combat with Do 17s over the Thames.

No 19 Squadron from Duxford, also engaged over the Thames Estuary, lost P9422 and its pilot, Sqn Ldr P. C. Pinkham, shot down by an Me 109. N3060 of No 66 Squadron suffered the same fate; Plt Off P. J. C. King baled out, but his parachute failed to open. No 72 Squadron, Croydon, lost three Spitfires, all destroyed by Me 109s; these were X4013 (Plt Off D. C. Winter killed); N3093 (Sgt M. Gray killed); and X4034 (Fg Off D. F. B. Sheen baled out wounded.) Sgt D. J. Chipping also baled out injured from X4057 of No 222 Squadron after being hit by the Dover AA

barrage while in pursuit of an Me 109, while No 603 Squadron lost X4261 (Flt Lt F. W. Rushmer killed) and X4264 (Plt Off W. P. H. Rafter wounded) in action against Do 17s and their Me 109 escort over Biggin Hill.

Fighter Command's weary pilots had no means of knowing it, but the next day, Friday 6 September, was to mark the end of the intensive phase of airfield attacks. On the night of 24/25 August, the *Luftwaffe* had inadvertently dropped some bombs on London, and Winston Churchill, correctly assessing Hitler's probable reaction to RAF bombing attacks on Berlin – he was expected to order retaliatory attacks on London to avoid losing face with the German people – seized the opportunity of this unintentional minor attack on the British capital to order bombing raids on Berlin, the object being to divert the *Luftwaffe* from its assault on the British fighter airfields. He had had a similar idea on 15 May 1940, when he ordered Bomber Command to attack targets east of the Rhine and in the Ruhr in an attempt to relieve *Luftwaffe* pressure on the Allied ground forces in France and Belgium.

On 31 August, in response to sporadic (and largely ineffectual) RAF raids on Berlin, the *Luftwaffe* Operations Staff ordered *Luftflotten* 2 and 3 to prepare a reprisal attack on London. On 4 September Hitler declared in public that his intention was to 'erase' Britain's cities, and on 5 September he gave orders to attack London and other large cities by day and night. London was to be raided in the afternoon of 7 September.

But the RAF as yet had no inkling of this change of policy, and 6 September was a day of furious fighting. German attacks on airfields, aircraft and armament factories and oil storage depots continued, Thameshaven being set on fire again. Reconnaissance aircraft reported steadily growing numbers of invasion craft in the Dutch, Belgian and French Channel ports, and Bomber Command was ordered to step up its night offensive against these targets. The British ordered Invasion Alert No 2 – attack expected within three days. For the first time, a Polish fighter squadron (No 303, Northolt) was committed to the battle. Fighter Command was now very close to exhaustion; in the two weeks from 24 August to 6 September the Command had lost 103 pilots killed and 128 badly wounded – almost one-quarter of its available trained personnel. For the first time, losses began to exceed replacements.

Of the twenty RAF aircraft destroyed on 6 September, seven were Spitfires. No 64 Squadron, resting at Leconfield in No 13 Group's area, lost K9903 in unknown circumstances on a routine patrol; at Croydon, No 72 Squadron lost N3070 in combat with an Me 109 over Maidstone, Plt Off R. D. Elliott baling out unhurt. At Middle Wallop, in No 10 Group's area, No 234 Squadron lost three aircraft, two shot down by Me 109s. They were X4036 (Plt Off W. H. G. Gordon killed); X4183 (Sgt W. H. Hornby baled out injured); and N3061, shot down by return fire from a Ju 88 over Portland (Plt Off P. W. Horton baled out slightly injured.) Me 109s also accounted for N3227 of No 602 Squadron (Sgt G. A. Whipps baled out unhurt) and X4260 of No 603 Squadron, shot down over the French coast. Its pilot, Plt Off J. R. Caister, was taken prisoner.

The offensive against London began in the late afternoon of 7 September, and was heralded by what has been described as the greatest serial armada ever seen until then. In all, 348 bombers and 617 fighters took part. Göring, dressed in his pale blue and gold uniform, stood on the cliffs above Calais and watched wave after wave of aircraft setting course for England. The coastal radar stations detected the approaching armada at 16.00, and first sighting by the Observer Corps was made about fifteen minutes later. The enemy formation towered in stepped-up echelons to a height of 23,000 feet on a twenty-mile front.

For the most part, the British defences were taken by surprise. The Fighter Command controllers had been expecting the massive enemy formation to split up and head for separate targets: instead, it flew straight on up the Thames towards London, where its bombs rained down on the East End of London and the docks. The widely scattered fighter squadrons of No 11 Group tried hard to intercept the raiders, but very few did so successfully.

Of the twenty-three RAF fighters lost that day (the *Luftwaffe* lost thirty-eight aircraft) eight were Spitfires. No 41 Squadron lost P9430 following a combat over Hornchurch, but Sgt J. McAdam got out without injury, while P9466 of No 234 Squadron crashed near Biggin Hill, killing Sqn Ldr J. S. O'Brien. The same squadron also lost Flt Lt P. C. Hughes in X4009. No 602 Squadron had two Spitfires shot down: N3198 (Fg Off W. H. Coverley died of burns) and X4256 (Plt Off H. W. Moody missing). No 603 Squadron lost P9467 in combat over the Thames, but Sgt A. R. Sarre baled out with slight wounds. The other two Spitfires lost on 7 September were not in the combat area at all, but at Catterick in

North Yorkshire, where No 54 Squadron was resting. P9560 crashed during a low-level training flight, killing Fg Off D. J. Sanders, and R6901 crashed in the sea off Flamborough Head, its pilot (Plt Off W. Krepski) being posted missing.

The attacks on London continued throughout the night, ceasing only at 04.30, and 448 civilians were killed along the nine miles of Thames waterfront, with many more injured. The code-word *Cromwell* – invasion imminent – brought the British defences to their highest level of readiness and action stations.

In contrast to the onslaught of 7 September, the next day was relatively quiet, with desultory fighting in which the RAF lost four fighters and the *Luftwaffe* thirteen aircraft. Only one Spitfire – R6756 of No 41 Squadron – was lost on this day, bounced by an Me 109, and its pilot (Fg Off W. J. Scott) killed.

On 9 September the enemy bombers returned, attacking Southampton and targets in the Thames Estuary. A major raid on London by 200 bombers was broken up by fighters of Nos 11 and 12 Groups, the latter now fully committed to the battle, but jettisoned bombs caused widespread damage in the suburbs, killing 412 people. The *Luftwaffe* lost twenty-five aircraft and the RAF seventeen, of which four were Spitfires: N3049 of No 66 Squadron was shot down by Me 109s over East Grinstead, Plt Off G. H. Corbett baling out; L1077 and P9372 of No 92 Squadron, which had moved to Biggin Hill from Pembrey on the previous day, were shot down over their base by Me 109s, but their pilots (Plt Off C. H. Saunders and Plt Off W. C. Watling) escaped with slight injuries; and K9910 of No 602 Squadron crash-landed in a wood after a combat with Me 109s over Bayfield, Fg Off P. C. Webb suffering nothing worse than a broken wrist. No 602 Squadron lost another Spitfire on the following day, when L1040 crashed during night-flying practice; its pilot, Sgt D. W. Elcome, escaped unhurt. Two more of the squadron's aircraft were damaged on the same exercise. The only combat loss of 10 September was Spitfire K9841, written-off in a forced landing after taking return fire from a Dornier. Plt Off E. E. Males was not injured.

On 11 September the *Luftwaffe* returned in strength, carrying out several co-ordinated attacks on London and on selected airfields. In the day's fighting the RAF suffered more heavily than the *Luftwaffe* – twenty-seven aircraft against twenty-two, and again it was the Hurricane squadrons that took the most punishment, losing nineteen aircraft with eight damaged. Eight Spitfires were lost and ten damaged. X4325 of No 41 Squadron went down during an attack on a Ju 88 over Sevenoaks, Plt Off G. A. Langley baling out unhurt; Plt Off I. J. A. Cruickshanks of No 72 Squadron nursed a badly damaged X4339 back to Croydon, where it was written-off; No 92 Squadron lost K9793, R6613 and P9464, together with two pilots, Fg Off F. N. Hargreaves and Plt Off H. D. Edwards (the third pilot, Flt Lt J. A. Paterson, was slightly injured.) P7313, a Mk II Spitfire of No 266 Squadron from Wittering, was shot down by return fire from a Heinkel He 111, Plt Off R. J. B. Roach baling out unharmed; Sgt M. H. Sprague of No 602 Squadron was shot down and killed in N3832 by Me 110s off Selsey Bill; and Spitfire Mk II P7298 of No 611 Squadron, Digby, went down in flames over Croydon. Sgt F. E. R. Shepherd baled out but was killed.

On 12 and 13 September air operations were hampered by bad weather, and the Spitfire squadrons suffered no losses during this 48-hour period. On 14 September the fighting flared up again, with attacks on south London and coastal radar stations – the latter a preliminary to a major onslaught on the capital scheduled for the next day. The *Luftwaffe* lost eight aircraft in combat on this day, the RAF thirteen, of which eight were Spitfires. No 19 Squadron lost R6625, which crashed during a patrol and killed its pilot, Sgt F. Marek, a Czech attached from No 310 Squadron; R6605 of No 41 Squadron was shot down by Me 109s, Sqn Ldr R. C. F. Lister baling out wounded; No 66 Squadron lost X4327, shot down by Me 109s near Maidstone (Plt Off R. H. Robbins seriously injured) and N3029, destroyed in a forced landing (Sgt P. H. Willcocks unhurt); K9960 of No 72 Squadron was shot down over Ashford, Sgt H. J. Bell-Walker baling out; No 92 Squadron lost R6642, shot down by Me 109s near Faversham (Sgt H. W. McGowan baled out wounded); and No 222 Squadron lost X4265 (Sgt S. Baxter killed) and X4249 (Sgt R. B. Johnson baled out), both in combat with Me 109s.

Sunday, 15 September 1940, was the day since remembered as the climax of the Battle of Britain. The *Luftwaffe* launched 200 bombers against London in two waves, and when the first wave attacked, such was the opposition put up by Nos 11 and 12 Groups that Fighter Command had no squadrons in reserve. If the second wave had come immediately, its bombers would have caught the

Spitfires and Hurricanes on the ground; but it was two hours before this wave attacked, and by that time the fighter squadrons were ready for it. A total of 148 bombers got through to bomb London, but fifty-six were shot down and many more limped back to their bases with severe battle damage. Fighter Command's loss was twenty-nine, of which twenty-two were Hurricanes; again, the Spitfire squadrons had escaped comparatively lightly. No 19 Squadron lost X4070, which ditched following combat off the French coast (Sgt J. A. Potter PoW) and P9431, wrecked in a forced landing after suffering battle damage (Sgt H. A. C. Roden slightly injured); No 41 Squadron lost P9324 and its pilot, Plt Off G. A. Langley; No 92 Squadron lost R6606 (Plt Off R. H. Holland baled out); No 603 Squadron lost X4324 and R7019 in combat with Dornier 17s, Fg Off A. P. Pease being killed and Sqn Ldr G. L. Denholm baling out; and No 609 Squadron lost R6690, shot down by Me 110s escorting enemy bombers over London. Its pilot, Plt Off G. N. Gaunt, was killed.

On 16 September the weather intervened, and there was only slight air activity in conditions of cloud and rain. Fighter Command lost only one aircraft – Spitfire L1036 of No 616 Squadron, Kirton-in-Lindsey – which ran out of fuel while chasing a Ju 88 over the North Sea and ditched twenty miles off Cromer. Its pilot, Sgt T. C. Iveson, was picked up unhurt by an MTB. Bad weather also reduced air operations on the 17th, although there were a number of fighter sweeps over southern England. During the night, RAF Bomber Command despatched 194 aircraft to attack the Channel ports; eighty-four barges were sunk at Dunkirk alone. During the day the *Luftwaffe* lost eight aircraft, the RAF five, one of which was Spitfire R6887 of No 41 Squadron, written-off after returning to Hornchurch with severe battle damage. Fg Off J. G. Boyle was unhurt.

On the orders of Adolf Hitler, Operation *Sea Lion*, the invasion of England, was postponed indefinitely; British Intelligence intercepted a secret German signal, ordering the dismantling of German invasion air transport facilities in Holland. It may be said that at this point, Fighter Command had won the Battle of Britain merely by staying in existence; but there was a lot of fighting still to come.

On 18 September the *Luftwaffe* resumed its attacks on oil storage facilities in the Thames Estuary and suffered heavily, losing sixteen aircraft, nine of them

Junkers 88s of KG 77, shot down in a combat lasting only minutes. RAF Fighter Command's loss was twelve aircraft, of which five were Spitfires. No 66 Squadron, Gravesend, lost R6603 and R6925, both shot down over the Estuary; Sgt D. F. Corfe and Plt Off J. R. Mather baled out, the former injured. Pilot Officer R. Mottram of No 92 Squadron also baled out with slight burns from N3193, while Sgt I. Hutchinson of No 222 Squadron escaped slightly injured from R6772 after a combat with Me 109s. The only Spitfire pilot killed that day was Plt Off P. Howes of No 603 Squadron, shot down in X4323 by Me 109s near Ashford. Nine Spitfires were damaged in the day's fighting.

After a lull caused by bad weather on the 19th, when there were no combat losses, the *Luftwaffe* launched several strong fighter sweeps over southern England on 20 September, both sides losing seven aircraft. Once again, five Spitfires went down. These were X4410 of No 72 Squadron, shot down over Canterbury (Plt Off D. F. Holland died of wounds); X4417 and N3248 of No 92 Squadron, both shot down by the German ace *Major* Werner Mölders of JG 51 (Plt Off H. P. Hill killed and Sgt P. R. Eyles missing); and N3203 and K9993 of No 222 Squadron, also shot down by Me 109s (Plt Off H. L. Whitbread killed and Plt Off W. R. Asheton baled out with slight burns).

The weather once again brought a respite on 21 and 22 September, Fighter Command's main losses on these two days being due to accidents. The sole exception was a Spitfire (X4351) of No 19 Squadron, destroyed in a bombing attack on Fowlmere in the afternoon of the 22nd. The weather cleared somewhat on the 23rd, and there were numerous small-scale combats between Fighter Command and enemy fighters carrying out sweeps over the Thames Estuary; the *Luftwaffe* lost thirteen aircraft, the RAF eleven. Once again, the Spitfire squadrons lost five aircraft: X4063 of No 72 Squadron, which crash-landed after combat with Me 109s (Plt Off B. W. Brown unhurt); P7362 of No 74 Squadron, Coltishall, abandoned for unknown reasons during a routine patrol (Sgt D. H. Ayers drowned); P9371 of No 92 Squadron, which crashed at West Malling following a combat with Me 109s (Plt Off A. J. S. Pattinson badly wounded); R7016 of No 152 Squadron, which failed to return from a sortie over the Channel (Plt Off W. Beaumont missing); and R6896 of No 234 Squadron, which vanished over the Channel on a patrol from St Eval in Cornwall (Plt Off T. M. Kane PoW).

On 24 September the *Luftwaffe* carried out a number of small-scale raids, one of which – by Me 110s of *Erprobungsgruppe 210* – damaged the Spitfire factory at Woolston. Two Spitfires were lost during the day, both in combat: N3118 of No 41 Squadron, shot down into the Channel off Dover (Sgt J. McAdam baled out), and X4037 of No 92 Squadron, shot down near North Weald (Plt Off J. S. Bryson killed). The day's losses were Fighter Command six, *Luftwaffe* nine. On the next day the *Luftwaffe* resumed its attacks on aircraft factories. The Bristol factory at Filton was badly damaged, with over 300 civilian casualties, in an attack by fifty-eight Heinkel 111s of KG 55. The day's operations cost the *Luftwaffe* thirteen aircraft, five in the Filton raid, and the RAF five. The attack on Filton meant that the fighters of No 10 Group were the most heavily involved, all the casualties were sustained by this Group. Three Spitfires were destroyed: No 152 Squadron, Warmwell, lost P9463, shot down over Portsmouth (Sgt W. G. Silver killed) and N3173, shot down near Bristol while attacking a KG 55 Heinkel (Sgt K. C. Holland killed); and X4182 of No 234 Squadron, St Eval, crashed near St Mawgan (Plt Off R. MacKay baled out seriously injured.)

On Thursday, 26 September, the *Luftwaffe* once again attacked the Supermarine works at Woolston, but Spitfire production was now well dispersed and although the factory was gutted the flow of aircraft to the MUs was not affected. The *Luftwaffe* lost six aircraft, Fighter Command eight, including two Spitfires; K9982, shot down off the Cornish coast by Me 109s (Flt Lt E. C. Deansley baled out and rescued) and K9882, shot down by Me 109s off Swanage (Sgt J. M. Christie picked up dead). Both aircraft belonged to No 152 Squadron.

The next day, Friday 27 September, cost Fighter Command more Spitfires than any other in the Battle of Britain. Following a night of heavy air attacks on the south and Midlands, the *Luftwaffe* launched a series of strong daylight raids, starting with an attack on London by bomb-carrying Me 110s. The latter suffered heavily, *Lehrgeschwader 1* alone losing seven aircraft. A second attack on London by fifty-five Junkers 88s of KG 77 ended in disaster when the bombers failed to rendezvous with their Me 109 escort; fifteen Ju 88s were shot down, and enemy fighters belatedly coming to the bombers' rescue were also badly mauled. In an attack on Filton, fighters of No 10 Group destroyed four Me 110s of *Erprobungsgruppe 210*. The day's losses were

Luftwaffe forty-nine, Fighter Command twenty-eight.

The RAF's loss included fifteen Spitfires. No 19 Squadron from Duxford, in action against Me 109s over Canterbury, lost X4352 (Plt Off E. Burgoyne killed) and X4237 (Sgt D. G. S. R. Cox wounded); an unidentified Spitfire of No 41 Squadron was shot down by Me 109s over West Malling, Sgt F. Usmar baling out with leg wounds; Sgt E. V. Darling of the same squadron also escaped wounded from a second unidentified Spitfire, the victim of the same 'bounce' by Me 109s over West Malling; and Flt Lt E. N. Ryder baled out of R6755 after being shot down during an evening patrol.

In the north, Spitfire X4032 of No 64 Squadron and its pilot, Sgt L. A. Dyke, went missing on a patrol from Leconfield, while at Biggin Hill No 72 Squadron lost X4340 and N3068 in combat with Me 109s over Kent; Plt Off E. E. Males and Fg Off P. J. Davies-Cooke were both killed. No 92 Squadron, also scrambled from Biggin Hill and fighting over Sevenoaks, lost X4422 (Flt Lt J. A. Paterson killed), R6767 (Flt Sgt C. Sydney killed), and R6622 (Sgt T. G. Oldfield killed). At Hornchurch, No 222 Squadron lost P9364, which vanished during an evening patrol with its pilot, Sgt E. Scott, and No 603 Squadron lost N3244; its pilot, Plt Off P. M. Cardell, baled out but was thought to have been too badly wounded to open his parachute. No 609 Squadron, Warmwell, lost X4107 which collided head-on with an Me 110 (Plt Off R. F. G. Miller killed); and R6702 of No 616 Squadron, Duxford, was shot down by Me 109s. Flying Officer D. S. Smith was seriously wounded and died the next day.

There were sporadic raids on 28 September, the bombers under strong fighter escort; the *Luftwaffe* lost ten aircraft and the RAF seventeen, of which eleven were Hurricanes. Of the six Spitfires lost, three belonged to No 41 Squadron: X4409 was shot down in combat over Charing and Plt Off H. H. Chalder baled out seriously wounded, to succumb to his injuries seven weeks later; Fg Off J. G. Boyle was killed in X4426, also shot down in flames over Charing; and Plt Off E. S. Aldous was slightly hurt when he crash-landed X4345 after the same battle. Plt Off A. B. Watkinson of No 66 Squadron managed to bale out of X4322 despite wounds in his leg

and shoulder, while Flt Lt H. K. MacDonald was killed in L1076 after being bounced by Me 109s over Gillingham. The other Spitfire loss was Mk II P7369 of No 611 Squadron, which crashed on landing at Ternhill in unknown circumstances; Plt Off J. R. G. Sutton was slightly injured.

Sunday, 29 September saw greatly reduced air operations over London and East Anglia; Liverpool was also attacked in daylight from the west, the bombers having detoured over the Irish Sea. The *Luftwaffe* lost six aircraft and Fighter Command seven (one of which was a Hurricane of No 79 Squadron that made a forced landing in Eire after attacking the Liverpool raiding force of Heinkel 111s; the aircraft was impounded). No Spitfires were lost.

By way of contrast, the last day of September was one of heavy air activity, beginning with an attempted attack on London by 200 enemy aircraft in two waves. The raids were intercepted by twelve fighter squadrons and the majority of the bombers were turned back over Kent with heavy losses. An attack on the Westland aircraft factory at Yeovil was also beaten off. The day's operations cost the *Luftwaffe* forty-five aircraft, the RAF twenty. Spitfire losses were six aircraft, of which one was P9564 of No 64 Squadron, in No 12 Group's area at Leconfield; it crashed near base on a routine sortie (Sgt A. F. Laws unhurt). X4069 of No 92 Squadron was wrecked in a forced landing after being badly damaged by an Me 109 of 4/JG 27, Plt Off R. Wright receiving slight wounds, and L1072 of No 152 Squadron was shot down into the sea off Portland (Sgt L. A. E. Reddington missing.) No 222 Squadron, Hornchurch, lost P9492, also wrecked in a forced landing after taking combat damage over London (Sgt I. Hutchinson wounded), and a second unidentified Spitfire which crash-landed after combat and blew up seconds after Flt Lt G. C. Matheson had got clear. The other Spitfire lost was an aircraft of No 610 Squadron, Acklington, which crashed at Alnmouth due to a flying accident. Fg Off C. H. Bacon was killed.

The rate of attrition suffered by the *Luftwaffe* in its operations against England had now reached an unacceptable level, an opinon that was now expressed by Air Chief Marshal Dowding. The next few days were to prove him right.

Spitfire Deliveries and Losses (All Causes), September 1940

	Into Service	Damaged (Repairable)	Destroyed	Hurricane Losses Damaged	Destroyed
1	18	5	5	4	9
2	7	8	5	10	9
3	12	1	4	10	10
4	1	8	8	7	8
5	12	7	13	9	7
6	20	5	7	10	13
7	7	17	8	12	15
8	11	–	1	3	3
9	5	7	4	8	13
10	18	2	2	–	1
11	2	10	8	8	19
12	7	–	–	–	1
13	15	–	–	1	1
14	10	3	8	6	5
15	6	7	7	20	22
16	3	1	1	2	–
17	5	5	1	3	4
18	12	9	5	3	7
19	10	–	–	1	–
20	9	2	5	2	3
21	2	1	–	–	–
22	3	–	1	4	–
23	6	1	5	–	6
24	11	5	2	3	4
25	8	5	3	3	2
26	18	3	2	6	6
27	6	13	15	19	13
28	10	2	6	3	11
29	13	1	–	3	7
30	1	5	6	18	14
Totals:	268	133	133	181	213

The beginning of October 1940 saw a major change in the *Luftwaffe*'s tactics. Attacks on southern England were now made by bomb-carrying Messerschmitts operating at high altitude, rather than by heavily-escorted bomber formations. To counter these new methods, No 11 Group instituted high-level standing patrols on a line covering Biggin Hill–Maidstone–Gravesend. The main bomber force of the *Luftwaffe* now operated almost exclusively at night against British targets; London was bombed by an average of 150 aircraft on every night in October except one. In the week 1–7 October the *Luftwaffe* lost seventy-eight aircraft, Fighter Command thirty-four Spitfires and Hurricanes, some of the RAF aircraft being destroyed accidentally.

Spitfire losses during the week were sixteen aircraft. On 1 October Plt Off G. H. Bennions of No 41 Squadron baled out of X4559 with serious wounds after a battle with Me 109s over Henfield (he survived and was still flying a civil-registered DH Tiger Moth many years later). On the following day No 41 Squadron also lost X4545 in a collision, Sgt J.

K. Norwell receiving slight injuries, and P9553 of No 603 Squadron was shot down by Me 109s over Croydon, Plt Off P.G. Dexter baling out with leg wounds.

There were no losses at all on 3 October, but on the 4th X4320 of No 66 Squadron was shot down into the Channel while intercepting a Heinkel 111; Flt Lt K. McL. Gillies was killed. On 5 October Plt Off N. Sutton, flying K9989 of No 72 Squadron, crashed and was killed following a mid-air collision with N3285, which returned to base; Plt Off J. S. Morton baled out with burns from K9087 of No 603 Squadron, shot down by Me 109s over Dover; and Fg Off T. Nowierski abandoned N3223 of No 609 Squadron over Salisbury Plain following an undercarriage failure. On 6 October, No 64 Squadron at Leconfield lost R6683, which went down into the North Sea during a routine patrol; Sgt F. F. Vinyard was posted missing.

On Monday, 7 October, the *Luftwaffe* stepped up its air activity, the day's operations including a heavily-escorted raid by Junkers 88s on the Westland factory at Yeovil. The *Luftwaffe* and Fighter Command both lost seventeen aircraft during the day, including seven Me 110s and seven Spitfires. No 41 Squadron lost N3267, shot down by return fire from a Dornier 17 over Folkestone (Plt Off D. A. Adams baled out unhurt); N3039 of No 152 Squadron crash-landed in flames after a combat over Lyme Regis, Plt Off H. J. Ackroyd dying from burns the next day; No 222 Squadron lost P9469 and its pilot, Plt Off J. W. Broadhurst, shot down during an attack on enemy bombers; X4160 of No 602 Squadron crash-landed after sustaining damage in combat with Junkers 88s (Sgt B. E. P. Whall died of injuries); Fg Off H. K. F. Matthews of No 603 Squadron was shot down and killed in N3109 during a fight with Me 109s; and No 609 Squadron lost N3238 and N3231, both bounced by Me 109s as they climbed to intercept the Ju 88 attack on Yeovil. Sgt A. N. Feary and Plt Off M. E. Staples both baled out, but the former pilot was too low and he was killed.

On 8 October the Germans made several small-scale fighter-bomber attacks on London and a daylight raid on Liverpool. The *Luftwaffe* lost six aircraft in combat and the RAF four, two of them Spitfires of No 66 Squadron: R6679 and N3043, Plt Off G. H. Corbett and Sgt R. A. Ward both being killed. No 74 Squadron at Coltishall also lost two pilots, Plt Offs D. Hastings and F. W. Buckland, when P7329 and P7373 collided during an air fighting exercise.

Cloud and rain dominated the scene on 9 October, but this did not deter enemy fighter-bombers from making sporadic attacks on RAF airfields in the south-east. The *Luftwaffe* lost nine aircraft, Fighter Command two, including Spitfire X4597 of No 92 Squadron, shot down by Me 109s near Ashford. Sgt E. T. G. Frith baled out badly burned and died the next day.

Enemy fighter-bombers came over south-east England in streams on 10 October, and Fighter Command pilots reported extreme difficulty in intercepting due to heavy showers interspersed with dazzling bright intervals. It may have been these conditions that caused Spitfires X4038 and R6616 to collide in mid-air over Tangmere while attacking a Dornier 17; Plt Off D. G. Williams and Fg Off J. F. Drummond were both killed. A third Spitfire, K9840 of No 152 Squadron, was wrecked in a forced landing after being hit by return fire from a Do 17; Sgt W. T. Ellis was unhurt. Fighter Command also lost five Hurricanes on this day; the *Luftwaffe* lost four aircraft.

Clearer weather on 11 October enabled the enemy to operate in greater strength, and in the various actions during the day Fighter Command lost eight aircraft, the *Luftwaffe* seven. Six Spitfires were among the RAF losses, and once again, two – X4042 and X4554 of No 41 Squadron – were lost in a mid-air collision. Sgt L. R. Carter baled out of the latter aircraft, but Fg Off D. H. O'Neill was killed when his parachute failed to open. No 66 Squadron lost N3121, shot down by an Me 109 of JG 51; Plt Off J. H. T. Pickering escaped with injuries. Another Me 109 claimed K9870, shot down in flames off Deal; despite wounds, Plt Off P. D. Pool managed to bale out. At Gravesend, No 421 Flight – recently formed on the instigation of Winston Churchill to patrol high over the Channel and report any build-up of enemy aircraft – lost Spitfire II P7303 and its pilot, Sgt C. A. H. Ayling, shot down over Hawkinge; and at Ternhill in Shropshire, Spitfire II P7323 crashed on returning from a sortie. Its injured pilot, Sgt K. C. Pattison, died two days later.

On Sunday, 12 October, on the orders of Adolf Hitler, the following directive was circulated to the German armed forces: 'The *Führer* has decided that from now until the spring, preparations for *Sea Lion* shall be continued solely for the purpose of maintaining political and military pressure on England. Should the invasion be reconsidered in the spring or early summer of 1941, orders for a renewal of operational readiness will be issued later. In the meantime, military conditions for a later invasion are to be improved'.

The pilots of Fighter Command, of course, knew nothing of this tacit admission of defeat, and on 12 October they were busy warding off attacks on Biggin Hill and Kenley, losing ten aircraft against the *Luftwaffe*'s eleven. No 421 Flight lost another Spitfire, P7441, bounced by Me 109s during a spotting mission at 20,000 feet over the south coast; Flt Lt C. P. Green baled out with wounds to the neck and arm. At Hornchurch, Sgt J. McAdam of No 41 Squadron walked unhurt from the wreck of his Spitfire (serial unknown) after engine failure on take-off, while at Biggin Hill Plt Off H. R. Case lost his life in P9338 of No 72 Squadron when it crashed through unknown causes near Folkestone. Also from Biggin Hill, X4591 of No 92 Squadron was shot down in combat over Hawkinge and Fg Off A. J. S. Pattinson killed.

Fog on 13 October cleared later in the afternoon to allow limited air operations that cost the Germans five aircraft and Fighter Command two, including

Spitfire X4543 of No 66 Squadron, which crash-landed at Hornchurch following a combat with Me 109s. Sgt H. Cook was unhurt. The next day saw heavy rain that restricted *Luftwaffe* operations to a heavy night attack on London and a lesser raid on Coventry; the only Fighter Command loss was a Hurricane of No 605 Squadron, believed to have been shot down by London's AA defences.

On 15 October the weather was fine, and a morning attack on London by Me 109 fighter-bombers wrecked the approach to Waterloo station and temporarily closed the railway lines. Factories on the south bank of the Thames were badly hit, and in the evening a major attack wrecked parts of the docks, Paddington, Victoria, Waterloo and Liverpool Street stations. Civilian casualties were 512 killed, with 11,000 made homeless. Fighter Command and the *Luftwaffe* each lost fourteen aircraft – the German loss including eight Me 109s, destroyed in a 'bounce' by RAF fighters. Spitfire losses were X4178 of No 41 Squadron, shot down by an Me 109 of 4/JG 51 (Sgt P. D. Lloyd killed); and R6838, X4418 and R6642 of No 92 Squadron, all shot down in combat with Me 109s over the Thames Estuary and Kent (Sgt K. B. Parker killed, Flt Lt C. B. F. Kingcome baled out wounded and Plt Off J. W. Lund rescued from the sea).

Cloudy conditions again curtailed operations on 16 October, the only Spitfire loss of the day being R6714 of No 65 Squadron, Turnhouse, destroyed in a flying accident. Sgt J. Pearson was killed. With the onset of the autumn weather, in fact, accident casualties on both sides would often exceed combat casualties from now on.

The next day, operating in showery conditions with bright intervals, the *Luftwaffe* lost fifteen aircraft in combat against Fighter Command's five. Two of these were Spitfires: R6800 of No 66 Squadron, shot down over Westerham by an Me 109 of JG 51 (Plt Off H. W. Reilley killed), and P7360 of No 74 Squadron, shot down over Maidstone by Me 109s (Fg Off A. L. Ricalton killed). One point worth noting about this day's fighting is that three Hurricanes were shot down, but fifteen returned from combat with repairable damage – an indication of the Hawker fighter's remarkably robust qualities.

There was only one Spitfire casualty on 18 October, when R6607 of No 152 Squadron crashed near Dorchester in unknown circumstances, killing Sgt E. E. Shepherd, and the next day Sgt L. C. Allton was killed in an accident involving R6922 of No 92 Squadron.

Enemy fighter-bombers again crossed the south coast in a stream attack on 20 October, and on this day No 74 Squadron – which had moved to Biggin Hill from Coltishall on the 15th, changing places with No 72 Squadron – lost three Spitfires in combat with Me 109s over the Thames Estuary or London. These were all Mk IIs, P7370 (Sgt T. B. Kirk baled out badly wounded and died in July 1941); P7426 (Sgt C. G. Hilken baled out wounded); and P7355 (Plt Off B. V. Draper unhurt). Throughout the Battle, the highest casualties were always sustained by fighter squadrons returning to the 11 Group combat area after resting and receiving replacement pilots.

There was only one Spitfire casualty on 21 October: X4265 of No 266 Squadron, which crashed on take-off from Stradishall after landing there to refuel. Plt Off W. S. Williams was killed. On 22 October the Me 109s claimed two more of No 74 Squadron's Spitfires in combat near Tonbridge: P7431 (Fg Off P. C. B. St John killed), and P7364 (Plt Off R. L. Spurdle baled out unhurt).

There were no Spitfire casualties on 24 October, but on the following day (one which, incidentally, saw the loss of eleven Hurricanes), X4170 of No 66 Squadron was shot down, Fg Off R. W. Oxspring baling out with slight injuries, and No 603 Squadron lost P7325 and P7309, Pilot Officers S. F. Soden and P. Oliver baling out wounded. It was on 25 October that England was attacked by Italian aircraft for the first time, sixteen Fiat BR.20 bombers carrying out an inconclusive night raid on Harwich. These aircraft belonged to the *Corpo Aereo Italiano*, established on Belgian airfields on 22 October 1940 at the request of the Italian leader Benito Mussolini (a move agreed to only with great reluctance by the Germans). Fiat BR.20s of the 13° and 43° *Stormo* carried out eight night attacks on east coast towns before the end of 1940, but only three daylight raids were attempted. These were escorted by Fiat CR.42s and G.50s of the 56° *Stormo*, but the Italians suffered heavily at the hands of the RAF's fighters. In all, between 25 October and 31 December 1940, the CAI despatched ninety-seven bomber and 113 fighter sorties against east coast targets.

Fighter Command lost two Spitfires on 26 October: R6839 of No 602 Squadron, which failed to return from a routine patrol from Westhampnett (Sgt D. W. Elcome missing), and R6773 of No 222 Squadron, which crash-landed as the result of an engine fire (Sgt P. O. Davis unhurt).

Sunday, 27 October, was the worst day for the Spitfire squadrons for three weeks, seven aircraft being lost. P7539 crashed near Tonbridge, killing Plt Off J. R. Mather of No 66 Squadron; the cause was never established. No 74 Squadron lost P7526 and its pilot, Sgt J. A. Scott, shot down by Me 109s over Maidstone, while R6721 of No 92 Squadron was wrecked in a forced landing, Sgt D. E. Kingaby escaping unhurt. Another crash-landing destroyed X4548 of No 222 Squadron and seriously injuring its pilot, Plt Off E. F. Edsall. No 603 Squadron, Hornchurch, lost Mk IIs P7439 and P7365, shot down by Me 109s over Maidstone; Fg Off C. W. Goldsmith was pulled from the wreck of the former aircraft but died the next day, and Plt Off R. B. Dewey was killed. A third Spitfire, P7286, was badly damaged in the 'bounce', but was repaired and returned to action. The other Spitfire loss of the day – which involved fighter-bomber attacks on seven RAF airfields, forcing Fighter Command to fly 107 defensive sorties – was P9503, abandoned by Plt Off P. A. Baillon after being damaged by return fire over Andover.

There was little or no action and no losses on 28 October, but the 29th was a very active day, with more heavy fighter-bomber attacks on RAF airfields and coastal targets. The Luftwaffe's combat loss of twenty aircraft included five Me 109s of JG 51, bounced by RAF fighters as a result of good tactical planning. The Hurricanes bore the brunt of the day's fighting, losing nine aircraft. Two Spitfires were destroyed: P7423 of No 19 Squadron, Duxford, shot down by an Me 109 over Chelmsford (Sub-Lt A. G. Blake killed), and P7385 of No 74 Squadron, wrecked in a forced landing (Sgt H. J. Soars unhurt).

Two Spitfires, both belonging to No 41 Squadron, Hornchurch, were shot down by Me 109s over Ashford, Kent, on 30 October; they were P7282 (Plt Off G. G. F. Draper slightly injured), and P7375 (Sgt L. A. Garvey killed). Three more Spitfires were also lost during the day; Plt Off A. E. Davies was killed in

N3119 of No 222 Squadron, bounced by Me 109s, while a similar fate overtook Plt Off H. P. M. Eldridge of the same squadron, who crashed in flames in K9939 and later died of injuries. X4542 of No 603 Squadron also crash-landed following a surprise attack by Me 109s and its pilot, Sgt W. B. Smith, was wounded.

That, virtually, was the end of the period officially designated as the Battle of Britain. From now on, because of increasingly bad weather and the fact that the Luftwaffe had exhausted its tactical options, the daylight offensive against Britain began to peter out. Although daylight incursions would continue for the rest of the year, weather permitting, to all intents and purposes the battle was over. The Luftwaffe had been firmly rebuffed, its tactical advantages ruined by inept political and military decisions.

The diversity of targets attacked right from the beginning of the German air war against the British Isles suggests that the whole air offensive was, from the outset, an attempt to win a war by bombing alone. This was a strategic objective, doomed to failure when attempted by means of a tactical air arm, which is what the Luftwaffe was. The attempt was based on exaggerated hopes and lack of experience – and also, perhaps, on the Luftwaffe's ambition to prove itself as an independent service.

The importance of the Luftwaffe's failure over Britain rests in the fact that the island could later be used as the base for the Allied air offensive against Germany and for the Allied invasion of the European continent, which decided the war. But it was fighter strength that decided the Battle of Britain; that, and the sacrifice of 537 young fighter pilots, flying the aircraft that rose to immortality in those summer and autumn weeks of 1940 – the Hurricane and the Spitfire.

Spitfire Deliveries and Losses, October 1940, All Causes

	In Service	Damaged (Repairable)	Destroyed	Hurricane Losses Damaged	Destroyed
1	–	1	1	1	5
2	9	1	2	1	–
3	1	–	–	–	–
4	–	1	1	3	–
5	7	6	3	3	3
6	1	1	1	3	1
7	9	5	7	4	9
8	9	4	4	–	2
9	5	2	1	–	1
10	–	1	3	–	5
11	10	4	6	4	2
12	1	2	4	4	6

13	9	2	1	–	1
14	3	2	–	2	1
15	10	6	4	11	10
16	1	–	1	2	2
17	7	–	2	15	3
18	1	–	1	4	5
19	–	–	1	2	1
20	2	3	3	3	–
21	10	–	1	1	1
22	2	–	2	2	4
23	5	1	–	–	–
24	16	–	–	3	3
25	5	2	3	5	11
26	5	1	2	2	6
27	5	3	7	–	7
28	5	2	–	–	–
29	8	4	2	10	9
30	4	4	5	3	2
31	1	–	–	1	–
Totals:	151	58	65	89	98

Cumulative totals, 1 July–31 October 1940

747	352	361	455	565

The above figures, of course, concern only Hurricanes and Spitfires; they do not take into account losses sustained by other types operated by Fighter Command during the battle, such as Defiants and Blenheims. It was the Hurricane squadrons that took the lion's share of the losses, but that was to be expected; Fighter Command began the battle with twenty-seven squadrons of Hurricanes, against nineteen squadrons of Spitfires. Bearing that in mind, the margin between the losses suffered by each type was not very wide.

But the losses sustained by Fighter Command, in terms of both aircraft and human life, must be seen in their proper context. From 1 July to 31 October 1940, Bomber Command lost 118 aircraft and Coastal Command 130, together with 998 aircrew, mostly in attacks on enemy-held ports, communications and airfields. It should never be forgotten that the Battle of Britain was a victory for the whole of the Royal Air Force.

Chapter 7
Development Interlude: the Spitfires Mk III, IV and V

THE SPITFIRE Mk III represented the first real attempt to achieve a major development of the basic Spitfire airframe, and had it gone into service it would have been a natural progression of the Mk I/II line. It was powered by the 2,240 hp two-speed Merlin XX engine, and other refinements included clipped wings, reducing the span from the original 36 ft 10 in to 32 ft 7 in, a retractable tailwheel, additional armour plating and the setting forward of the undercarriage legs by three inches. In fact, the aircraft was intended to be an air superiority fighter, embodying all the service experience gained in combat with the earlier marks.

The prototype Mk III, N3297, was taken from the Mk I production line and, after modification, made its first flight from Eastleigh on 15 March 1940. In July, it underwent trials with No 11 Group Fighter Command, and these produced an excellent report, apart from two points: it was felt that the landing run was dangerously long and would probably seriously restrict night flying, and that the square-cut wings would lead

to confusion in combat with the Me 109, with the danger of losses through friendly fire.

The Air Ministry decided to place an order for 1,000, to be built at Castle Bromwich, but this was never taken up and the Mk III remained an experimental aircraft. The fact that this came about, and that a compromise Spitfire – the Mk V – was rushed into service instead, was entirely due to new tactics adopted by the *Luftwaffe* in the autumn and winter of 1940.

Late in November 1940, small numbers of a new model of the Messerschmitt Me 109 – the F-1 – began to appear at high altitude over southern England. This variant, which featured rounded wingtips, an improved DB 601E engine, an engine-mounted 20mm cannon and two MG 17 machine-guns, was clearly superior to the Hurricane and had an advantage at altitude over the existing marks of Spitfire. In fact, the Me 109F was undergoing operational trials at this stage, and suffered from technical problems that would cause its withdrawal early in the new year; it would be May 1941 before the

The Spitfire Mk III, intended for the air superiority role, was the first attempt to achieve a major development of the basic Spitfire airframe.

Luftwaffe received an improved version, the Me 109F-2.

The Air Staff, naturally, was unaware of this; but it was clear that an improved version of the Spitfire was needed to counter the new Messerschmitt, and on 25 December representatives of the Royal Aircraft Establishment, Supermarine and Fighter Command met at Boscombe Down to discuss the problem, which in essence was quite simple: the Spitfires then in service were being out-manoeuvred at altitudes above 25,000 feet, and the new air superiority Spitfire, the Mk III, was nowhere near ready for service.

The key to the whole question was the Rolls-Royce Merlin engine. The Merlin XX had the necessary power, but it was optimised for low- and medium-level operation and was fitted with a low-level blower that made it more difficult to manufacture quickly in quantity and also impaired its high-altitude performance. Since the latter was now the principal requirement, Rolls-Royce suggested that the blower be deleted; this was done, and the less complex engine that emerged was the Merlin 45, which increased the Spitfire's ceiling by about 2,000 feet.

By January 1941 three Spitfire Mk I airframes, K9788, N3053 and X4334, had been fitted with the modified engine and were undergoing speed and altitude trials at Boscombe Down. These were a success, and since there was no hope of the planned Spitfire III – orders for which had now risen to 1,500 – being brought into service quickly, it was decided to allocate this serial batch to a new Spitfire variant designated Mk V, which was basically a Mk I airframe with strengthened longerons married to the Merlin 45.

Production of the Mk V started in March 1941, and Mk I and II airframes were also converted to Mk V standard as they were withdrawn for repair or overhaul. The Spitfire Mk VA was fitted with what was known as the 'A' wing, mounting the original armament of eight .303-in Browning machine-guns; the Mk VB had the 'B' wing, with four Brownings and two 20mm cannon. Only ninety-four aircraft had the 'A' armament, production soon switching to the 'B' configuration. Later, the so-called 'Universal' or 'C' wing was adopted; this was capable of mounting either four machine-guns and two cannon in each half, or one cannon and two machine-guns, and the Spitfire variant fitted with it was the Mk VC. The Spitfire V was built in larger numbers than any other version of the Supermarine fighter, production totalling 6,479 examples. The clipped-wing version of the Spitfire VB was specially adapted to the low-level air combat role, serving in all theatres of war.

Long before the Mk V Spitfire came along, Supermarine and the Ministry of Aircraft Production had been giving serious thought to the possibility of introducing a more powerful engine to the Spitfire airframe. At the outbreak of war such an engine already existed: the Rolls-Royce RR-37 V-12, developed from the Type R that had powered the later models of the Schneider racers and known as the Griffon. Work on an advanced version of the Spitfire powered by the Griffon proceeded throughout 1940 and the prototype, DP845, was built in the following year, making its maiden flight from Worthy Down on 27 November 1941. Designated Spitfire Mk IV, the aircraft underwent extensive trials but did not go into production. However, as we shall see later, it served as the prototype Spitfire XII, which was the first Griffon-engined Spitfire to go into squadron service and which proved to be a very successful low-level air superiority fighter.

Spitfire Mk VB BM448 of No 234 Squadron.

Chapter 8
Spitfire Squadron, 1940–41: a Pilot's Story

T O BE posted to a fighter squadron in the summer of 1940 was the dream of every newly-qualified RAF pilot, and if the squadron happened to be equipped with Spitfires, there was definitely icing on the cake. One such young pilot was Sergeant (later Flight Lieutenant) Jim Rosser, who describes the transition from FTS to an operational squadron during this period.

'I was awarded my pilot's brevet at RAF Sealand in North Wales, having passed out of No 5 Flying Training School. There was no formal parade with a VIP pinning the badge on my chest; I was simply given a piece of paper authorising the issue from stores of two brevets (Pilot Type). Stores had run out, so I had to go into Chester and buy some from a shop.

I was now Sergeant Rosser, W. J., General Duties (Pilot). After a most hectic party at the Blossoms Hotel in Chester, I waited the next day with most of the other pilots for news of our postings. I prayed for a posting to fighters, and if the prayer was granted, then please let it be Spitfires! When the postings were at last read out there seemed to be an awful lot of people whose names began with the initials A to Q, but eventually my turn came. My heart leapt; I was posted to Hawarden, which was a Spitfire OTU.'

Hawarden was about ten miles from Sealand and was the home of two operational training units, one of which, No 7 OTU (Wing Commander J. R. Hallings-Pott, DSO) specialised on the Spitfire. In August 1940 the OTU had fifty-eight Spitfires on

Spitfire VBs of No 243 Squadron, which reformed at RAF Ouston in June 1942 after service in the Far East.

strength, together with seventeen Miles Masters and six Fairey Battles, the latter used for target-towing. Trainee pilots underwent a two-week course of intensive flying; this was concerned mainly with conversion work, with a little basic tactical instruction thrown in; the compressed nature of the course was indicative of Fighter Command's desperate shortage of pilots, for the Battle of Britain had taken a heavy toll.

The OC Hawarden also maintained a Battle Flight of three Spitfires at armed readiness, and these could be used by any of the instructors in the event of an air raid alert coming through from No 7 Group of the Observer Corps at Manchester. This arrangement paid dividends; on 14 August 1940 one of the Flight's Spitfires shot down a Heinkel 111 which had bombed Sealand, and in September two more enemy aircraft, a Junkers 88 and a Dornier 215, were also destroyed, the crew of the former being taken prisoners.

Jim Rosser was soon caught up in the hectic tempo of OTU life.

'No time was wasted. There was a lull in the Battle of Britain, but the Germans could start up again at any time. We did about a dozen circuits and bumps, squadron formation, battle climb to about 30,000 feet, some aerobatics, and I fired my guns once into a sandbank in the estuary of the River Dee. Such was the desperate shortage of pilots that everything had to be rushed, and when I was posted to a squadron to go into action I had 11 hours 15 minutes' flying time on Spitfires.

The Spitfire Mk I had a pump-up undercarriage, so to begin with the initial climb from take-off was very undulating, as the left hand holding the stick kept pace with the right hand operating the pump. Each aircraft had a facility for transmitting an IFF identification signal; one aircraft only in a squadron or flight operated this for

Servicing a Spitfire VB of No 332 Squadron, the first Norwegian Spitfire squadron to form, at RAF Catterick on 16 January 1942.

fifteen seconds in each minute, and for that fifteen-second period he could not be warned if the formation came under attack, as he could not receive any R/T messages while transmitting. This was later corrected. As a matter of interest, the first take-off in a Spitfire was disappointing in a way, because there was no thump in the back on opening the throttle, as with the Miles Master on which I had trained. The latter had a Rolls-Royce Kestrel engine in a very light wooden frame. The Spitfire's performance after take-off, of course, was very different from the Master's.

At the end of the OTU course I received my posting notice and joining instructions. I was given three days' leave and was then to report to No 72 Squadron. This was at RAF Coltishall in Norfolk and I joined it on 5 November 1940. The Squadron had played its full part in the Battle of Britain, flying from Biggin Hill, and had suffered very heavy losses before being pulled back to Coltishall, in the No 12 Group area.

I was one of nine or ten replacement pilots. Having reported to Station HQ I was directed to 'A' Flight crew room, or the 'Dispersal Hut' as such buildings were then called. It was a long, single-storeyed building about thirty-six feet by ten; there was an office at one end for the flight commander, and down the centre of the room there ran a long, linoleum-covered table which I think had once been used for parachute packing. Against the walls were the now familiar wooden-armed easy chairs; I little realised at the time how many hours I would spend sitting in such chairs at readiness. The table was covered with parachutes, leather flying jackets, Mae Wests, maps and all sorts of assorted junk. At one end was a well-preserved shove ha'penny board, and woe betide anyone who left so much as a fingermark on it.

The room was crowded with pilots, some in chairs in their flying kit, others standing around. In one corner was a crowd who were clearly new boys, like myself; they were distinguished by the fact that they were wearing ties, for most of the others wore silk scarves of varying hues. I was suddenly grabbed by someone I recognised; it was Pilot Officer Bob Elliott, who had been a fellow member of the RAFVR at Sywell before the war. He had joined very much earlier than I had and was therefore a good deal further ahead in flying. He had been in the Battle of Britain, and I very quickly learned that he was no longer "Bob

Elliott" but "Pilot Officer Robert Deacon-Elliott".

He introduced me to my new flight commander, Flight Lieutenant Desmond Sheen, who was an Australian and still wore the dark blue uniform of the RAAF with gold rank braid instead of the blue RAF braid. I was to find him a very pleasant, undemonstrative man; because of his uniform, I learned that he was very often mistaken for a member of the Air Transport Auxiliary, and when that happened his sense of humour completely deserted him. He was later to command the Squadron, and subsequently the Biggin Hill Wing.

I was introduced to the other members of the Flight and stood around with the other new boys. To the best of my memory there was only one officer amongst us and that was Pilot Officer Fordham, who was a Canadian; all the rest were sergeant pilots. Within a year all were to be killed except myself and one other, Bill Lamberton.'

Rosser's friend Bill Lamberton, in fact, was shot down and taken prisoner during a fighter sweep over France in the summer of 1941. Jim Rosser remembers the occasion very well; he should have been flying on that sortie himself, but was feeling unwell, and Lamberton offered to take his place.

After a few weeks at Coltishall, No 72 Squadron moved to Leuchars, in Scotland, at the end of November 1940. Jim Rosser recalls that the move was not a particularly happy one, at least for the sergeant pilots.

'We found that the Sergeants' Mess, with the support of the Station Commander, refused to accommodate sergeant pilots, and arrangements had been made for us to eat and sleep in rather poor spare accommodation. The other squadrons, one of which was a Dutch unit, went along with this, but our CO, Squadron Leader Grey, did not. After a clash with the Station Commander, and several calls to Group HQ, the Station Commander was ordered to admit us to the Sergeants' Mess, as was our undeniable right. This of course generated quite a bit of bad feeling, so we took only breakfast and lunch in the mess and spent our evenings in Dundee. Fortunately it was only a few miles away, and there was a rail halt on the edge of the airfield. We would catch the most convenient train after we came off readiness at dusk, and return in time for readiness in the morning!

We were not long at Leuchars, and soon moved

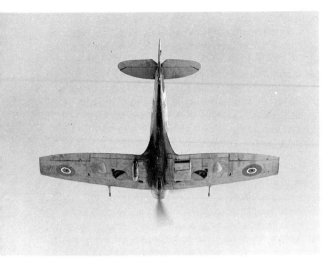

This photograph shows the Spitfire VB's clipped wings to good advantage.

It was almost always a false alarm, but in poor weather it could be a Hun securely hidden in the cloud. One day, the whole Squadron was released from readiness to fly up and down the Northumberland coast in formation while a party of American photographers followed us in a Wellington and took our picture for the *Chicago Times*. We flew up and down until the CO had to call a halt because we were getting short of fuel. As we were returning to the airfield, Bill Lamberton's engine suddenly cut and he had to land in a field quite close to the airfield. It would have been quite a good landing but for the fact that some sheep in the field panicked and ran in front of him; he hit them and this caused the aircraft to tip on to its back, but Bill crawled out unscathed and unperturbed. A year or so later, we were much amused to see a photograph of our formation over the north-east coast appear in a London magazine with the caption: "A squadron of Spitfires returning from a sweep over France!"

One afternoon in March 1941 – I was a section leader by this time – the flight was at readiness. It was a filthy, cloudy day and we did not really expect very much 'trade'. But we were scrambled and another sergeant and I were first off, with me leading. As soon as we were airborne I was given a vector to fly due east, out to sea. The cloud was in layers, and the base was at 1,000 feet. Apparently the Ops room had a firm plot, because they constantly changed the vector and height. Suddenly, I saw my first German aircraft, a Dornier 17.

As we chased after it it went into cloud. I quickly noted the reading on my directional gyro and followed the Dornier into the cloud. As I broke into the next bit of clear sky I saw it again. I dropped back into cloud and opened the throttle, and about ten seconds later gingerly pulled the

to Acklington in Northumberland. This was to be our home for the rest of the winter. The Squadron was well-known in the district, and we were royally welcomed in pubs from Morpeth to Alnmouth. The days were spent in training of various sorts: simulated dog-fights, air-to-air firing, and of course there was always a flight of three or four aircraft at constant readiness, from half-an-hour before first light until dusk. Readiness meant that you had about five minutes in which to scramble – to get from armchair into the air – but it was invariably done in much less. As a general rule one of the flights would have four aircraft at five minutes' readiness, four at fifteen or thirty minutes, and the other flight would have four aircraft at one hour. Those at thirty minutes or more could fly on local training.

Two aircraft used to be scrambled fairly often.

Spitfire Vs of No 485 (New Zealand) Squadron, which formed at Driffield in March 1941.

nose up, picking up the enemy aircraft again as I re-emerged. It was at extreme range, but I opened fire and gave it a long burst. I was gaining on it all the time, and saw some hits on the port engine nacelle. Then the Dornier dived into cloud, and I thought I could never be lucky enough to find it again. But I pushed the nose down, and as I broke cloud there, incredibly, was the enemy machine, with its port engine smoking badly. I knew I had very little time and I had lost touch with my number two, so I opened the throttle, closed in and gave the starboard engine a long burst. Smoke streamed from it, and as it went down into cloud I saw that the starboard propeller had stopped. I couldn't find it again, but I knew deep down that I had got my first Hun. Unfortunately the powers that be were not in agreement, although I was awarded one enemy aircraft 'damaged'.

Early in July 1941 there came a day of great rejoicing; we were informed that the Squadron was to move south to join the Biggin Hill Wing. We had now exchanged our Spitfire Is for Mk IIs with two 20mm cannon and four Brownings; the performance was better and the radio had been much improved.

Biggin Hill had been so knocked about during the Battle of Britain that there were facilities for only two of the three squadrons, so the third was based at Gravesend, and that was where we went initially – on 8 July – until our turn came to move to the main airfield. We took over all the airport buildings, which became the Squadron offices.

'A' Flight was lucky in that we had the old aero club premises for our dispersal point, whereas 'B' Flight were in some huts on the other side of the field. Incidentally, Gravesend was a grass airfield with a nasty slope on it.

The day after our arrival we had a visit from the people at Biggin, including Group Captain Barwell, the Station Commander, and the Wing Leader, Wing Commander 'Sailor' Malan. We were officially welcomed, and the CO was told that we were to fly over to Biggin the following morning for a briefing in preparation for our first sortie over France as part of the Biggin Hill Wing. On reaching Biggin, we went straight to the briefing room. The wall at one end was covered with a map showing the south-east of England and the enemy coast from Cherbourg to the Dutch border. On this map were strings, fixed with drawing pins, running from various airfields to points over which the Wings taking part in the mission were to rendezvous, and then following our route into France and out again.

After take-off we crossed the Channel in sections, line-astern, climbing all the time. We climbed into the sun, which was absolute hell; my eyes felt as though they were burning down into my head and within a few minutes I was saturated in sweat. It may have been just co-incidence, but every subsequent sweep we flew always seemed to head for Lille, which I soon learned to hate. It was our deepest penetration at that time, and there was flak all the way.

Spitfires of No 611 Squadron setting out on a fighter sweep.

I shall never forget my first operation. 72 Squadron was flying top cover; I was "Yellow Two", in other words the number two aircraft in Yellow Section, and quite honestly I hadn't a clue what was going on. We flew a sort of semi-circle over France, still in sections line-astern, and then came out again. I never saw a single enemy aircraft; but we must have been attacked, because when we got home three of our Spits were missing.'

The mission described by Rosser was a *Rodeo*, an offensive sweep into occupied Europe that usually involved one or two Fighter Command Wings, each of thirty-six aircraft. The other main offensive fighter operation of 1941, called a *Circus*, was a much larger affair, involving a small number of bombers – usually Blenheims, and occasionally Stirlings – making short penetrations into Europe under very heavy fighter escort.

According to Air Marshal Sholto Douglas, who assumed the leadership of RAF Fighter Command on 25 November 1940, the seeds that led to the implementation of large-scale fighter sweeps were sown at the tail-end of the Battle of Britain by Marshal of the Royal Air Force Sir Hugh Trenchard, who had continued to be a powerful force in Service matters long after his retirement as Chief of the Air Staff in 1930. With the German air offensive against the British Isles broken, Trenchard thought that the RAF should 'lean towards France', and advocated a system of offensive sweeps across the Channel in much the same way that the Royal Flying Corps had swept deep into enemy territory over the Western Front in the First World War. Douglas later said that at first he harboured grave doubts about such a policy, fearing that likely casualties would outweigh any positive results; but he changed his mind, and the idea was wholly supported by Air Vice-Marshal Trafford Leigh-Mallory, who took command of No 11 Group on 18 December 1940.

Within two days of Leigh-Mallory's appointment, on 20 December 1940, two Spitfires of No 66 Squadron, flown by Flight Lieutenant G. P. Christie and Pilot Officer C. A. W. Brodie, took-off from Biggin Hill on Fighter Command's first offensive sortie over enemy territory since the Battle of France. Crossing the enemy coast at Dieppe, they continued to Le Touquet airfield and shot up some buildings before returning to base, having encountered no opposition. This type of operation, by fighters working in pairs, was known as a *Rhubarb*.

Three weeks later, on 10 January 1941, the first *Circus* operation took place when six Blenheims of No 114 Squadron, escorted by six squadrons of Spitfires and Hurricanes, bombed an ammunition dump in the Foret de Guines. All the bombers returned safely; one Hurricane was lost in a skirmish with German fighters and two Spitfires crash-landed on return, one pilot being fatally injured.

Subsequent *Circus* and *Rodeo* operations in the first half of 1941 produced results that were far from encouraging. They involved, from January to June, a total of 190 bomber and 2,700 fighter sorties, in the course of which Fighter Command lost fifty-one aircraft and claimed forty-four enemy aircraft in return. Later analysis showed even this to be an

Spitfire Mk VB of the Air Fighting Development Unit. As a matter of interest, No 607 Squadron's Spitfires also carried the code AF in the Far East.

exaggeration, the true figure of German aircraft destroyed rising not much beyond twenty.

It was only the German invasion of the Soviet Union, with its attendant pressures for more intense British action in the west, that brought *Circus* and *Rodeo* operations a reprieve, and within a matter of weeks *Circus* operations had become very large affairs indeed, with as many as eighteen squadrons of fighters covering a small force of bombers. Getting six Wings of Spitfires airborne, to the rendez-vous at the right time and place, and shepherding them into and out of enemy territory, was something of a nightmare for everyone concerned, and it began on the ground. Three squadrons of Spitfires – thirty-six aircraft – might make an impressive sight as they taxied round the perimeter of an airfield, but with propellers flicking over dangerously close to wing-tips it was all too easy to make a mistake. A late starter would add to the problem as its pilot edged around the outside of the queue, trying to catch up with the rest of his squadron.

Making rendezvous with the bombers – usually over Manston – was another critical factor. A Spitfire's tanks held eighty-five gallons of fuel, and every minute spent in waiting for the Blenheims to turn up reduced a pilot's chances of getting home safely if he found himself in trouble over France. And over enemy territory the *Luftwaffe* always seemed to have the advantage. No matter how high the Spitfires climbed, the Me 109s usually managed to climb higher, ready to dive on the weavers, or 'tail-end Charlies' of the fighter formations and pick them off. Fighter Command was still employing its outdated fighter tactics in 1941, and continued to suffer as a consequence. There was no dog-fighting in the original sense of the word; the Messerschmitts fought on the climb and dive, avoiding turning combat with the more manoeuvrable Spitfires wher-ever possible, and the difference between life and death was measured in no more than seconds.

Much depended on skill and experience – but equally as much on leadership, and in the summer of 1941 the RAF had some very fine fighter leaders. No 72 Squadron, for instance, was commanded by Squadron Leader Desmond Sheen, an Australian who had begun his operational career before the war. In April 1940 he had been posted to No 212 Squadron, flying photographic reconnaissance Spit-fires, and during the next couple of months he had flown sorties all over Europe, returning to No 72 Squadron just in time to take part in the Battle of Britain. He was to lead the squadron on sweeps over occupied Europe for eight months, from March to November 1941.

Sheen's opposite number with No 92 Squadron – which had been the first to receive Spitfire VAs, all converted Mk Is, in February 1941 – was Jamie Rankin, a Scot from Portobello, Edinburgh, who had originally joined the Fleet Air Arm but later transferred to the RAF. When he was appointed to command No 92 Squadron in March 1941 it was the top-scoring unit in Fighter Command, and its score

Spitfire VB of No 316 (Polish) Squadron, based at Northolt in early 1942.

increased steadily under Rankin's leadership. Rankin himself opened his score with No 92 Squadron by destroying a Heinkel He 59 floatplane and damaging an Me 109 on 11 April. This was followed by another confirmed 109 on the 24th, and in June – a month of hectic fighting over France – he shot down seven more 109s, together with one probable.

It was Jamie Rankin who provided Jim Rosser with the latter's first Me 109. Rosser was now commissioned, with the rank of pilot officer.

'We didn't always fly operationally with our own squadrons. On this occasion Jamie Rankin was leading the Wing and I was flying as his number two, which was a considerable privilege. The *Luftwaffe* was up in strength and there was an almighty free-for-all, during which the Wing got split up. I clung to Jamie's tail like grim death, and as we were heading for the Channel he suddenly called up over the R/T and said: "There's a Hun at two o'clock below – have a go!" I looked down ahead and to the right and there, sure enough, was a 109, flying along quite sedately a few thousand feet lower down. I dived after him, levelled out astern and opened fire. He began to smoke almost at once and fell away in a kind of sideslip. A moment later, flames streamed from him.

In general terms, when the Squadron was attacked it tended to split up into pairs, but in practice a lot of people ended up on their own. On my third or fourth sweep – it was somewhere well up into Holland – we ran into a lot of trouble, and I ended up all by myself with about five 109s around me. There were no clouds to escape into,

and the position was very dicey. I collected a few holes and got off a few shots, but the situation would have been really serious if some other Spitfires had not appeared and seen off the Huns. Nevertheless, quite a scrap developed, and one of the Huns got off a deflection shot which put my propeller out of gear. Fortunately we were at about 20,000 feet, out to sea off the Dutch coast, and I was able to glide home, scraping into Martlesham Heath by the skin of my teeth.

Dog-fights never really lasted very long, consisting of very fast passes, quick 'squirts' and so on. I remember being involved in only one 'classical' dog-fight with a 109; I was alone and the scrap took place at about 8,000 feet twenty miles or so into France. He came down on to me out of the sun; fortunately I spotted him in time and pulled hard round to meet him, seeing his tracer go past me as he opened fire. He was turning fast, but I knew that the Spitfire would out-turn him so I hauled back on the stick to get behind him, momentarily blacking out with the 'g'. When my vision cleared I saw that he was in position for me to take a deflection shot at him, so I let him have it with cannon and machine-guns. I hit him around the cockpit area as he went down; I think I probably killed the pilot.

I always found it very difficult to see enemy aircraft. The second time I was technically shot down, the Squadron was split up into four flights after being attacked and I was Yellow Two, and we got into a gaggle of about eighteen 109s. The scrap only lasted a couple of seconds and I got in

Spitfire VBs of No 340 *Ile-de-France* Squadron preparing to take off on a sortie.

a burst at a 109, but whether I hit him or not I don't know. But while I was engaged with this Hun another had a go at me and hit me in the skew gear on top of the engine, which put the whole thing out of action. There I was, engineless, so I just stuffed the nose down. Fortunately I was not followed, and I was well out to sea, so I flattened out and headed for home. Once again I just managed to scrape in, making a forced landing literally on top of the cliffs.'

One of the biggest fighter sweeps of 1941 – code named *Circus 62* – was mounted on 7 August, when eighteen squadrons of Spitfires and two of Hurricanes accompanied six Blenheim bombers in an attack on a power station at Lille. The whole force made rendezvous at Manston, with the North Weald Wing, comprising the Hurricanes of No 71 (American Eagle) Squadron and the Spitfires of Nos 111 and 222 Squadrons providing close escort for the bombers. Behind and above, as immediate top cover, came the three Spitfire squadrons of the Kenley Wing: Nos 452 RAAF, 485 RNZAF, and 602. High above this beehive of nearly eighty fighters and bombers came the target support Wings, flying at 27,000 feet. There was the Biggin Hill Wing, with Nos 72, 92 and 609 Squadrons; the Hornchurch Wing, with Nos 403 RCAF, 603 and 611 Squadrons; and the Tangmere Wing, with Nos 41, 610 and 616 Squadrons. The target support force's task was to assure air superiority over and around Lille while the attack was in progress.

On this occasion, the *Luftwaffe* refused to be drawn into the battle in any large numbers; the invasion of Russia a few weeks earlier had seriously depleted German fighter strength in the Channel area, and the units that remained, seriously outnumbered in the face of Fighter Command's growing strength, had been ordered to conserve their resources. The 109s stayed well above the Spitfire formations, shadowing them. From time to time, small numbers of Messerschmitts broke away and darted down to fire on the odd straggler, always disengaging when the rest of the Spitfires turned on them.

The bombers, meanwhile, had found Lille obscured by cloud, so had turned back towards the Channel to attack St Omer airfield. A fierce air battle was already in progress over the coast, where the two Polish Spitfire squadrons of the Northolt Wing – Nos 306 and 308 – had been waiting to cover the Blenheims' withdrawal. No 308 Squadron was suddenly bounced by about eighteen Me 109s, and in the ensuing fight two Spitfires were shot down. The Blenheims made their escape unmolested, but the rear support Wing, comprising Nos 19, 257 and 401 Squadrons, lost two Spitfires and a Hurricane. Since No 41 Squadron had also lost a Spitfire, *Circus 62* had therefore cost the RAF six aircraft, a result which, set against a claim for three Me 109s de-

Spitfire VB BM252 *Bombay City*, which served with Nos 122, 222, 316 and 130 Squadrons during its career.

stroyed, could hardly be considered favourable, set against the far smaller numbers of enemy aircraft involved.

Another large operation – *Circus 63* – was mounted two days later, on Saturday 9 August. This time, the Blenheims' objective was a supply dump in the Béthune area. Once again, the Tangmere Wing formed part of the target support force, but things went wrong right from the start when No 41 Squadron failed to rendezvous on time. The remainder, unable to wait, carried on across the Channel. For a while, all was peaceful; then, just a few miles short of the target, the 109s hit them hard. For the next few minutes, the Tangmere pilots were hard put to hold their own, the Wing becoming badly dislocated as the Messerschmitts pressed home determined attacks. The Wing Leader, Wing Commander Douglas Bader, misjudged an attack on a 109 and found himself isolated. Six enemy fighters closed in on him and, by superb flying, he destroyed two. The end came soon afterwards, when a third 109 collided with him and severed his Spitfire's fuselage just behind the cockpit. Bader managed to struggle clear of the plunging debris, leaving one of his artificial legs still trapped in the cockpit. His parachute opened, and he floated down to a painful landing and captivity.

As August gave way to September, some senior Air Staff members began to have serious doubts about the value of *Circus* operations. Fighter Command losses were climbing steadily, and the results achieved hardly seemed to compensate for them. The AOC No 11 Group, Air Vice-Marshal Leigh-Mallory, claimed that between 14 June and 3 September 1941 his pilots had destroyed 437 German fighters, with another 182 probably destroyed. As the *Luftwaffe* never had any more than 260 single-engined fighters in France and the Low Countries at any one time during this period, of which only about 200 were serviceable, it is hardly surprising that the actual figure turns out to be 128 destroyed and seventy-six damaged – while Fighter Command lost 194 pilots during those three months. The RAF's claim for the six and a half months from 14 June to 31 December 1941 – 731 enemy aircraft destroyed – was equally as exaggerated; the actual German loss was 154, including fifty-one not attributable to combat. Fighter Command's admitted loss, on the other hand, was 411.

With the trend going the way it was, it was only a matter of time before large-scale fighter sweeps over the continent were halted; and halted they were, in November 1941, on the orders of Winston Churchill. The sweeps had done little, in fact, except to ensure that Fighter Command remained in a state of combat readiness; they had also shown that the Spitfire Mk V was no match, one-to-one, for the Me 109F.

And before the sweeps were halted, Fighter Command had received yet another damaging blow to its morale. On 21 September 1941, Polish Spitfire pilots of No 315 Squadron, on their way home after *Circus 101*, reported having been attacked by an 'unknown enemy aircraft with a radial engine'. All sorts of wild rumours began to circulate in Fighter Command, the favourite among them being that the strange aircraft were Curtiss Hawk 75As, captured by the Germans and pressed into service.

A few days later, Jim Rosser and his fellow pilots of No 72 Squadron were providing medium-level cover to a formation of bombers attacking Le Havre.

'As we turned to come away the top Wing suddenly broke up because they were being attacked. A few seconds later some enemy fighters came down on us, very fast. I turned after one, pouring on the coals, and got off a burst at very long range with cannon and machine-guns before he disappeared into the safety of the Le Havre flak barrage. I made to follow him, but my flight commander, Ken Campbell, called me back as it was not worth risking my neck. When we got back my photographs were hurriedly developed and, long range though they were, they gave us the first clue as to what the new fighters really were.'

The Focke-Wulf 190 had arrived in France, and the Spitfire squadrons were about to face their sternest challenge so far.

Spitfire Squadrons in the RAF Fighter Command Order of Battle, 31 December 1941

Squadron	Mark	Location	Remarks
19	VB	Ludham	
41	VB	Westhampnett	
54	VB	Castletown	Left for Australia, June 1942
64	VB	Hornchurch	
65	VB	Debden	
66	IIA	Portreath	
72	VB	Gravesend	
74	VB	Llanbedr	
79	VB	Martlesham Heath	Formed 19.9.40 as the first 'Eagle' squadron with US personnel.
91	VB	Hawkinge	Formed from No 421 (Recce) Flight, 11.1.41.
92	VB	Digby	Left for Middle East, 12.2.42.
111	VB	Debden	
118	VB	Ibsley	
121	VB	North Weald	The second 'Eagle' squadron, formed 14.5.41.
122	IIA/B	Scorton	
123	IIA	Castletown	Left for Middle East, 11.4.42.
124	VB	Biggin Hill	
129	VB	Westhampnett	
130	VA	Perranporth	
131	IIA, VB	Atcham	
132	IIB	Peterhead	
133	IIA	Eglinton	The third 'Eagle' squadron, formed 1.8.41.
134	VA	Catterick	Moved to Eglinton, 1.1.42. Left for Middle East, 10.4.42.
145	VB	Catterick	Left for Middle East, 11.2.42.
152	IIA	Coltishall	
154	IIA	Fowlmere	
222	VB	North Weald	
234	VB	Ibsley	
266	VB	King's Cliffe	Began conversion to Typhoons, January 1942.
302 (Polish)	VB	Harrowbeer	Name: *Poznanski.*
303 (Polish)	VB	Northolt	Name: *Kosciuszko.*
306 (Polish)	IIB/VB	Churchstanton	Name: *Torunski.*
308 (Polish)	VB	Woodvale	Name: *Krakowski.*
310 (Czech)	IIA	Perranporth	First Czech fighter squadron in RAF, formed 10.7.40.
312 (Czech)	IIA	Ayr	Moved to Fairwood Common, 1.1.42.
313 (Czech)	VB	Hornchurch	
315 (Polish)	VB	Northolt	Name: *Deblinski.*
316 (Polish)	VB	Northolt	Name: *Warszawski.*
317 (Polish)	VB	Exeter	Name: *Wilenski.*
331 (Norwegian)	IIA	Skaebrae	First Norwegian-manned fighter squadron in the RAF, formed 21.7.41.
340 (Free French)	IIA	Ayr	First Free French fighter squadron in the RAF, formed 7.11.41. Name: *Ile-de-France.*
350 (Belgian)	IIA	Valley	First Belgian fighter squadron in RAF, formed 12.11.41.
401 (RCAF)	VB	Biggin Hill	
403 (RCAF)	VB	Debden	
411 (RCAF)	IIA	Hornchurch	
412 (RCAF)	IIA	Wellingore	
416 (RCAF)	IIA	Peterhead	
417 (RCAF)	IIA	Charmy Down	
421 (RCAF)	IIA	Fairwood Common	
452 (RAAF)	IIA	Kenley	
457 (RAAF)	VB	Jurby, Isle of Man	
485 (RNZAF)	VB	Kenley	
501	VB	Ibsley	
504	IIA/B	Ballyhalbert	
602	VB	Kenley	
603	VB	Dyce	
609	VB	Digby	
610	VB	Leconfield	
611	VB	Drem	
616	VB	Kirton-in-Lindsey	

Chapter 9
The Air Superiority Challenge, 1942

FIGHTER COMMAND entered 1942 with sixty squadrons of Spitfires, a threefold expansion achieved over little more than eighteen months. More squadrons would be formed in the course of the year, as the demands of the Middle East and Far East, where a new theatre of hostilities had just opened up against Japan, made inroads into these home-based assets. Despite these inroads into its resources, it seemed that the Command, in 1942, was strong enough not only to fulfil its primary task of defending Britain from air attack, but also to renew its offensive against the enemy.

The swordthrust of disillusionment was quick to come, and it was delivered by the Focke-Wulf 190. A team from *Jagdgeschwader 26* was given the job of introducing the fighter into *Luftwaffe* service; the first Fw 190A-1s were delivered to 6/JG 26 in August 1941, and aircraft of this Le Bourget-based unit clashed with Spitfires on 27 September, the day Pilot Officer Jim Rosser of No 72 Squadron secured his photographs of the type, and from that moment on it was clear that the Spitfire V was outclassed in every aspect of combat except turning radius. This fact was hammered home early in 1942, by which time the Fw 190 equipped two *Gruppen* of JG 26.

In the early weeks of 1942, much of RAF Bomber Command's effort was directed against the German battle cruisers *Scharnhorst* and *Gneisenau* and the heavy cruiser *Prinz Eugen*, sheltering in Brest harbour. The fear was that they would attempt to break out and join up with the latest addition to the German fleet, the powerful battleship *Tirpitz*, which had put to sea and taken temporary refuge in a Norwegian fjord. In January, air reconnaissance revealed that a breakout by the cruisers appeared imminent, and on 4 February every available aircraft of Bomber Command was bombed up and placed on two hours' readiness. At the same time, Nos 10, 11 and 12 Groups of Fighter Command stood ready to provide air cover, while Coastal Command stepped up its reconnaissance sorties over the Channel area. After a week, however, the state of readiness was downgraded and squadrons released for other operations, with the proviso that they could immediately be released for attacks on the warships as required.

As the torpedo-bomber resources of Coastal Command and the Royal Navy were very limited, the main hope of inflicting damage on the warships rested with Bomber Command. When the German vessels finally did break out on the night of 11/12 February, however, it was in bad weather, with a cloud base of only 600 feet, which rendered level-bombing operations useless. It also concealed the movements of the cruisers and their escorting vessels for some time, and – allied with some effective radar jamming – meant that they were within twenty miles of Boulogne before they were discovered. In fact, the discovery itself was accidental, the fleet being sighted in passage through the Channel by the pilots of two Spitfire sections, one from No 91 Squadron, Hawkinge, and the other from No 602 Squadron, Kenley, led respectively by Sqn Ldr Bobby Oxspring and the other by Gp Capt Victor Beamish. It was later said that they did not report what they had seen until they were on the ground, having previously been warned to keep radio silence, but this is untrue. The Germans themselves later confirmed that R/T silence was broken by one or more of the pilots at the time they sighted the ships, so what happened subsequently was hardly their fault.

The Germans had assembled a formidable array of fighters to cover the naval force; ninety Me 109Fs of JG 2 and twelve of the *Jagdfliegerschule* (Fighter School), Paris, covering the sector Le Havre-Cherbourg; ninety Fw 190s of JG 26, covering the Channel narrows from Abbeville to Calais; and sixty Me 109s of JG 1, covering the final sector from the river Scheldt to Wilhelmshaven, the warships' destination.

Of the RAF's available striking force, only two units – the Beauforts of No 217 Squadron at Thorney Island and six Swordfish of No 825 Naval Air Squadron at Manston – were in a position to attack more or less immediately, and it was decided that the Swordfish would attack in conjunction with an assault by Ramsgate-based MTBs. No 11 Group undertook to provide five squadrons of Spitfires, three to cover the Swordfish and two to make diversionary attacks, but stated that it would be difficult to get them to the rendezvous at Manston by the required time of 1225. In fact, the controllers at both Biggin Hill and Hornchurch passed word to Manston that their squadrons would be a few minutes late.

At 12.20, the commander of No 825 Squadron, Lieutenant-Commander Eugene Esmonde – having received word that the enemy warships were travelling faster than previously estimated – decided that he could delay his take-off no longer and circled over Manston, waiting for the fighter escort. At 12.28 the Spitfires of No 72 Squadron arrived, three minutes late, but there was no sign of the other two.

Jim Rosser, one of the 72 Squadron pilots, disagrees that there was any time discrepancy.

'It was an absolutely foul day – even the sparrows were walking, as they say – and we were told to take-off and rendezvous with a strike of Fleet Air Arm Swordfish torpedo-bombers which were to attack the warships from Manston. We arrived overhead exactly on the time we had been given according to our Ops Room clock. You couldn't see from one side of the airfield to the other, conditions were so bad, but we flew one circuit around Manston and were then told over the R/T that the Navy aircraft had gone, so we set course for the action at very low level.

We eventually sighted the warships just as the Swordfish were going in, and we were too late; they were mown down. Our whole squadron made a rather abortive attack on the warships, strafing their superstructures, and it was remarkable that no-one was shot down. It was a very tragic affair, and it was ghastly to see the Swordfish going into the water, but there was nothing we could do about it, because it was the flak that was getting them. Why we didn't lose at least half our own aircraft from the flak, I shall never understand.'

All six Swordfish were destroyed, with the loss of all but a handful of their aircrew. Lt-Cdr Esmonde was later awarded a posthumous Victoria Cross.

The other two Spitfire squadrons detailed to escort the Swordfish, Nos 121 and 401 (RCAF), had cut straight out over the coast at Deal in an attempt to locate their charges en route. Failing to find them, they flew back to Manston and headed out to sea again, reaching the combat area a few minutes after the Swordfish had made their attack. The Spitfire pilots soon found themselves engaged in savage combats with the enemy fighter umbrella, as did other Spitfire squadrons that were despatched to provide cover for the 242 aircraft of Bomber Command that went out to attack the warships in the course of the day. In spite of the fact that the *Scharnhorst* and *Gneisenau* were damaged by mines, all ships reached their bases in Germany without loss.

The action cost the RAF and Fleet Air Arm dearly: thirty-one aircraft failed to return, mostly bombers (including the six FAA Swordfish). The *Luftwaffe* lost seven aircraft.

March 1942 saw a limited resumption of *Circus* operations, the vulnerable Blenheims of No 2 Group now being replaced by the faster, more modern Douglas Boston. The number of Bostons involved in these operations was never more than thirty, but they were often escorted by twenty-five, -six or -seven Squadrons of Spitfires – nearly half Fighter Command's available strength. On one occasion – 30 April 1942 – no fewer than thirty-eight Squadrons of Spitfires were involved in escorting twenty-four Bostons on four separate missions. Only six Bostons were lost during April but Spitfire losses were heavy as the Fw 190s and Me 109Fs continued to show their superiority (albeit marginal, in the case of the latter aircraft) over the Spitfire V. For example, eleven Spitfires failed to return on 4 April, fifteen on 12 April, and twelve on 25 April, Spitfire losses for the whole of the month being fifty-nine aircraft. To make matters worse, in May 1942 a newly-formed *Luftwaffe* unit, 11/JG 2 *Richthofen*, took delivery of a new model of the Me 109 – the G-1, optimised for high-altitude interception.

As far as the Focke-Wulf Fw 190 was concerned, two aspects in particular gave this excellent fighter the edge in air combat: the power of its BMW radial engine and its superlative rate of roll. If a Spitfire variant could be produced with powerplant and aerodynamic characteristics to match those of the Fw 190, the balance would be restored.

When the Fw 190 entered service in the late summer of 1941, the only RAF fighter with the potential of matching it was the Hawker Typhoon, which had just been delivered to No 56 Squadron at Duxford in September 1941. But the Typhoon was bedevilled by all sorts of technical troubles to do with its airframe and the Napier Sabre engine, and although it was fast and handled well at medium and low altitudes, its performance at high altitude

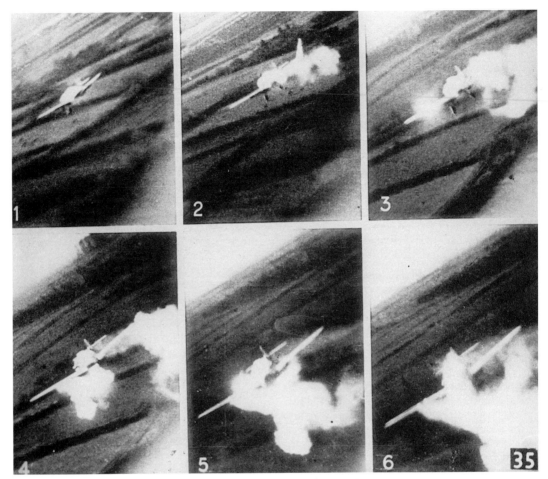

A Messerschmitt Me 109F falls to a Spitfire's guns over France early in 1942.

was inferior to that of both the Fw 190 and the Me 109F, and its rate of climb was poor. Teething troubles kept the squadron non-operational with the type until the end of May 1942, and at one time there was talk of cancelling the Typhoon programme altogether.

While the Typhoon was undergoing its trials in 1941, another Spitfire variant had made its appearance. This was the Mk VI, the first of the high-altitude Spitfires and the first to be fitted with a pressurised cockpit. The prototype was a Mk I, R7120, which was taken off the production line and partially dismantled. Two airtight bulkheads were fitted into the fuselage, the forward one being installed as close as possible to the rear of the fuel tanks and the rear one immediately behind the

Perspex window aft of the pilot's seat. The sliding hood was deleted and replaced by a specially designed hood of strengthened Perspex that was clamped down on to a sponge rubber seal before take-off. The pilot's side door was blanked off.

Despite some initial difficulty in making the cockpit completely airtight, the pressurisation system worked well, the Marshall IXa cabin blower providing a maximum pressure of 2 lb per square inch and an air temperature of over 60°C, resulting in a cabin temperature of 8°C at an outside air temperature of minus 55°C. The system gave a pressure equivalent to 28,000 feet apparent altitude while the aircraft was at 40,000 feet.

Fitted with a Merlin 47 engine of 1,415 hp, R7120 went to RAE Farnborough for pressurisation trials in

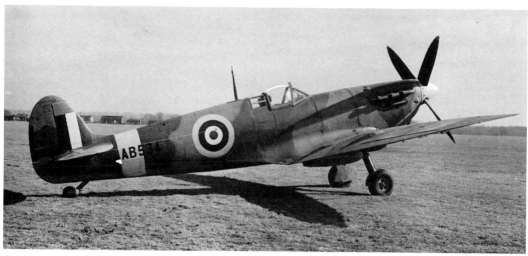

Spitfire Mk VI AB534, a Mk V conversion.

June 1941. In the meantime a second aircraft, X4942, had been coverted from a Mk VA, and Jeffrey Quill flew this at Eastleigh with the hood off on 4 July. Two days later he reached an altitude of 38,000 feet from Worthy Down. The other aircraft, R7120, flew on 25 August, and on 7 September Sqn Ldr H. J. Wilson took it to 39,500 feet.

Both aircraft were fitted with the extended wingtips that were to be a feature of all the high-altitude Spitfires, increasing the wing area from 242 sq ft to 248.5 sq ft. This was a notable recognition feature,

and the type appeared in the Air Ministry aircraft recognition lists as 'Experimental Aircraft No 152'.

One hundred Mk VI Spitfires were ordered, the first entering service with No 616 Squadron at King's Cliffe, Northamptonshire, in April 1942. Over the next eighteen months or so the type was also allocated to Nos 124, 129, 234, 310, 313, 504, 519 and 602 Squadrons. All of these except No 519, which was a meteorological squadron, were assigned to home defence, and generally one flight of each squadron had the Mk VI specifically to

A converted Spitfire Mk I with extended wingtips, X4942 was a Mk VI trials aircraft. One hundred Mk VIs were built.

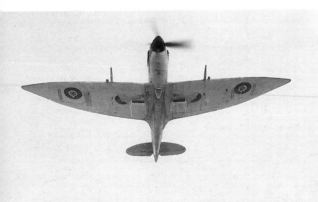

The prototype Spitfire Mk VIII, AB450, a converted Mk V.

Mk VIs were gradually relegated to training and communications duties.

Much of the technology that went into the Mk VI Spitfire's pressurised cockpit had been developed for another Vickers project, the high-altitude Wellington V and VI bombers. Also specified for this aircraft was the Rolls-Royce RM 6SM Merlin 60 engine, a two-stage, two-speed, inter-cooled powerplant which was to take Merlin development to its ultimate. Here, the Air Ministry felt, was an engine that would give the Spitfire an edge over the Focke-Wulf 190, and at a meeting held on 16 December 1941 representatives of all the bodies concerned discussed the production of a variant fitted with the new engine, the aircraft to be designated Spitfire Mk VII.

The Merlin 60/Spitfire combination had already flown on 27 September 1941 – the day, coincidentally, when Spitfires and Fw 190s first met in combat. The Spitfire involved was Mk III N3297, now used by Rolls-Royce as a test-bed at Hucknall. By the end of the year a second Spitfire, Mk I R6700, had also been fitted with a Merlin 60-series engine (Merlin 61) and this flew on 6 January 1942.

Air Staff planning now envisaged production of both the Spitfire VII and, in large numbers, the Spitfire VIII, which was basically an unpressurised version of the Mk VII and intended for low-level air superiority operations. But the Mk VIII design needed a lot of refinement, including a general strengthening of the fuselage, which meant that production would be delayed for an unacceptably long time, and Air Staff thoughts consequently turned to an interim aircraft: a Mk V Spitfire air-

A fine air-to-air study of Spitfire Mk VIII MD351. Unfortunately, no record appears to exist of this aircraft's operational career.

intercept high-flying enemy reconnaissance aircraft. Five examples, BS106, BS124, BS133, BS134, and BS149, were sent to the Middle East in October 1942 to help counter incursions by Junkers Ju 86Ps. As the activities of German high-altitude reconnaissance aircraft diminished from 1944, the

Spitfire Mk VIII JG204 was the tropical trials aircraft, undergoing extensive testing at Farnborough before the mark was cleared for service in the Far East.

frame combined with a Merlin 61 engine.

Two Mk Vs, AB196 and AB197, were delivered to Hucknall for conversion in December 1941, and these flew respectively on 26 February and 26 March 1942 with their new engines. Four more Mk Vs were selected as development aircraft; these were AA837 (the first production Spitfire VC with four 20mm cannon), AB501, AB505, and AB507. Trials were successful, and on 18 April 1942 Supermarine and Rolls-Royce were instructed to install Merlin 61 engines into 100 Spitfire Mk VC airframes, deliveries to Fighter Command to be completed by the end of June. Designation of the new Spitfire variant was F Mk IX.

For an aircraft intended as a stop-gap, the Spitfire IX was a resounding success. In all, 5,665 were built, more than any other mark except the Mk V. No 64 Squadron at Hornchurch was the first to equip with the new variant in June 1942, followed by No 611 in July and Nos 401 and 402 (RCAF) in August.

In the early months of 1942, however, the Spitfire IX was still in the future, and the Mk V-equipped squadrons continued to suffer at the hands of the Focke-Wulfs. *Circus* operations to France and the Low Countries continued as the main activity, although there were frequent anti-shipping armed reconnaissance patrols over the English Channel and the North Sea. In July, the air defence task once

more assumed priority for the Spitfire squadrons in south-east England, for Focke-Wulf Fw 190s of JG 2 and JG 26 began carrying out hit-and-run attacks on coastal targets in growing numbers. All the raids were carried out at very low level to avoid radar detection and were usually flown by a *Schwarm* of four aircraft. They were highly successful, and it was fortunate for the British that the *Geschwader* never had more than about twenty Fw 190A-3 fighter-bombers available for operations at any time. The *Luftwaffe* pilots made full use of the contours of the South Downs, flying what would nowadays be called 'nap of the earth' to pop up and attack coastal targets from the rear.

The sternest test for Fighter Command during this period was the Dieppe operation of 19 August 1942 (Operation *Jubilee*), one object of which was to battle all the forces of the *Luftwaffe* on northern France and the Low Counties. Control of the RAF part of the operation was given to Air Vice-Marshal Trafford Leigh-Mallory of No 11 Group, and fifty-six squadrons of Spitfires, Hurricanes and Typhoons were placed at his disposal, as well as five Blenheim and Boston squadrons of No 2 Group and four Mustang squadrons of Army Co-operation Command.

The story of that ill-fated venture, and of the gallantry of the Canadian troops who took appal-

One that didn't get back: a Focke-Wulf Fw 190 shot down during a hit-and-run raid on the south coast.

ling casualties in the landing, is well known. Dieppe was a disaster for the RAF, too; in the day's operations the British lost 106 aircraft against the *Luftwaffe*'s forty-eight. Of the RAF losses, eighty-eight were fighters, and the majority of these were Spitfires.

Tuesday, 29 September 1942, was a significant day for the officers and men of Nos 71, 121 and 133 'Eagle' Squadrons at Debden. At a formal parade, they were handed over to VIII Fighter Command, United States Army Air Force, to become the 334th, 335th and 336th Fighter Squadrons of the 4th Fighter Group. From now on, the primary task of the pilots would be bomber escort to the Boeing B-17s that had become operational in the United Kingdom that summer. The pilots of No 133 Squadron had already had an unhappy taste of this type of mission on 4 September, when twelve brand-new Spitfire IXs had accompanied a formation of B-17 Fortresses in an attack on Morlaix. A serious navigational error, compounded by bad weather, had resulted in eleven

of the twelve Spitfires running out of fuel over the Brest peninsula on the return flight. Four pilots were killed and the rest taken prisoner; only one Spitfire made it home. The physical casualties were bad enough, but it was followed by a severe blow to the Americans' pride; re-equipment arrived in the shape of Spitfire Vs.

The fiasco proved that whatever else the Spitfire might be, it was not an escort fighter, and that was precisely what the American bombers were going to need as they penetrated deeper into enemy territory. It had never been envisaged as one – although it might have become one, with improvements to the Merlin engine's fuel consumption and the addition of long-range tanks. The formula worked later, with the Merlin-engined North American P-51 Mustang, but in its early operations the USAAF's VIIIth Bomber Command made its deep-penetration missions virtually unescorted, with disastrous consequences.

The Americans did have one long-range escort

Posed photograph of British, Dominion and American Spitfire pilots who took part in the ill-fated Dieppe operation of August 1942. RAF Fighter Command suffered heavy losses.

fighter in 1942; this was the Lockheed P-38 Lightning, which equipped two fighter groups. In November, however, these were diverted to the Mediterranean Theatre to take part in the North African campaign. So were several of Fighter Command's valuable Spitfire squadrons, which were to play a major role in turning the tide of Axis success in an environment vastly different from that of north-west Europe.

Pilots of the 4th Fighter Group, VIIIth Fighter Command USAAF, put on a scramble for the benefit of the camera at Debden.

Chapter 10
Spitfires over the Desert

THE FIRST Desert Air Force Spitfire squadron to become operational in North Africa was No 145, which embarked for the Middle East in February 1942 and became established at Heliopolis, Egypt, in April. In the following month it equipped with Spitfire Mk VBs fitted with Vokes tropical filters and moved up to Gambut, from where it flew its first mission – an escort for Hurricane fighter-bombers – on 1 June. During the next few weeks No 145 was joined by two more Spitfire squadrons deployed from the United Kingdom, Nos 92 and 601, which formed No 244 Wing of No 211 Group together with the Hurricanes of No 73 Squadron.

One of the most important aspects of the Spitfire's arrival in the North African theatre was that it led to the complete denial of photographic reconnaissance intelligence to the enemy. During the first half of 1942, a German reconnaissance unit, 2(F)/123, had been overflying the Suez Canal Zone with Junkers Ju 86P-2 aircraft, based at Kastelli in Crete. Operating at altitudes of more than 42,000 feet, these aircraft were unchallenged; even when the first Spitfire VCs reached the theatre in May, the Germans could not have seriously regarded them as a threat to their reconnaissance activities, for the Mk VC's ceiling was only about 33,000 feet.

Three test pilots at the Aboukir Aircraft Depot, however, were determined that something ought to be done about the Ju 86 nuisance. They were Flying Officer G. W. H. Reynolds and Pilot Officers A. Gold and G. E. Genders, all of them veterans and among the most experienced pilots in the Middle East. With the help of the depot's technical staff, they set about stripping down one of the Spitfires, cutting out all extra weight such as armour plating. A new four-blade Rotol propeller was fitted, and the Spitfire's Merlin 46 engine specially modified to give more power at high altitude. The standard armament of two 20mm cannon and four .303-in machine guns was also removed and replaced by two .50-in machine-guns.

After several abortive attempts, it was Fg Off Reynolds who made the first successful intercep-

tion on 24 August 1942. He sighted a Ju 86P a few miles north of Cairo, flying at 37,000 feet, and went in pursuit. The Germans saw him and climbed in an effort to escape, but Reynolds – frozen stiff and suffering from anoxia – clung doggedly to the Junkers' tail and opened fire from astern at 42,000 feet. His aim was good and the Junkers fell away in a diving turn, one engine smoking. Then 38-year-old Reynolds, utterly exhausted, blacked out and the Spitfire went out of control. He came to 10,000 feet lower down, regained control and landed safely with only five gallons of petrol in his tanks. Later, he learned that the Junkers had made a forced landing in the desert and that its crew had been taken prisoner.

A few days later it was Genders' turn to score. Since the stripped-down Spitfire carried no radio, he flew in company with a standard Spitfire VC whose job was to act as a marker aircraft. If Genders succeeded in damaging the Ju 86, the marker – flying several thousand feet lower down, but always in sight of Genders' aircraft – would hopefully be able to finish off the enemy machine.

The Junkers was duly sighted, right on time as usual, and Genders managed to catch it at 45,000 feet a long way out to sea. He fired most of his ammunition at it and had the satisfaction of seeing it start to go down – it was subsequently destroyed, as planned, by the marker Spitfire – but he ran out of fuel shortly after turning back towards Aboukir. At 1,000 feet, still far out over the Mediterranean, Genders baled out. He had no dinghy – that, too, had been left behind to save weight – and so, with only his Mae West lifejacket for support, he started swimming for the Egyptian coast. Twenty-two hours later, half dead with fatigue, he crawled ashore and, after a short rest, set out to thumb a lift back to Aboukir.

After a delay of over a week while a second Spitfire (BR114) was stripped down, the Aboukir test pilots scored their third victory. It was Reynolds' turn once again, and on this occasion the chase took him to 50,000 feet, a record altitude for 1942. The whole flight proved agonizing, for the temperature in the cockpit was 67 degrees below zero and Reynolds, who was wearing the minimum of flying clothing, suffered severe pain and was partially paralyzed. Nevertheless, he caught the Junkers 86 eight miles out to sea and shot it down. After that, there were no more high-level reconnaissance flights over the Canal Zone, although 2(F)/123 continued to operate its Ju 86Ps until May 1943, when they were withdrawn.

Although the Spitfires of No 244 Wing made an important contribution to Desert Air Force operations, the main effort throughout the summer of 1942 continued to be sustained by the Hawker Hurricane and Curtiss P-40 Kittyhawk squadrons of the RAF, RAAF and SAAF – joined, later in the year, by the three squadrons of the 57th Fighter Group, USAAF, which was also equipped with P-40s. All these units were fully committed when, on the night of 22/23 October 1942, General Montgomery's Eighth Army launched its major counter-offensive against the Axis forces at El Alamein.

On 8 November, while the Eighth Army's drive from the east rolled the Axis forces steadily back through Cyrenaica, Anglo-American forces carried out a series of simultaneous landings in Morocco and western Algeria under the code-name Operation *Torch*. Apart from the tragic and abortive Dieppe operation of August 1942, Operation *Torch* was the first large-scale amphibious operation undertaken by the Allies, and was supported by seven British and four American aircraft carriers.

Two Fleet Air Arm squadrons on the carrier HMS *Furious*, Nos 801 and 807, were equipped with Supermarine Seafires; this navalised version of the Spitfire was about to see action for the first time. Originally known as the Sea Spitfire, the Seafire Mk I was basically a Mk VB/C Spitfire fitted with an arrester hook; the first aircraft to be modified, in January 1942, was Mk VB AB205. In February 1942 Mk VB AD371 was fitted with an arrester hook and also catapult spools, receiving the designation Seafire Mk II.

The first forty-eight Seafires, without catapult spools, were redesignated Mk 1Bs; the only FAA squadron to be completely equipped with them was No 801, which embarked on HMS *Furious* in June 1942. In the summer of 1943 Seafire IBs partially equipped No 842 Squadron, embarked on HMS *Fencer*. About 140 Seafire IBs were eventually converted, the variant being regarded as a stop-gap until the Seafire Mk IIC (which featured catapult spools, a strengthened fuselage and undercarriage, a

Merlin 32 engine and a four-blade Rotol propeller) became available in sufficient numbers. Production of the Seafire Mk IIC totalled 372; No 807 Squadron had begun to equip with the type in September 1942, and was roughly at half strength at the time of Operation *Torch*.

Air cover during the initial phase of the landings and the subsequent consolidation was undertaken by the naval fighters, with the exception of the Hurricanes of No 43 Squadron, which flew into Maison Blanche, Algiers, less than an hour after the airfield had been captured by an American combat team. They were quickly followed by the Hurricanes of No 255 Squadron, the Spitfires of Nos 72, 81, 93, 111, 152 and 242 Squadrons and the Beaufighters of No 255, which had assembled at Gibraltar. On the first day of the landings stiff opposition was encountered in some areas from Vichy French forces, and there were several combats with Dewoitine D.520 and Curtiss Hawk 75A fighters. Lt G. C. Baldwin of No 801 Squadron scored the Seafire's first kill on 8 November, destroying a D.520.

The USAAF's 31st Fighter Group, also equipped with Spitfire VBs and operating from Gibraltar, was tasked with providing air cover for American ground forces approaching the airfield of Tafaraoui, Oran. As they approached their objective the Americans, flying through scattered showers,

Spitfire VBs of the 31st Fighter Group, USAAF, North Africa, 1943.

sighted what they took to be four Hurricanes orbit-
ing the airfield; the Hurricanes, however, turned out
to be D.520s, and these shot down one of the Spitfires. The remaining four Spitfires, led by Major
Harrison Thyng, fell on the Vichy fighters and
destroyed three of them, leaving the survivor to
flee for home. One of the D.520s was shot down
by Thyng; it was the start of a combat career that
was to end in the cockpit of an F-86 Sabre over
Korea, where he destroyed five MiG-15 jets.

Once the Vichy French airfields in Algeria had
been secured, the build-up of Allied fighter squadrons proceeded at a fast rate. On 9 November,
the Hurricanes of No 43 Squadron and the Spitfires of Nos 81 and 242 were scrambled to
intercept an unescorted force of Junkers 88s.
'The RAF pilots', it is recorded, 'appreciated the
experience'.

Although the Allied landings had taken the Germans completely by surprise, their reaction was very
swift, and the *Luftwaffe* units in North Africa – of a
very high calibre already – were quickly reinforced.
The Vichy French, who had fought to keep the Allies
out of Morocco and Algeria, allowed the Germans
into Tunisia without opposition. On 10 November,
Allied air reconnaissance detected 115 Axis aircraft
on the ground at El Aouina; while at Sidi Ahmed,
outside Bizerta, transport aircraft were flying in at
the rate of fifty a day. On 11 November, Allied
shipping offloading vital supplies was heavily attacked, losing several of their number. Among other
things, these attacks had the effect of slowing down
deliveries of aviation fuel to the Allied forward
airfields, so that when the Spitfires of No 154
Squadron flew in to Djidjelli in the early morning
of 12 November no stocks of fuel were waiting for it.
It managed to put up one patrol of six aircraft by
draining the tanks of the rest, and was then
grounded for twenty-four hours until the fuel arrived.

On 12 November the important harbour and
airfield at Bone were seized by British commandos
and paratroops, and the next day the Spitfires of No
81 Squadron flew in, followed on the 14th by those
of No 111 Squadron. Unfortunately, the new arrivals
were immediately attacked by enemy aircraft, which
caused substantial casualties to both men and machines.

As the Allies began their advance into Tunisia, the
lack of suitable forward airfields became a serious
problem. Existing airfields became overcrowded,
and their ever-increasing distance from the front

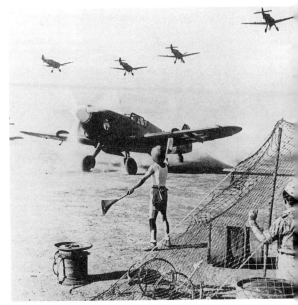

The Desert Air Force's main opponent in the North African
campaign was JG 27, whose Me 109Fs are seen here at a desert
airstrip.

line meant that the fighters could spend only ten
minutes, or even less, in the combat area. In an
attempt to remedy the situation, the Spitfires of
No 93 Squadron were deployed forward to a mud-
dy airstrip at Medjez el Bab early in December, but
they had barely arrived when Me 109s swept down
on them and shot them up.

A new challenge to Allied air superiority had now
arrived in North Africa in the shape of the Focke-
Wulf Fw 190, which mainly operated in the fighter-

An Me 109F meets its end in combat over North Africa.

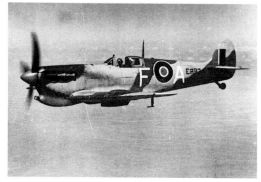

Desert Air Force Spitfire VCs over Tunisia, early 1943.

bomber role under the control of *Fliegerführer* Tunis. The first unit to equip, in November 1942, was I/ *Schlachtgeschwader 2*, based at Zarzun. The deployment of the Fw 190s posed a serious threat to the Allied airfields, crowded as they were; in mid-December, for example, five Spitfire squadrons – Nos 72, 81, 93, 111 and 152 – were crammed into Souk el Arba, sixty miles behind the front line.

Compounding the overall problem was the fact that serviceability was very poor through lack of maintenance facilities, the five squadrons barely being able to muster forty-five aircraft between them. Also, the torrential December rains turned the airstrips into quagmires and bogged down the Allied advance on Tunis. The *Luftwaffe*, on the other hand, was able operate from hard ground – at El Aouina its aircraft took-off from the road between the airfield and Tunis docks – and so remained comparatively unaffected.

For the Allied squadrons, December was a miserable month. As the official RAF history records:

'Apart from a good meal there was little cheer for our airmen that Christmas. "A pretty miserable day", recorded No 111 Squadron at Souk el Arba; "raining all the time and bogging the aircraft. The pilots spent the day trying to get them out and came back at dusk dead to the world". "Rained most of the day", recorded No 152 (Hyderabad) Squadron at the same place; "kites bogged, pilots spent most of the day trying to unbog them . . . in fact a shambles for Christmas Day". On this airfield, as elsewhere, efforts were being made to lay steel matting; but some 2,000 tons of this – or two days' carrying capacity of the entire railway system in the forward area – were required for a single runway. And when laid, it tended simply to disappear into the mud. Like everything else on our side, the provision of hard runways suffered from the long, thin line of communication and the appalling weather.'

Appalling weather or not, the Focke-Wulf 190s continued to be a nuisance, making hit and run attacks on the Allied airfields and other key targets at every opportunity. To counter them, some Spitfire Mk IXs were shipped to the theatre late in December 1942 and attached to No 145 Squadron; they were flown by a highly experienced group of Polish fighter pilots led by Squadron Leader Stanislaw Skalski and collectively known as the Polish Fighting Team, or more popularly as 'Skalski's Circus'. In eight weeks of operations their exploits became legendary. During that two-month period (January–February 1943) they shot down more enemy aircraft than any other Polish unit in the whole of that year, and the pilots were subsequently offered

Spitfire VB QJ-E of No 92 Squadron comes to grief in the desert. Many forced landings were caused through engine failure.

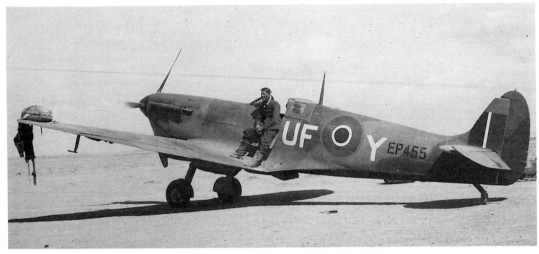

Spitfire VB EP455 of No 601 Squadron. This aircraft was lost on 2 November 1942.

appointments as commanding officers of other RAF fighter squadrons. Skalski, who shot down two Me 109s and a Junkers 88 over Tunisia, became the first Pole to command an RAF fighter squadron, No 601. Later in 1944, he was promoted wing commander and led No 2 (Polish) Wing for the rest of his career, flying Mustangs. He ended the war with a score of nineteen enemy aircraft destroyed, four of them over his native Poland in 1939.

In February 1943, sufficient Spitfire Mk IXs had arrived in North Africa to permit the re-equipment of No 72 Squadron, just in time for the Allied offensive that would end, on 7 April, with the link-up of the American II Corps and the British Eighth Army; the essential preliminary to the final Allied push northwards into Tunisia. At the same time, the Allied air forces began an all-out campaign to destroy the remnants of the *Luftwaffe* in

Spitfire VB of No 601 Squadron in a bomber escort mission over North Africa, late 1942.

North Africa; they also launched a series of heavy attacks on enemy airfields in Sicily and southern Italy, where the enemy was assembling fleets of transport aircraft – Junkers Ju 52s and six-engined Messerschmitt Me 323s – in a desperate attempt to get supplies and reinforcements through to the *Afrika Korps*.

Some enemy transports managed to slip through under cover of darkness. When they came by day, however, they were shot down in large numbers by the Allied fighters. On 18 April 1943, for example, forty-seven P-40 Warhawks of the US Ninth Air Force, together with twelve Spitfires of No 92 Squadron, intercepted a formation of ninety Junkers 52s escorted by fifty German and Italian fighters and destroyed seventy-seven enemy aircraft for the loss of six Warhawks and a Spitfire. This great air battle, known as the 'Palm Sunday Massacre', resulted in the destruction of more enemy aircraft than the RAF shot down at the height of the Battle of Britain. On 22 April, RAF Spitfires and SAAF Kittyhawks followed up this success by shooting down fourteen Me 323s, all laden with fuel, and seven of their escorting fighters. When night fell, the coastal waters off Cape Bon were still ablaze with burning petrol, and of the 140 aircrew of *Transportgeschwader* TG 5 who took part in the operation, only nineteen survived. According to Allied estimates, 432 enemy transports had now been destroyed since 5 April, for the loss of thirty-four fighters. This wholesale waste of transport assets, coming hard on the heels of severe losses at Stalingrad, was to have a profound

Spitfire VC EP688 of No 40 Squadron, South African Air Force. The aircraft went on to survive the campaigns in Sicily and Italy.

effect on German air re-supply operations later in the war.

For the *Afrika Korps*, it was the end. Yet, right up to the last, the Germans persisted in their reckless efforts to fling reinforcements into the cauldron of Tunisia. The few who did get through were sacrificed on the battlefield or were captured when the final offensive rolled over them in May 1943.

With the enemy eliminated from North Africa, the stage was now set for the next phase of the Allies' plans: the invasion of Sicily. In the early summer of 1943, the bomb-battered island of Malta underwent a complete transformation. It was now that the gallant resistance of the island's people and garrison bore fruit, for in June 1943 Malta swarmed with aircraft and personnel, all standing ready for the coming operation. The whole of the Desert Air Force

Towards the end of the Tunisian campaign, Spitfire and Warhawk squadrons caused massive destruction among Messerschmitt Me 323 transports ferrying fuel to Axis forces.

flew in, together with much of the 1st Tactical Air Force from Tunisia; to accommodate the influx, another airstrip was bulldozed on Gozo and the overspill went to the newly-captured airfields of Pantelleria and Lampedusa.

At the beginning of July, forty Allied squadrons were in position on the Mediterranean islands. Many of them were now equipped with Spitfires, and the fighters were to play a prominent part in the campaign ahead.

Spitfire Squadrons in the Mediterranean Air Command Order of Battle, 10 July 1943

Air HQ, Gibraltar
No 544 Squadron (Spitfire IX), detached from RAF Benson for PR duties.

AHQ Malta
Nos 40 (SAAF), 126, 185, 229 and 249 Squadrons (Spitfire VB/C, IX).
No 683 (PR) Squadron (Spitfire XII).
No 1435 Squadron (formerly 1435 Flight) (Spitfire IX)

Northwest African Tactical Air Force (Desert Air Force)
No 285 Wing RAF:
  No 40 Squadron SAAF (Spitfire VB, attached).
No 7 Wing SAAF:
  Nos 2 and 4 Squadrons SAAF (Spitfire VB/C).
No 244 Wing RAF:
  Nos 1 (SAAF), 92, 145, 417 (RCAF), 601 (Spitfire VB/C, IX).
No 322 Wing RAF:
  Nos 81, 152, 154, 232, 242 Squadrons (Spitfire VB/C, IX).
No 324 Wing RAF:
  Nos 43, 72, 93, 111, 243 Squadrons (Spitfire VB/C, IX).
US XII Air Support Command:
  31st Fighter Group (three squadrons, Spitfire VB/C, IX)
Tactical Bomber Force:
  No 225 Squadron (Spitfire VC: had previously provided tactical reconnaissance
  support in Tunisia, flying Hurricanes and Mustangs.)

Northwest African Coastal Air Force
No 323 Wing RAF:
  No 73 Squadron (Spitfire VC)
  Groupe de Chasse GC 11/7 (Spitfire VC)
No 328 Wing RAF:
  52nd Fighter Group, USAAF (Spitfire VC)

Northwest African Photographic Reconnaissance Wing
No 682 Squadron (Spitfire IV/XI)

HQ Air Defences, Eastern Mediterranean
No 209 Group:
  No 127 Squadron (Spitfire VC, Hurricane IIB: based at Ramat David, Palestine).
No 212 Group:
  No 80 Squadron (Spitfire VC, IX: based at Idku, Egypt).

Chapter 11
Spitfire Operations in Sicily, Italy and the Balkans

FOLLOWING AIRBORNE landings on the night of 9/10 July 1943, the seaborne landings that began on Sicily at dawn were covered by a massive fighter umbrella of Spitfires and Warhawks, which between them flew 1,092 sorties on the first day of the invasion. The landings were also covered by the two fleet carriers HMS *Formidable* and HMS *Indomitable*, with Seafires of 807, 880, 885 and 899 Squadrons providing cover over the warships while their strike aircraft were in action. However, they were unable to prevent a dusk attack by a lone Junkers 88, which took the British force completely by surprise and torpedoed the *Indomitable*, causing considerable damage that put her out of action for

almost a year. Small numbers of Ju 88s sank twelve ships of the invasion force in the course of the day, but apart from that the *Luftwaffe* made no attempt to interfere with the landings. Initial opposition to the landings was left to the *Regia Aeronautica*, whose 165 aircraft already on the island were rapidly reinforced.

First into action were the Reggiane Re 2002 fighter-bombers of the 5° *Stormo Assalto*, which attacked the invasion fleet and sank the transport *Talambra* before losing four of their number to Spitfires. The Italians did the best they could, but suffered appalling losses both on the ground and to Allied AA fire and fighters. Nevertheless, reinfor-

Far more Seafires were wrecked in accidents than through enemy action. This Mk III has ended its career at the base of a carrier's island.

cements continued to arrive, and by 19 July sufficient new Re 2002s had been received to enable the 5° *Stormo* (which had damaged the battleship HMS *Nelson* on the second day of the invasion) to mount an attack by fifteen aircraft on shipping in Augusta Bay. Once again the Spitfires pounced, and six Reggianes were shot down. After that, only a few Italian fighters battled on in Sicily as shattered units were gradually withdrawn. By 27 July, the last *Regia Aeronautica* units had been pulled back to the Italian mainland.

The first Spitfire to land on Sicily, on the morning of 11 July, was an aircraft of No 72 Squadron piloted by Fg Off D. N. Keith. Running out of fuel after shooting down two enemy aircraft, Keith spotted the airfield at Pachino, which had been captured in a ploughed-up state and was being prepared for occupation by Royal Engineers and No 3201 RAF Servicing Commando Unit, and went down to land on the furrowed runway. The Spitfire was refuelled, rearmed and dragged to a nearby road from which Keith took-off.

By 13 July the airfield was serviceable and the Spitfire squadrons of No 244 Wing arrived from Malta; six more Spitfire squadrons, together with six USAAF fighter units, flew to the island on the 16th and were respectively installed at Comiso, Licata and Ponte Olivo. 'Thereafter', says the official history, 'the transference of Tactical Air Force squadrons to Sicily in accordance with the Air Plan occurred at regular intervals, and full air support to our advancing land forces was continued without a break.'

As they had done in Tunisia, the Germans made determined attempts to keep the Axis force supplied and reinforced by flying in personnel and equipment – and, as was the case in Tunisia, these near-suicidal operations often met with disaster. On 25 July, for example, thirty-three Spitfires of No 322 Wing intercepted a formation of fuel-laden Junkers 52 transports attempting to land on a coastal strip near Milazzo, in the north of the island. Within ten minutes the Spitfires destroyed twenty-one Ju 52s and four Me 109s of their fighter escort. 'Flames, flashes, explosions and aircraft dropping into the sea made up the picture before the eyes of the Spitfire pilots, and the range was so close that fragments of the disintegrating transports struck the attackers

Spitfire Mk V of the Desert Air Force on a Sicilian airfield.

Spitfires of No 241 Squadron with Mount Vesuvius in the background.

and smoke filled their cockpits with acrid fumes', says the official history.

Despite the overwhelming Allied air superiority, the Germans succeeded in withdrawing the bulk of their forces from Sicily in an orderly manner, using tanks and any other means to bulldoze a path through demoralized Italian columns that were streaming back towards the Straits of Messina. It was hardly surprising that when the battle for Sicily ended in mid-August, the bulk of the 162,000 prisoners taken were Italians. In the air, the Allies had lost fewer than 400 aircraft; on the credit side, they had destroyed or captured 1,850 Axis aircraft and had killed or wounded 32,000 men.

On 3 September British forces landed at Reggio in Calabria, and on the 9th – the day after the Italian government surrendered unconditionally, a move that resulted in the Germans seizing full control of all defensive measures – a second Allied landing was made at Salerno, with the object of capturing the port of Naples and cutting off the German forces retreating before the British advance from Reggio.

Spitfires on patrol over southern Italy.

But things went badly from the start; the Germans, under *Generalfeldmarschall* Kesselring, counter-attacked ferociously, and for a time it seemed that the Anglo-American forces might be pushed back into the sea. This time, because of the distance of Salerno from the recently-captured airfields on Sicily – which meant that the Allied Spitfire and Warhawk squadrons could only patrol the invasion area for less than thirty minutes at a time, and then only in small numbers – much of the air cover was provided by the USAAF's longer-range Mustangs and Lightnings and by Seafires of the Royal Navy.

Combat air patrols were flown by over 100 Seafires operating from the escort carriers *Attacker*, *Battler*, *Hunter*, *Stalker* and *Unicorn*, which formed part of Force V under the command of Rear-Admiral Sir Philip Vian. As before, the Fleet carriers of Force H, the *Formidable* and *Illustrious* – which had been brought in to replace the damaged *Indomitable* – were positioned out to sea well clear of the beaches as a screen against enemy surface vessels. Initially, it was thought that the Fleet Air Arm's commitment would be brief; hopes were pinned in the rapid capture of Montecorvino airfield, which would enable air support operations to be taken over by shore-based fighters.

By the end of the first day, however, during which the Seafires flew 265 sorties, the airfield was still in enemy hands, and for the hard-pressed Allies the situation showed no sign of improving. The Seafire pilots were forced to continue operating without respite for a further two and a half days, until the Americans succeeded in levelling out a rough airstrip in their sector. At the end of that time the escort carriers could muster only twenty-three serviceable Seafires between them. In all sixty Seafires were lost in five days, the majority in landing accidents; a rough sea was running, and several aircraft bounced into the sea on touch-down. On the credit side, only two enemy fighter-bombers had been shot down and another four damaged, largely because the Seafires were not fast enough to catch the Me 109Fs used by the *Luftwaffe*.

The surviving Seafires were flown to the rough-and-ready American airfield at Paestum, from which they continued to operate until 15 September, while their carriers returned to Palermo. Five days later, Force V was disbanded, and soon afterwards, with the Allied air forces now firmly in control of the Mediterranean skies and the Italian Fleet immobilised, the task of Force H also came to an end. For three years or more, it had borne the brunt of the enemy onslaught by sea and air; now it was disbanded and its warships dispersed to other theatres of war.

Meanwhile, on 12 September, three squadrons of Spitfires of No 324 Wing had flown into Paestum, operating alongside the Seafires until the latter withdrew and also a squadron of P-38 Lightnings, which had arrived the previous day, so that continuous air cover over the beaches was assured. In fact, although the *Luftwaffe* made small-scale attacks with Me 109Fs and Fw 190s, it was never in a position to offer a really serious challenge to Allied air superiority; its airfields had taken far too much punishment.

The crisis of battle came on 14 September, a day that saw 700 sorties flown by the fighters and fighter-bombers of the 1st Tactical Air Force, the Desert Air Force being employed mainly in strafing German transport near Eboli. By 16 September the Salerno beach-head was secure, and on 1 October the 7th Armoured Division – the 'Desert Rats' – entered Naples. The 5th and 8th Armies now began

Landing the Spitfire still produced problems. The aircraft shown are both of No 92 Squadron.

a steady advance; by 6 October the former was on the line of the Volturno river and the 8th was facing Termoli, so completing the second phase of the campaign. The third phase envisaged the capture of Rome, to be followed by a rapid advance on Livorno (Leghorn), Florence and Arezzo.

While these operations were in progress, the Allies had launched a separate operation in the eastern Mediterranean, its objective to secure a foothold in the Aegean. The principal target was the island of Rhodes, but this was very strongly garrisoned and the Allied commanders decided instead to capture Kos, Leros and Samos, isolating Rhodes and other islands in the Archipelago. Since August, the whole area had been photographed by the PR Spitfires of No 680 Squadron, and following an attack on enemy airfields by B-24 Liberators of the Northwest African Strategic Air Force, a British force landed on Kos on 13 September and occupied the port and airfield at Antimachia, which was found to be serviceable. The next day the Spitfires of No 7 Squadron, South African Air Force, flew in, and from first light on 15 September two aircraft maintained a standing patrol over Kos to cover transport aircraft and ships bringing in reinforcements. Within the next forty-eight hours, the islands of Leros and Samos were also occupied without opposition.

On 17 September the *Luftwaffe* began a series of heavy attacks on the Kos garrison, and by the end of the month reinforcement of the Aegean area had increased its strength to over 350 aircraft, including ninety Ju 88s and He 111s, fifty Me 109s and sixty-five Ju 87s. Antimachia was severely damaged and by 26 September only four of No 7 Squadron's Spitfires were airworthy. Reinforcements in the form of nine Spitfires of No 74 Squadron arrived from Nicosia, Cyprus, but they were too few to prevent the determined enemy air attacks. The Germans soon achieved complete air superiority over the islands and on 3 October they landed on

Spitfire VC of No 2 Squadron, South African Air Force, armed with 250lb bombs.

Spitfire VB AB320 was used for trials with overload fuel tanks designed for operations in the Mediterranean theatre.

Kos, which was defended by 800 soldiers and 235 men of the RAF Regiment. Within twenty-four hours the island had been recaptured, the remnants of its garrison taking to the hills to carry on a guerrilla war, and Leros and Samos were also retaken in November, despite heavy air action against enemy shipping by Beaufighters, Liberators and Mitchells.

In Italy, October and November 1943 saw the Allies across the Volturno River and advance on the Garigliano and Sangro, all of which involved bitter fighting against a determined enemy. This, in essence, was the continuing story of the Italian campaign: one swift-flowing river after another, each one more heavily defended than the one before. There were to be no brilliantly-executed armoured dashes here, as there would be later in north-west Europe. Italy was a hard slog from beginning to end, and in many instances an advance of a few miles was only accomplished thanks to overwhelming tactical air support.

It was amid the mountains and rivers of Italy that tactical air power was brought to a fine art. In the desert, a request for air support had been passed through a mobile operations room, which allotted the target to a particular Wing. This had worked quite well in an area where there was a good deal of room for manoeuvre, and where considerable time often elapsed between enemy forces being sighted and engaged. In Italy, however, it was a different story; army units fighting in close country usually

needed air support very quickly indeed. A system known as *Rover David* was therefore instituted, under which fighter-bombers maintained standing patrols over the battle area. When a call for assistance was received, aircraft were detached from the overhead 'cab rank' to attack whatever target was designated. The system worked in conjunction with an RAF Forward Air Controller, but the fact that it worked at all was due entirely to the absence of enemy fighters over the front line.

On 10 December 1943, all Allied air units in the Mediterranean came under the aegis of a new organization, the Mediterranean Allied Air Forces. One of the first major operations under the control of the new Command was mounted in support of the Allied landings at Anzio and Nettuno on the west coast of Italy, a move designed to outflank the formidable enemy defences at Monte Cassino, which commanded the coastal road approach to Rome. As a preliminary to the landings, which took place on 22 January 1944, the Allied air forces struck hard at enemy airfields in central Italy, and it was not until several hours after the troops went ashore that *Luftwaffe* reconnaissance aircraft were able to give Kesselring a clear picture of what was happening.

Unfortunately, the invasion forces failed to exploit their success for a variety of reasons, and although the Allied air forces dropped 12,500 tons of bombs on enemy airfields and communications between 22 January and 15 February 1944, they could not

Named Spitfire Mk Vs that served in the Mediterranean Theatre included:

JK640 *Central Provinces and Berar No VII*

EP829 *Malta's 1,000th*

prevent the Germans launching a fierce counter-attack. With the help of strong air support, including the dropping of more than 10,000 fragmentation bombs on enemy troop concentrations, the counter-attack was contained. It had, however, come perilously close to succeeding, and the forces at Anzio were as yet in no state to break out.

During this critical period there was some re-shuffling of the Spitfire Wings operating in Italy. For example, No 7 Wing SAAF, whose four squadrons – Nos 1, 2, 4 and 7 – were now all equipped with Spitfires, crossed the Appennines to support the US Fifth Army, and on 30 January its Spitfires escorted 215 Fortresses and Liberators which dropped 29,000 fragmentation bombs on four enemy airfields, causing much damage among enemy fighters assembling there for the dual purpose of reinforcing Kesselring's air force and of intercepting the long-range Allied bombers operating from Foggia against Austria and southern Germany.

The spotlight now fell on Monte Cassino, where the ancient monastery was reduced to rubble by USAAF bombers on 15 February 1944. It is not within the scope of this book to discuss the necessity for, or the implications of that action; but a month later the town of Cassino itself was also

destroyed, and RAF and SAAF bombers played a part in its destruction. Subsidiary attacks were made by about 200 aircraft of XII Air Support Command, USAAF, on enemy positions to the south and south-west, and by fifty-nine Desert Air Force Kittyhawks on gun positions to the north of Aquino. To cover the advance of the infantry, 200 USAAF P-38 Lightnings and seventy-four RAF Spitfires patrolled the battlefield, but encountered no enemy aircraft. Spitfires also joined North American Mustangs in spotting for Allied artillery. The bombing attacks created exactly the opposite effect to that required, the tumbled blocks of masonry and piles of rubble forming excellent defensive positions where none had previously existed. Not until two months later, after one of the most bitter and prolonged close-quarter battles of the war, did Cassino fall.

In the meantime, during March 1944, the Mediterranean Allied Air Forces made a determined effort to paralyze the enemy communications network in Italy by mounting Operation *Strangle*, in which 19,460 tons of bombs were dropped on the road and railway system. A further 51,500 tons were dropped in a subsequent operation, code-named *Diadem*, but although severe damage was inflicted on the Italian railway system the attacks lacked

Adamawa Province (serial unknown)

North Western Railway II (ER762)

concentration; with hindsight, it would have been more profitable to select a limited number of very important targets, such as repair and maintenance facilities, and subject them to continual heavy attacks. As it was, the enemy managed to carry out the majority of repairs quickly and efficiently. Although the supply of material to troops at the front was undoubtedly slowed down, the flow never ceased.

During these operations the Spitfire squadrons in Italy flew many ground-attack sorties against pinpoint targets such as railway and road bridges, with considerable success. There was a good deal of flak, and losses were not light. Some of the squadrons were now equipped with three marks of Spitfire – Mk V, Mk VIII and Mk IX. Production of the Spitfire Mk VIII had got under way in 1943; 1,658 examples were built, and most of these went to Italy and the Far East.

Luftwaffe fighters put in occasional appearances, but they were frequent enough to make bomber escort a necessity, and there were a number of air combats during this period. On 24 April 1944, for example, No 451 Squadron RAAF – which had arrived at Poretta in Corsica with its Spitfire Vs a week earlier, having spent some time in Palestine before returning to North Africa – was escorting twenty-four Mitchell medium bombers in an attack on Orvieto when it was engaged by ten Fw 190s and four Me 109s. No Spitfires were lost and the Germans were beaten off, although no claims were made by the Australians. On 25 May, No 451 Squadron destroyed three Fw 190s near Roccalbenga.

On 4 June 1944 the Allies entered Rome, which had been declared an open city. Within two weeks, the Allied invasion of Normandy had brought about a profound change in the situation in Italy, at least insofar as air operations were concerned. *Luftwaffe* units were hurriedly transferred to north-west Europe from northern Italy, leaving *Luftlotte 2*'s com-

Spitfire IXs of No 225 Squadron, Italy, mid-1944.

mander, *General* Ritter von Pohl, with only three *Staffeln* of Me 109s for tactical reconnaissance, about 100 fighters of all types, a long-range reconnaissance group and and three *Staffeln* of night bombers.

The enemy fighter assets included aircraft of the *Aeronautica Nazionale Repubblicana* (ANR), composed of personnel who had elected to continue fighting on the side of the Germans after the armistice of 1943. The ANR had two fighter units, the *I Gruppo Caccia* equipped with Macchi C.205, *Veltros* and the *II Gruppo Caccia* equipped initially with Fiat G.55s. In the early months of 1944 the *I Gruppo* suffered heavy losses, some inflicted by the *Luftwaffe*, whose pilots often mistook the C.205s for Mustangs, and in

June the *II Gruppo* turned over its G.55s to its sister unit to make good some of these casualties, itself re-equipping with Messerschmitt Me 109Gs. Most of the ANR's actions were against American heavy bombers and their P-47, P-38 and P-51 escorts heading for Austria and Germany, but in July the Italian pilots shot down five Spitfires. In total the two *Gruppi* engaged in twenty-three combats during July 1944, shooting down twenty-six Allied aircraft (including the Spitfires) for the loss of twenty-three Italian fighters.

In support of the Allied advance into northern Italy that followed the capture of Rome, the Allied Tactical Air Force flew an average of 1,000 sorties daily, with roads, railways and supply dumps still the main objectives. Despite this overwhelming weight of air power, there was no prospect of a rapid Allied victory; Field Marshal Alexander, the Allied commander, had lost seven divisions which had been withdrawn to take part in the invasion of

Normandy, while his opponent, *Generalfeldmarschall* Kesselring, had been reinforced by eight. Moreover, in August 1944 a large part of the Allied effort in the Mediterranean was diverted to the support of Operation *Dragoon*, the invasion of the French Riviera, which began on the night of 14/15. Much of the tactical support and the airborne part of the operation was undertaken by the USAAF, although the transport aircraft were escorted by Spitfires and Beaufighters and the Coastal Air Forces covered the approach of the seaborne convoys.

The Spitfire squadrons of No 7 Wing SAAF were included in the *Dragoon* order of battle, as was No 451 Squadron RAAF. The latter began fighter sweeps over Marseille and Toulon on the first day of the landings and by 31 August was operating from Cuers-Pierrefeu. It continued to operate in support of American and French forces until 18 October 1944, when it moved back to Foggia. A month later it left for the UK, re-forming at Hawkinge on 2 December. The South African squadrons, meanwhile, had returned to their base at Foiana by the end of August, taking part in the Allied advance through Rimini to Ravenna on the Adriatic coast.

Other Spitfire squadrons involved in *Dragoon* were Nos 237, 238 and 253, all former Hurricane units. Another such was No 213 Squadron, which had converted to Spitfires in February 1944 and used them until May, when it converted again, this time

Spitfire VC BR166 was ferried to Takali, Malta, in June 1942.

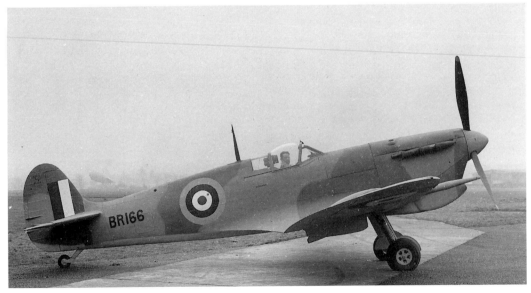

to the Mustang Mk III, in preparation for transfer to the Balkan Air Force. This organisation, created to support partisan operations in Yugoslavia and Greece, included several squadrons of Spitfires, among them Nos 335 and 336 (Hellenic) and 351 and 352 (Yugoslav) Squadrons, all formed previously in North Africa. In November 1944 the two Greek Spitfire squadrons moved to Greece, while the Yugoslav squadrons continued to operate from Italian airfields, sending detachments to the Adriatic island of Vis in order to fly fighter sweeps over Yugoslavia. In April 1945 both squadrons moved to the captured airfield of Prkos, on the Yugoslav mainland.

Another Spitfire squadron to exchange the Supermarine fighter for the Mustang, in September 1944, was No 249, which was also assigned to the Balkan Air Force. Most of the long-range Mustangs, however, went to squadrons equipped with the P-40 Kittyhawk, although there were two notable exceptions. In April 1944, P-51 Mustangs were assigned to the USAAF's 31st and 52nd Fighter Groups, which had flown Spitfires throughout the Tunisian campaign and which had brought these aircraft to Italy. The 31st FG was now assigned to the bomber escort role with the Fifteenth Air Force, while the 52nd FG went over to the tactical role with the Twelfth Air Force.

The re-equipment of the Spitfire squadrons in Italy with the Mk VIII and IX meant the release of numbers of Mk Vs in the summer of 1944, and in September fifty-three examples were allocated to the 20° Gruppo of the 51° Stormo of the Italian Co-Belligerent Air Force, which, fighting on the side of the Allies, had been using a mixture of Macchi C.202s and C.205s. The Spitfires, understandably, were not in very good condition, and only thirty-three could be made serviceable. After training, the Gruppo moved to Lecce-Galatina on 20 October, beginning ground attack operations alongside Italian-manned Bell P-39 Airacrobras against German lines of communication. One Spitfire was shot down over Scutari on 4 November.

Early in 1945 the Spitfires, Airacobras and Macchis went to Canne, taking part in offensive operations over Yugoslavia as part of No 281 Wing, Balkan Air Force. Bad weather curtailed operations in January, but in February many attacks were carried out on roads, railways, coastal gun emplacements and ports. The Italian Spitfires flew their last mission of World War Two on 5 May 1945, when two aircraft of the 20° Gruppo reconnoitred the

Zagreb area. By that time, the Gruppo was reduced to eight serviceable Spitfires.

In the meantime, the last great air offensive of the Italian campaign had been launched on 9 April 1945 against seventeen Axis divisions on the Apennine-Senio line, when more than 1,700 heavy, medium and fighter-bombers dropped 2,000 tons of bombs on the enemy positions. This massive air attack was followed by an equally devastating artillery barrage, which was lifted for four-minute intervals to allow fighter-bombers to attack strongpoints. On the following day, when the Eighth Army launched its assault, the line began to crumble, and by 21 April, after the Fifth Army had also attacked in the centre, it was completely broken. There was no stopping the relentless advance of the Allied armies now; the remaining objectives fell in rapid succession, and on 24 April German representatives signed the instrument of unconditional surrender at Field Marshal Alexander's headquarters. To all intents and purposes the war in the Mediterranean Theatre was over, and the Spitfire – together with its naval counterpart, the Seafire – had played no small part in the Allied victory.

The Malta Spitfires
None of it – neither the victory in North Africa nor the subsequent landings in Sicily and Italy – would have been possible without one factor: the tenacious resistance, under months of almost ceaseless air attack, by the garrison and people of the island of Malta, deservedly awarded the George Cross in 1942.

Although the Spitfire tends to be regarded as Malta's saviour, it should not be forgotten that it was the Hawker Hurricane that took the full weight of the early onslaught against the island by the Luftwaffe and Regia Aeronautica for over a year before the first Spitfire reinforcements arrived in March 1942, at a time when only thirty serviceable Hurricanes were left. Code-named Operation Spotter, the first reinforcement, on 7 March, involved the flying-off of fifteen Spitfires from the aircraft carriers HMS Eagle and HMS Argus at extreme range; all arrived safely, as did nine aircraft on 21 March (Operation Picket I) and seven more on 29 March (Operation Picket II), both reinforcements beings flown in from HMS Eagle. These precious assets were divided between the three Hurricane-equipped squadrons defending the island, Nos 126, 185 and 249.

By the middle of April 1942 the position was once

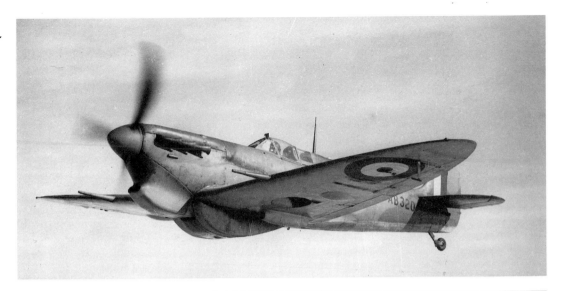

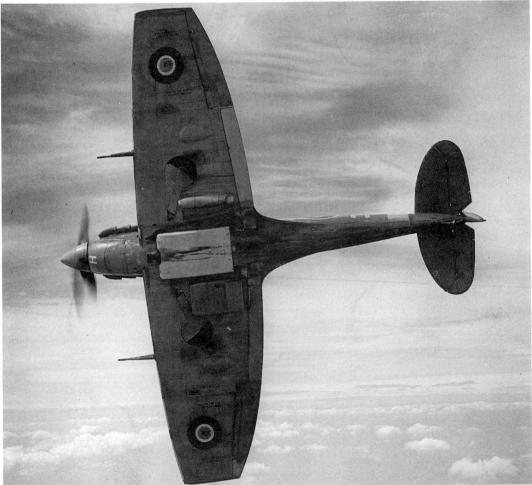

Two views of Spitfire Vs (one AB320, the trials aircraft) showing the installation of the under-fuselage fuel tank needed to ferry aircraft to Malta.

This remarkable snapshot shows newly-arrived Spitfires blazing at Takali following enemy air attacks on 21 April 1942. Malta victims of the RAF, 1942, right, from the top, a Messerschmitt 109, Me.110, Junkers Ju 87, and a Dornier Do 17 reconnaissance aircraft.

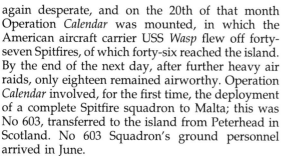

again desperate, and on the 20th of that month Operation *Calendar* was mounted, in which the American aircraft carrier USS *Wasp* flew off forty-seven Spitfires, of which forty-six reached the island. By the end of the next day, after further heavy air raids, only eighteen remained airworthy. Operation *Calendar* involved, for the first time, the deployment of a complete Spitfire squadron to Malta; this was No 603, transferred to the island from Peterhead in Scotland. No 603 Squadron's ground personnel arrived in June.

On 9 May the USS *Wasp* returned, together with HMS *Eagle*, and between them the carriers flew off sixty-four Spitfires (Operation *Bowery*). Of these, sixty reached Malta, and the next day they played an important part in a major air battle that developed over the island when the *Luftwaffe* made a determined effort to sink the fast minelayer HMS *Welshman*. The defending Spitfires and Hurricanes flew 124 sorties, destroying fifteen enemy aircraft. Three Spitfires were lost, two pilots were picked up by the air-sea rescue service, and the *Welshman*, with her vital cargo of supplies and ammunition, escaped.

On 18 May 1942 Operation *L.B.* brought seventeen more Spitfires to Malta, again flown from the carriers *Eagle* and *Argus*, and all arrived safely. On

3 June the same carrier launched thirty-one more, of which twenty-seven arrived (Operation *Style*), and she returned on 9 June in Operation *Salient* to fly off another thirty-two, all of which reached the island.

Among the replacement pilots who reached Malta that day was a Canadian, Flight Sergeant George Frederick Beurling, posted to No 249 Squadron. He was to become Malta's best-known and top-scoring fighter pilot, and his story is worth re-telling, for it represents that of all the pilots who fought in that epic battle.

Beurling's arrival on Malta was dramatic. Seconds after he taxied his Spitfire clear of the runway at Luqa a big enemy raid developed and he was bundled unceremoniously into a slit-trench while waves of Junkers 88s and Italian bombers pounded the airfield. Beurling watched the action unfolding all around him, and craved to be part of the action. His craving was satisfied sooner than he expected. At 15.30 he was strapped into the cockpit of a Spitfire on immediate readiness, with eleven other Spitfires of No 249 Squadron ready to taxi from their dispersals. The pilots, even though they wore only shorts and shirts, were dizzy with the heat as the sun beat down mercilessly; although it would be up to thirty degrees below freezing at 20,000 feet, to don heavier flying clothing would be to risk sunstroke on the island's baked surface.

It came as a relief when the Squadron was ordered to scramble to intercept an incoming raid over Gozo, Malta's neighbouring island. The Spitfires climbed in sections of four, their pilots searching the sky to the north. Suddenly they saw the enemy: twenty Ju 88s, escorted by forty Me 109s and Macchi C.202s.

Beurling's section went for the fighter escort while the remaining Spitfires tackled the bombers. There was no time for manoeuvre; the opposing sides met head-on at 18,000 feet over the sea and within seconds a fierce battle spread out across the sky. George loosed off an ineffectual burst at a Messerschmitt that flashed across his nose; a moment later he got another enemy fighter in his sights, but at the last instant the Messerschmitt skidded out of the line of fire and dived away.

The next moment, Beurling himself came under fire and brought his Spitfire round in a maximum-rate turn. His adversary shot past him; it was a Macchi C.202, and now it hung squarely in Beurling's sights as the Canadian turned in behind it. The Macchi shuddered as the Spitfire's cannon shells struck home and then went down in a fast spin.

There was no time to see whether the Macchi had crashed; the sky was still full of aircraft and Beurling went after a section of Ju 88s which was diving in the direction of Valletta harbour. Closing to within fifty yards of the nearest bomber he opened fire; it burst into flames and the crew baled out.

As he was preparing to select another target, Beurling heard a frantic call over the R/T from a fellow pilot who, short of fuel, was being prevented from landing on Safi airstrip by Messerschmitts. Beurling at once dived over the island towards Safi, squeezing off a short burst at an Me 109 on the way. It was a lucky shot; the German fighter spun down and crashed. Arriving over Safi, Beurling quickly assessed the situation. A lone Spitfire, desperately trying to land, was being menaced by an Me 109, closing in on its tail. Beurling came down and opened fire, roaring over the top of the landing Spitfire and attacking the Messerschmitt head-on. The enemy fighter flashed past him and vanished. A moment later, more Spitfires arrived and circled watchfully overhead as Beurling himself went in to land.

An hour later Beurling was airborne once more, together with every available fighter on the island, intercepting thirty Junkers Ju 87s which were attacking HMS *Welshman*, once again unloading a vital cargo of fuel and ammunition. The Spitfires and Hurricanes ran the gauntlet of their own AA fire to get at the *Stukas* as they dived over Valletta, and a free-for-all developed over the harbour as no fewer than 130 enemy fighters joined the fray. Beurling shot down a 109 and severely damaged a Junkers; pieces from the enemy bomber whirled back and damaged his propeller, but he made a successful belly landing near the clifftops.

During the remainder of June there was a comparative lull in the air fighting over Malta. The Germans and Italians had suffered considerable losses in their air offensive of April and May, which had all but beaten the island to its knees, and were now gathering their strength for a renewed offensive. In July, however, the fighting flared up again, and on the 11th Beurling destroyed three Macchi C.202s in the course of a single afternoon, an exploit that earned him the award of the Distinguished Flying Medal. From then on, his score began to mount with remarkable speed. On the 18th he shot down a Reggiane 2001 fighter-bomber, on the 27th he destroyed two Macchis and two Messerschmitts, damaging two more; and on the 29th he shot down another Me 109. He opened his August score on the

8th with yet another 109, and on the 13th he shared a Ju 88 with two other pilots.

Meanwhile, HMS *Eagle* had brought more Spitfire reinforcements to Malta. On 16 July she flew off thirty-two, of which thirty-one arrived (Operation *Pinpoint*) and on the 21st she despatched thirty, two of which failed to reach the island. (Operation *Insect*).

On 3 August 1942 No 229 Squadron, which had flown Hurricanes in the defence of Malta until it became non-effective in April, reformed with the replacement Spitfires (Mk VC) and absorbed the remaining aircraft and aircrew of No 603 Squadron, the latter's ground echelon having been evacuated to Cyprus in June. No 603 reformed with Beaufighters at Idku, Egypt, early in 1943.

The air battles of July 1942, in which the RAF fighters claimed 149 victories (much exaggerated) for the loss of thirty-six, saw the end of the Hurricane's combat career over Malta; from now on, the defence of the island rested solely upon the Spitfire. August and the early part of September passed fairly quietly, but towards the end of the month, with Malta's torpedo-bombers and submarines taking a growing toll of Rommel's vital supply

lines to North Africa, the *Luftwaffe* made a last attempt to knock out the island's offensive and defensive capability.

Prior to this, further Spitfire reinforcements had reached Malta in August. On the 11th, the aircraft carrier HMS *Furious* had flown off thirty-eight aircraft, all but one of which arrived safely (Operation *Bellows*); and on the 17th the same carrier flew off thirty-two more in Operation *Baritone*, twenty-nine reaching the island. On the day of the first reinforcement, 11 August, HMS *Eagle*, which had served the island so well, was sunk by U-73 while escorting a large Malta convoy (Operation *Pedestal*).

On 25 September there was a fierce air battle over the island, and Beurling, now commissioned as a pilot officer, shot down two Me 109s. On 9 October he shot down three more, together with a Junkers 88, a score that was repeated three days later. On the 13th he got another Me 109, bringing his score to twenty-four. His last day of combat came on 15 October. He engaged a Junkers 88 and shot it down, but not before the enemy gunner had hit his Spitfire and wounded him in the heel. Despite this, he managed to shoot down two Messerschmitts before taking to his parachute. He landed in the sea

Spitfire LF IXEs of No 43 Squadron at Zeltweg, Austria, in September 1945, four months after the end of the Italian campaign.

and was picked up by an air-sea rescue launch. He was repatriated to the United Kingdom a fortnight later.

The last Spitfire reinforcements to Malta – Operation *Train* – took place on 25 October, when HMS *Furious* flew off thirty-one aircraft; twenty-nine reached the island. Enemy air attacks continued into November, but by that time the Battle of El Alamein and the Eighth Army's subsequent offensive in North Africa, in concert with the Allied landings in the western Mediterranean, was sending the Allies rolling towards victory. Malta's crisis was over.

It was in Malta that the Spitfire was first used as a fighter-bomber, attacking enemy airfields on Sicily. It was a role that Reginald Mitchell had never envisaged for it, but one in which it was to prove highly successful.

Chapter 12
North-West Europe, 1943

I N MANY ways, 1942 had been a disastrous year for RAF Fighter Command, committed as it now was to offensive rather than defensive action. Losses had been high – unacceptably high, in cases such as the Dieppe operation – and they had been measured against very little in the way of achievement, in view of the fact that the Command had carried out 43,000 offensive cross-Channel sorties during the year.

Lessons were being learned, however, and one of the most important was that fighter aircraft had a definite application in the tactical role. This had already been ably demonstrated in North Africa, and the practical experience gained there by the Desert Air Force would later be amply reinforced in Sicily and Italy.

In the United Kingdom, the Spitfire squadrons had their first real chance to function in this role under relatively realistic conditions in March 1943, when the Home Forces conducted a large-scale manoeuvre called Exercise *Spartan*. The assumptions for this exercise were that Allied forces had

Spitfire IXs of No 611 Squadron, Biggin Hill, early 1943.

gained marked air superiority, established a bridge-head on enemy territory, captured a number of airfields and were now preparing a further advance. It drew on all the lessons of the war in North Africa and of Dieppe, and was in fact a dress-rehearsal for the liberation of North-West Europe.

Already, on 10 March, it had been decided that the so-called 'Composite Group' designated to give air support to the land forces in a cross-Channel invasion should be named a Tactical Air Force, and that this was to be formed within the framework of Fighter Command. The force could consist of No 2 Group (light bombers, transferred from Bomber Command); No 83 Composite Group (fighters, fighter-bombers and fighter-reconnaissance aircraft, already part of Fighter Command); No 84 Group, not yet formed; No 38 Airborne Wing, transferred from Army Co-operation Command; and No 145 Photo-Reconnaissance Squadron. On 1 June 1943, Army Co-operation Command ceased to exist with the formation of the Tactical Air Force, which was to be designated 2nd Tactical Air Force later in the year. Later still, in August 1943, Air Marshal Trafford Leigh-Mallory, the controversial figure who had commanded No 12 Group during the Battle of Britain, was appointed to command an as yet non-existent Allied Expeditionary Air Force.

Meanwhile, the Spitfire squadrons of Fighter Command devoted much of its effort in 1943 to escorting the medium bombers of No 2 Group in attacks on fringe targets in France and the Low Countries, or to fighter sweeps in conjunction with such attacks, the aim being to draw the *Luftwaffe* to battle. Most of the squadrons in No 11 Group were now equipped with

Mk IX Spitfires, but some in No 12 Group still had the Mk V, and suffered accordingly when they met Focke-Wulf 190s.

The war diary of No 118 Squadron, which moved from Ibsley to Coltishall on 3 January 1943 with its Spitfire VBs, gives a typical day-by-day account of the life of an East Anglian Spitfire squadron in the early weeks of that year, when much of the activity involved shipping reconnaissance and bomber escorts to the Low Countries. No 118 generally operated in concert with No 167 Squadron, which also had Spitfire VBs and was based at Ludham, a few miles away and nearer the coast. No 118 Squadron shared Coltishall with No 68 Squadron, which had just begun to receive Beaufighter VIs to replace its Mk Is, and No 278 (ASR) Squadron, with Walrus amphibians.

'21.1.43. Twelve flights by thirty-six aircraft; Boston escort, practice interception, flight formation, camera gun practice and cannon tests. During the night fourteen Lancasters and Halifaxes, a Wellington, a Hampden and other aircraft landed from operations on the Other Side. The big bombers were from the Berlin raid, and all seemed very pleased with the results.

The sweep was a complete fiasco. The Squadron was supposed to make rendezvous with 167 Squadron and twelve Bostons at 14.30 hours; it arrived over the appointed place at the correct time and orbited. The leader of 167 Squadron was heard to say 'hold-on' and the CO thought he meant us; however, he was addressing the bom-

Spitfire Mk IX formates with a Lancaster during an affiliation exercise, 1943.

Spitfire Mk IX EN133, unit unidentified. No record appears to exist of this aircraft.

ber leader. Cloud was on the deck, and visibility less than a mile. As there was no sign of the bombers and escort, the CO got in touch with Ops and asked them what was happening. They replied that our friends had set course ten minutes ago. We followed, and met the bombers and escort returning from an attack on Flushing. They had not been engaged, so no harm was done. They had apparently made rendezvous out to sea and not over Orfordness, which was the cause of all the trouble.

22.1.43. Nine flights by sixteen aircraft. Shipping recce, camera gun practice, cannon tests, reflex tests and local flights in cloudy but fine weather. Shepherd, Croall, Buglass and Smith did the recce, which was to Texel. All they saw was the fishing fleet out off Ijmuiden and two floating mines, which were duly reported.

23.1.43. Six flights by nine aircraft. Cannon tests and shipping recce in cloudy weather. The recce was carried out by Stan Jones, Beer, Smith and Brown, who sighted a large convoy off Texel consisting of about twenty ships steaming in two lines ahead, some ships carrying balloons. Here again we have no further information as to what happened when Coastal Command took over.

25.1.43. Twelve flights by twenty-six aircraft. Shipping recce, practice *Rhubarb*, camera tests,

camera gun practice and section attacks in fine weather. Shepherd, Cross, Watson and Lax carried out the shipping recce which was to Texel. Only the usual fishing fleet was sighted.

26.1.43. Nineteen flights by thirty-three aircraft in sunny and comparatively warm weather. The day's exercises included a beat-up of gun positions at Watton, practice interception, Army co-operation, beating-up searchlight posts, practice *Rhubarbs*, camera gun practice and local formation flying. There was no operational flying.

27.1.43. Sixteen flights by forty-one aircraft. 'A' Flight went to Matlock for air firing, and as usual shot some big lines when they returned. There was also a practice bomber escort in preparation for a big 'do' in the near future, as well as drogue towing, air-to-air firing, sector recces and camera gun practice. Weather was fine, sunny and remarkably warm for January.

28.1.43. Four flights by sixteen aircraft. This was a great day in the Squadron's history for the King and Queen visited the station. We spent the morning preparing ourselves. Dispersals were cleaned and a large number of pilots, having been turned out of their dispersal during this operation, visited the Intelligence Officer and signed on the dotted line for the Fighter Command 'A' list of aircraft. There is an awful flap in 12 Group on this aircraft

Spitfire Mk IXs of No 611 Squadron at Biggin Hill, 1943. EN133 also appears in this photograph.

recognition business, as 12 Group holds the record for attacks on friendly aircraft.'

The diary describes the royal visit at length, and concludes with an interesting paragraph.

'After the King and Queen left here, they went on to Ludham. During this visit we had up a standing patrol, putting up two flights of four aircraft each. During these patrols a Ju 88 appeared off Lowestoft, but instead of vectoring 118 on to it, a section of 167 Squadron was sent up from Ludham and they had the extraordinary good luck to shoot down this Ju 88 almost at the King's feet. The pilot was of course the hero of the day and had the honour of taking tea with the King and Queen, who were most interested in his experience.'

The Junkers 88, in fact, was an aircraft of KG 6 from Soesterberg in Holland, out to attack shipping off the East Anglian coast. The pilots scrambled to intercept it were Pilot Officer Code and Sergeant Nash, and it was Code who destroyed the enemy aircraft. The two Spitfires had been airborne for only nine minutes.

'29.1.43. Misery (the Squadron Intelligence Officer) went on a forty-eight and of course things happened; there were four flights by twenty-seven aircraft in fine weather. In the morning there was drogue towing, air-to-air and air-to-sea firing, camera gun practice, camera tests and in the afternoon a sweep over Ijmuiden. There was a most unfortunate accident in the morning when de Courcy, taking off for drogue towing, apparently did so in coarse pitch. The Martinet crashed into a tree, and de Courcy and his passenger were injured. The aircraft caught fire and was burnt out. De Courcy soon recovered from his injuries but his passenger died a few days later, which is very bad luck indeed. A Court of Inquiry is pending.

In the afternoon the Squadron made rendezvous with 167 and twelve Venturas over Mundesley, and flew at sea-level to within a few miles of the Dutch coast, then climbed to 9,000 feet over Ijmuiden. As we crossed the coast four Fw 190s were seen breaking cloud below at 2,000 feet. Our allotted task was to give top cover to the bombers which, instead of bombing immediately, went inland for ten minutes then turned round and bombed from east to west on an outward heading. Squadron Leader Wooton decided not to go down for the 190s until the bombers had carried out their task, or while they were still in danger of being attacked.

Spitfire Mk IX of No 316 (Polish) Squadron, 1943. This aircraft failed to return from an operation in July that year.

While the bombers and escorts were making their incursion the 190s climbed up and were joined by others, but before they could attack the bombers they were engaged by 118 Squadron. In the resultant dog-fight, of which no-one seemed to have a very clear picture, Sgt Lack destroyed a Fw 190 which he followed down to sea-level and set on fire; it was eventually seen to crash into the sea by Hallingworth.

Hallingworth was attacked and his aircraft hit, and he in turn claimed a 190 damaged. The CO, who engaged the leading Fw 190, also claimed one damaged, the enemy aircraft breaking away after being hit by cannon fire and going down followed by Sgt Buglass, who lost sight of it. Shepherd went to Hallingworth's rescue when he was being attacked, and was himself fired at head-on by two Fw 190s. Flight Sergeant Cross is missing from this engagement; no-one saw what happened to him, but as he was flying number two to Shepherd it is believed that he must have been hit during the double attack on his section leader. The Squadron got split up during the engagement, seven aircraft coming back together with the other four in two pairs, one in company with the Venturas and 167 Squadron.

No-one saw Cross crash. He was a very nice, quiet Canadian and will be very much missed, particularly by his friend, Flight Sergeant Croall.

The weather was seven-tenths at 1,000 feet over the target. The day's work brings our Squadron total to fourteen enemy aircraft destroyed, six probably destroyed and thirteen damaged.

30.1.43. One flight by two aircraft, carrying out a *Rhubarb.* Cloud was on the deck and Brown and Smith carried out an attack on trains. They found a goods train; Brownie took on the engine and blew it up, while Smith hit the goods waggons with cannon and machine-guns. Two Fw 190s were seen over Ijmuiden, but as they were at 800 feet over the flak area and our aircraft were short of ammunition our pilots decided to call it a day.

31.1.43. There was no flying, and the month ended in heavy rain and a howling gale . . . It has been a strange month for us; we have been on three stations (Ibsley, Wittering and Coltishall), made lots of new friends and said goodbye to many old ones. We have added to our score of Huns, lost a good pilot in Cross, and been better fed than at any time in the Squadron's history.

3.2.43. Eight flights by twenty-seven aircraft; camera gun and low-flying practice, with an extremely shaky sweep over Imjuiden in foul weather.

Rendezvous was made over Mundesley and course set for Ijmuiden. On reaching the Dutch coast the weather had deteriorated to such an extent that the bomber leader decided to return, the target being obscured. We, by the way, were top cover and 167 close escort. Something went wrong with the bomber leader's navigation on the way back, and he followed a course of 300 to 310 magnetic. This would have brought the formation in over the Humber. When forty miles off the English coast, the bombers suddenly turned south; 167 didn't like the look of this at all, and headed north. Our CO decided to keep going west, and eventually crossed the coast over Manby at 2,500 feet. Donna Nook was sighted through a gap in the cloud and eight of our aircraft put down there, while four others landed at Manby.

Arrangements to receive visiting aircraft at Donna Nook seem very bad indeed, and the Flying Control Officer, a very lackadaisical Canadian, seemed to have no idea of how to do his job. The ground crews made no effort to wave-in our aircraft, and as a result Sgt Beer taxied over a rough bit of ground and went over on his nose, damaging the airscrew of his kite. Luckily he was unhurt, and can in no way be blamed for an accident which was entirely due to the finger trouble at Donna Nook.

167 also had a rough time on landing, eight of their aircraft coming down at Manby and four at Watton. We spent a very anxious time with Operations trying to find out what had happened to everyone, and were greatly relieved to hear that all was well. Some aircraft were airborne 2 hours and 35 minutes. Weather was 10/10ths at 2,000 feet most of the way over and back and our aircraft flew through hailstorms and rainstorms and encountered cloud layers of varying density throughout.'

In fact, Donna Nook, right on the Lincolnshire coast a few miles south of North Coates, had no flying units of its own; it had been opened in 1940 as a relief landing ground for the neighbouring airfield, and facilities there were very primitive. Its main function was to co-ordinate practice bombing at the adjacent coastal range. The Flying Control Officer and his staff must have got a shock when most of a Spitfire squadron landed there.

13.2.43. Nine flights by thirty-two aircraft. There were two sweeps to Ijmuiden, and some cannon and air tests.

The first sweep was carried out without opposition. As the CO had not returned from his forty-eight, Dicky led the Squadron. No results of bombing were observed and it is thought that the Venturas may not have dropped their bombs, as a second sweep was laid on after lunch.

The CO, looking surprisingly fit, turned up from his forty-eight at lunchtime, and despite the fact that he had been on the train all morning went on the second sweep. This time, Focke-Wulf 190s attempted to frustrate the bombing. As the coast was crossed by the bombers and their escort ten miles south of Imjuiden, the enemy put up eight aircraft who made a head-on attack on the bombers and escort from extreme range as they made their sweep towards the target. 118 positioned themselves in the sun and approached Ijmuiden parallel to the coast at 12,000 feet, the bombers and escort being at 9,000. After making their run, the bombers and escort dived down to sea-level. Further attacks were made by the 190s and we sent down Red and Yellow Sections, Blue Section remaining above as top cover.

Four enemy aircraft were seen climbing to attack the bombers on their port side; they were engaged by our aircraft and three dived rapidly for the coast, but the fourth pressed home its attack with explosive ammunition. It was later pursued by Red Section and climbed away very steeply, but not before Shepherd, Smith and Watson had got in short bursts from quarter astern as they climbed after it. The 190 got away in cloud at full throttle with black smoke coming from it, but no claim was made. The 190 completely outclimbed our poor Spit 5s.

Some of the enemy aircraft bore night fighter camouflage, which looks as though the enemy are running short of day fighters in this particular area. (*Authur's Note*: in 1943, both I and II/ *Nachtjagdgeschwader 1*, based in north-west Europe, were experimenting with the use of the Fw 190 in the night fighter role.)

This time the bombing looked very successful and the bombs fell in the docks area, a direct hit being made on an 8,000-ton MV, the rearmost of three ships moored along the southern quay.

Weather was 4/10ths at 3,000, otherwise good visibility. Flak was fairly intense and accurate for the bombers' height.'

(To put the raid into its proper perspective, the Venturas' primary target on this occasion was the iron works at Ijmuiden, and there is no record of any damage to enemy shipping – *Author*).

There were better results a few days later, as the 118 Squadron Diary records.

19.2.43. Nine flights by thirty-one aircraft. The main item of the day was a sweep to Ijmuiden. We made rendezvous over Mundesley with twelve Venturas and 167 Squadron at under 500 feet and set course for Den Helder, climbing to 10,000 feet after twenty-three minutes at sea-level. The target was approached from north to south, with 118 as top cover.

The objective was the torpedo workshops. The Den Helder defences were caught with their pants down. There was some moderate, heavy, fairly accurate flak and tracer. Bombing was highly successful, the bombs being seen to fall on the torpedo workshops and the north-east corner of the port, where there was a mighty explosion which rocked the top cover aircraft at 10,000 feet and started a petrol type of fire, according to the bomber boys.

After bombing the Venturas split into two boxes, and as these were very far apart, the top cover squadron was called down to escort one of them. One of the Venturas had been hit by flak in the port engine and was lagging, so blue section, led by Dicky Newbury, was detached and escorted the aircraft safely across the coast, leaving it plodding along slowly at Ludham.

24.2.43. Fourteen flights by twenty-four aircraft. Shipping recce, *Rhubarb*, air-sea rescue, cannon tests, camera gun practice, D/F homings, air tests and local flying.

The *Rhubarb* met with disaster. After a shipping recce in the Hook/Texel area, during which nothing was seen, Croall and Buglass took-off to attack either barges or trains in the Mennisten Beut/Zand area. They were originally briefed to make landfall between the two shipwrecks to the north of Petun. At the last moment the Group Controller decided that owing to flak at Petun, it would be advisable to make the penetration further south in the Bergen area. It seems a pity that this was done, as it meant a much longer time over land and as the coast is defended along the whole area from Texel to the Hook there was really nothing to be gained.

The course given brought our aircraft just off Bergen aan Zee, where visibility was barely 1,000 yards. The leader, Flt Sgt Buglass, decided to call off the operation. As he was turning for home, something – presumably flak – hit his aircraft in the spinner as the Dutch coast loomed into view out of the haze. No gun flashes were seen, and it would appear that this was one lucky burst. Buglass's cockpit and windscreen were immediately drenched in oil and there was a considerable loss of airspeed. He called up Croall and asked him if he could see what had happened, and Croall verified that the spinner was damaged.

The two aircraft continued slowly towards base at sea-level. A few miles out to sea, Croall passed underneath Buglass to take another look at the damage. His starboard wing was dipped and must have touched a wave. The aircraft turned over on its back, plunged into the sea and disintegrated. There can be little doubt that poor Croall was killed instantly.

Buglass, considerably shaken at losing his number two, continued homeward for a while, but when about ten miles out from the Dutch coast he decided that he hadn't a dog's chance of getting home. He therefore returned to the coast, intending to climb and bale out. He recrossed over Bergen aan Zee, but could not induce his aircraft to climb to more than 400 feet. Below him he saw a number of farm houses; near them was a canal, running east and west, with trees along the northern bank and a road or towpath adjoining. After fruitless efforts to try and gain height, during which some German soldiers fired at him with rifles from a camouflaged dump, his engine at last began to pick up a little and – spurred on by visions of his girl friend in Edinburgh – he decided to have another shot at getting home.

There was a parting shot from a gun post as he left the coast, but he was in no mood to plot its position and he was unable to return the fire as he could not see through his oil-spattered windscreen. After ten minutes on 278 degrees magnetic at sea-level his engine became considerably steadier and he began to climb unsteadily at 140 knots IAS, finally reaching 8,500 feet about fifty to sixty miles off the Dutch coast. He then contacted Coltishall Control, telling them that he was in

distress and would probably have to bale out. Oil was now pouring from the port side of his engine, which was again running rough.

He decided to try and glide back as near the English coast as possible. As he came down through cloud he spotted the Newarp lightship below him and ditched half a mile from it at 100 knots indicated, with flaps up. The tail wheel hit the water first and the aircraft made a graceful landing, skimming the water and remaining afloat for ten to fifteen seconds. The pilot disengaged his oxygen and wireless plugs, but unfortunately undid the clip fixing his dinghy to his Mae West. He then attempted to climb out of the aircraft, but his parachute got entangled with the back of the cockpit and he was trapped. The aircraft sank, taking Buglass with it. Holding his breath, he crouched down and, getting his hands behind his back, managed to wriggle free, shooting up to the surface.

His troubles were by no means over, for, after blowing up his Mae West and releasing his parachute harness, he tried to grip the parachute in order to disentangle the dinghy – but it was carried away by the current and sank. Buglass, who is not a very strong swimmer, now had only his Mae West to rely on.

Shortly after entering the water – which was bitterly cold, although he did not feel it at the time – he heard Spitfires overhead. They were two aircraft from 167 Squadron and two of ours, Shep and Watson. The latter got there first and spotted Buglass immediately, vectoring a Walrus of 278 Squadron to the scene. Within a quarter-of-an-hour Buglass had been picked up and was soon back in Station Sick Quarters. It was a near thing for him and he was exceptionally lucky to have got away with a ditching, a procedure not recommended to others, despite the success of this effort.

We failed to mention that when Buglass was first hit he jettisoned the hood, which gave him a nasty crack on the head. He felt very cold in the Walrus and was not very pleased with the way they knocked him about on the floats when getting him out of the sea. Nevertheless, the air-sea rescue was a very fine effort and reflects the greatest credit on all concerned, including the Controller.'

From the spring of 1943, the fighter Wings of No 11 Group equipped with the Spitfire IX were assigned to escort missions with the US Eighth Air

Force, which had begun deep-penetration missions into Germany in March. The Spitfires' limited range meant that escort could only be provided for part of the way, leaving the bombers to continue unescorted into Germany, and the *Luftwaffe* soon shattered the myth that large formations of heavy bombers, without fighter escort and relying entirely on their defensive armament, could operate deep inside enemy territory without suffering serious losses. The USAAF fitted P-47 Thunderbolts with long-range fuel tanks, enabling the fighters to penetrate as far as the German border, but it was not long before the German fighter leaders developed new combat techniques that went a long way towards eliminating the Americans' advantage; the Focke-Wulfs and Messerschmitts would attack the Thunderbolts as they crossed the Dutch coast, forcing the P-47s to jettison their auxiliary tanks to increase manoeuvrability. As a consequence the Fortresses and Liberators took appalling casualties in 1943, particularly on two major raids, the first against Regensburg on 17 August and the second against Schweinfurt on 14 October. On the latter day the *Luftwaffe* flew over 500 sorties and destroyed sixty of the 280 bombers taking part, more than twenty per cent.

Group Captain J. E. Johnson, leading a Wing of Spitfires across the Channel to escort the bombers home, described the aftermath of this terrible encounter, and summed up the frustrations of the RAF pilots.

'It was a clear afternoon, and we first saw their contrails many miles away, as well as the thinner darting contrails of the enemy fighters above and on either flank. As we closed the gap we could see that they had taken a terrible mauling, for there were gaping holes in their precise formations. Some Fortresses were gradually losing height, and a few stragglers, lagging well behind, were struggling to get home on three engines.

We swept well behind the stragglers and drove off a few 109s and 110s, but the great air battle was over, and what a fight it must have been because more than half the bombers we nursed across the North Sea were shot up. One or two ditched in the sea, and many others, carrying dead and badly injured crew members, had to make crash landings. How we longed for more drop tanks, so that some of the many hundreds of Spitfires based in Britain could play their part in the great battles over Germany.'

Spitfire Mk IX of No 302 *Poznanski* Squadron on a bomber escort mission, 1943. Because of its limited range, the Spitfire's usefulness in this role was severely restricted.

The problem was not that the Spitfire was not equipped to carry drop tanks, but that the latter were in short supply. Both the Mk V and Mk IX Spitfire had provisions for auxiliary blister-type drop tanks of 45, 90 or 170 gallons, or a cigar-shaped 'slipper' tank of fifty gallons. An additional twenty-six-gallon tank could be carried in the rear fuselage for long-range reinforcement flights, such as those to Malta in the summer of 1942.

Although the Hawker Typhoon was coming increasingly into play as an interceptor in the early months of 1943, countering the troublesome Focke-Wulf fighter-bombers, the latter also found a formidable opponent in the shape of the Griffon-engined Spitfire Mk XII. Only 100 examples of this aircraft were built, but it represented an important step forward in Spitfire development. On 20 January 1943 the third Mk XII, EN223, flew to Manston in Kent from the Air Fighting Development Unit at Duxford, where it had been undergoing trials. At that time the Typhoons of No 609 Squadron were based at Manston, and the Spitfire's arrival co-incided with a daylight raid on London by twenty-eight Fw 190s and Me 109Gs. The balloon barrage had been grounded before the raid, and so little warning was received of the approaching enemy fighters that the defences were taken almost completely by surprise. Eight bombs were dropped on Lewisham, two on Poplar and twelve at Dept-ford, Bermondsey and Greenwich, causing heavy damage to a large warehouse in the Surrey docks and inflicting severe civilian casualties. However, the Typhoons of 609 Squadron and the Spitfire – which was flown by Sqn Ldr R. H. Harris of No 91 Squadron, one of the units selected to equip with the new variant – were scrambled in time to intercept the raiders on the way out. The RAF pilots destroyed four Fw 190s and three Me 109s, one of the Focke-Wulfs being shot down by Harris.

In the following month No 41 Squadron began to re-equip with the Spitfire Mk XII at High Ercall, Shropshire, moving to Hawkinge in April. No 41 Squadron shot down its first Fw 190 on 27 April and continued to operate from Hawkinge until 21 May, when it moved to Biggin Hill on the arrival of No 91 Squadron, which had also equipped with the Spitfire XII. On 25 May, No 91 Squadron shot down five enemy fighter-bombers in a running battle over the Channel.

In June 1943, following a marked decline in enemy fighter-bomber activity, and with the Typhoons well able to cope with what there was, the two Spitfire XII-equipped squadrons moved to Westhampnett to form a bomber support wing. No 41 Squadron, the first to arrive, shepherded sixty B-17s home from Le Mans on 26 June, and with the arrival of No 91 Squadron a couple of days later the Wing began escorting the medium bombers of No 2 Group and also Typhoon fighter-bombers.

In late August and early September 1943, the Tactical Air Force's Spitfire squadrons flew intensively in support of Operation *Starkey*, which was designed to test the strength of the *Luftwaffe* in the Channel area. The main activity was airfield strafing, a hazardous business at the best of times and one which now cost Fighter Command too many pilots, particularly veterans with a lot of action behind them. Fatigue, coupled perhaps with over-confidence, tended to make them 'push their luck'; instead of being content with one strafing run over an enemy airfield they would often attempt a second, and get themselves shot down. In any case, *Starkey* was a failure in that the Allies were left little wiser as to the enemy's true air strength.

In November 1943, Fighter Command – a name associated with a proud, if brief, tradition and much heroism – was suddenly re-named the Air Defence of Great Britain, reverting to its pre-1936 title. It was a considerable psychological blunder on the part of the Air Ministry, and one that did nothing for morale. Fortunately, the new designation was to last less than a year; in October 1944, Fighter Command re-assumed its proper identity.

The closing weeks of 1943 saw the Spitfire squadrons participating in *Noball* operations, attacks on V-1 flying bomb sites that were under construction in the Pas de Calais. These were made initially by the Hurricane IVs of Nos 164 and 184 Squadrons armed with rocket projectiles, and losses were dreadful. Squadron Leader (later Wing Commander) Jack Rose was No 184 Squadron's CO, and he has this to say about the task.

'The Hurricane IV's low speed in comparison with contemporary fighter aircraft, and its poor armament after the rockets had been released (one .303 Browning in each wing) meant that operations could only be carried out in selected circumstances: Spitfire fighter cover, when this could be arranged, good low cloud cover or the use of semi-darkness. Spitfire escorts were un-popular with the Spitfire pilots as all our opera-tions were at low level, and to maintain effective contact with us this meant flying lower, slower and longer than they would have liked.

Cloud cover was useless unless we could escape into it quickly, so this ruled out medium and higher cloud. My log book records a number of instances (usually entered in the log book as Operation *Twitch*) when we started out, mostly from Manston, but were recalled before reaching the enemy coast as cloud cover was reported by the Met. people to have lifted. Firing the rockets at low level in the dark was not on, as a regular practice, so we made use of darkness to approach the enemy coast, timing our arrival for about first light so that, with eyes by then accustomed to the gloom, we could attack and make a quick get-away while there was still half-an-hour or so to dawn.'

In December 1943, much to the relief of the pilots, No 184 Squadron re-equipped with Typhoons, and No 164 Squadron followed suit shortly afterwards. By this time the V-1 sites were the target of a major bombing offensive. It was during these operations that two Spitfire squadrons, Nos 132 and 602, pioneered precision-bombing techniques with the aircraft, a task that was not greeted enthusiastically by the pilots. As Pierre Clostermann, a French pilot flying with No 602 Squadron, explained:

'Dive-bombing with Spitfires is a technique on its own, as the bomb is fixed under the belly of the machine, in the place of the auxiliary tank. If you bomb vertically the propeller is torn off by the bomb. If you bomb at forty-five degrees aiming is very difficult. After various attempts Maxie (Wng Cdr R. A. Sutherland, DFC) evolved the following method:

The twelve aircraft of the squadron made for the objective at 12,000 feet in close reversed echelon formation. As soon as the leader saw the target appear under the trailing edge of his wing he dived, followed by the remainder, at seventy-five degrees. Each pilot took the objective individually in his sights and everyone came down to 3,000 feet at full throttle. At that point you began to straighten out, counted three and let go your bomb. It was rather rudimentary, but after a fortnight the squadron was landing its bombs inside a 150-yard circle.'

On 12 April 1944, the Spitfires of the two squadrons, each armed with a 500 lb bomb, attacked the V-1 site at Bouillancourt, twelve miles south of Le Tréport; they were the first bombs to be dropped by Spitfires in north-west Europe.

Meanwhile, the component parts of the massive machine that was soon to take the war to France were gradually being assembled, and the men and women responsible for their individual segments of it were studying, day by day, the thousands of aerial photographs that revealed the enemy's movements and dispositions in the most minute detail.

Most of the vast photographic coverage was the work of the Spitfire, for it was in the realm of photographic reconnaissance that Mitchell's versatile aircraft was making one of its most valuable contributions to the war effort.

Chapter 13
The Photographic Reconnaissance
Spitfires

NOT LONG before the outbreak of the Second World War, *Generaloberst Freiherr* Werner von Fritsch, an officer of the old school and a former cavalryman, who was Commander-in-Chief of the German Army during the early years of the Nazi regime in Germany, let fall a prophetic

The Spitfire XII equipped Nos 41 and 91 Squadrons and proved effective against enemy low-level fighter-bomber raids.

remark. 'The next war', he said, 'will be won by the military organisation with the most effective photographic reconnaissance'.

In 1938–39 it seemed that the Germans had a clear lead in this field. They had better scientific instruments, they had better cameras fitted with those splendid Zeiss lenses, and they had a very promising photographic aircraft in the Heinkel He 119, a highly streamlined design that was one of the fastest aircraft produced by the German aviation industry before the war. In the event, the He 119 never went into production for the *Luftwaffe*, and at the outbreak of war the German strategic PR task was undertaken by the Dornier Do 17 and, later, by versions of the Junkers Ju 86 and Ju 88.

Throughout the war, there was an extraordinary contrast between the amount of PR the Allies carried out over Germany and the very small amount the Germans performed over the United Kingdom. In fact, the Germans did a great deal of PR from 1941, but much of the effort was directed to the Eastern Front.

During the 1930s, the Germans paid far more attention to the development of strategic photographic reconnaissance than did the British, and put their techniques to the test in the Spanish Civil War with aircraft like the Do 17 and the Heinkel He 70. In Britain, however, the concept was sadly neglected between the wars.

In the First World War, most aerial photography had been connected with the land battle, and in the years that followed had remained the prerogative of RAF Army Co-operation Command. In practice, this meant, usually, taking hand-held obliques from the open rear cockpit of a slow aeroplane – which, in 1939, was the Westland Lysander. Bomber Command used air photography to some extent, but only to check the results of practice bombing attacks. Perhaps the most profitable use of air photography during this period was overseas, where the RAF carried out extensive photographic surveys of dependent territories such as Iraq.

The RAF's air reconnaissance structure in the Second World War was to become something very far removed from this, and the basic initiative for change came from Wing Commander F. W. Winterbotham, Chief of Air Intelligence in the Secret Intelligence Service. Winterbotham had been receiving the results of some clandestine flights made over German territory in the late 1920s and early 1930s, and he began looking around for someone to undertake similar work on behalf of the British Government.

He was steered towards a very remarkable man called Sidney Cotton, once described rather aptly as a 'buccaneering entrepreneur', who agreed to undertake a series of clandestine photographic missions over Germany for the British and French intelligence services, who were co-operating very closely at the time. The aircraft selected by Cotton for the purpose was the Lockheed 12A, two of which were purchased with funds provided jointly by the UK and French governments. The purchase was concluded in September 1938, with Imperial Airways acting as the agent, and one aircraft – painted pale green overall – was positioned at Heston in Middlesex in November. To maintain secrecy, the aircraft was registered under a company called the Aeronautical Sales and Research Corporation.

The first sortie was carried out on 10 March 1939, when Mannheim was photographed. In the event of the Lockheed being intercepted by German fighters, its installation of three cameras could be jettisoned through a hole in the cabin floor. A Leica camera, concealed behind a sliding panel, was also installed in each wing leading-edge; Cotton planned to use these for low-level photography.

During the months that followed, Cotton ranged far and wide over Germany, usually taking his photographs from 20,000 feet, and also went to Malta to photograph Italian naval installations.

Meanwhile, the embryo photographic reconnaissance organisation at Heston had begun to expand. In the course of 1939 Cotton was joined at Heston by Squadron Leader A. Earle (photographic officer), Flight Lieutenant R. H. Niven (a Canadian on a short service commission in the RAF, who was well known to Cotton), Flying Officer H. Blyth (liaison officer), Pilot Officer H. G. Belcher (equipment officer) and Flying Officer M. V. Longbottom. Maurice Longbottom, predictably known as 'Shorty', joined the organisation for flying duties; Cotton had met him in Malta during one of his visits and had enlisted him as an assistant, not without having to overcome a few administrative problems with the AOC Malta! Eighteen other ranks were also posted to Heston.

In August 1939, as a result of working with the dynamic and determined Cotton, Longbottom produced a memorandum entitled *Photographic Reconnaissance in Enemy Territory in War*, which he submitted to the Air Ministry. It divided reconnaissance into two categories: tactical work in the immediate vicinity of the front line and strategic reconnaissance of enemy territory behind the zone of conflict. What was remarkable about the document was the way in which Longbottom foresaw the problems of reconnaissance – more dangerous than bombing, in his opinion – and suggested the solution. In his words: 'This type of reconnaissance (strategic) must be done in such a manner as to avoid the enemy fighter and aerial defences as completely as possible. The best method of doing this appears to be the use of a single small machine relying solely on its speed, climb and ceiling to avoid detection.' What Longbottom was in effect advocating was a small, stealthy aircraft, relying on speed and altitude for its survival, rather than on any ability to fight its way out of trouble.

Between 26 July 1939 and the end of August the Lockheed made a number of trips to Berlin, landing at the capital and, of course, photographing installations en route. John Weaver, one of the earliest members of what was to become the Photographic Reconnaissance Unit, flew with Cotton several times and recalls that 'On one occasion he (Cotton) flew over to Tempelhof, and Göring and his lieutenants were there. Seeing the aircraft, they made a number of enquiries as to whom it belonged. On finding out, they approached Cotton for a flight and asked where he would take them. Cotton was a very clever chap and said, "I have a dear old aunt who lives in such an area, and if you have no objections we could fly over there". It was agreed and off they set, but what they didn't know was that dear old Sidney was pressing the tit the whole time, taking photographs.'

Cotton's last clandestine flight before the outbreak of war was in the afternoon of 2 September 1939, when, at the request of the Admiralty, he carried out a reconnaissance of the Elbe Estuary, where units of the German fleet were at anchor. The action did not endear Cotton to the Air Ministry, who knew nothing about the mission until after it had taken place; nevertheless, valuable photographs of the German fleet's dispositions were in the hands of the Director of Naval Intelligence that same evening.

On the outbreak of war Heston airfield was requisitioned by the RAF, becoming a satellite of Northolt under No 11 Group, Fighter Command, and the Heston Flight – as the PR organisation was now known, with Sidney Cotton in charge of it as an acting wing commander – also came under Fighter Command. The Flight actually came into existence officially on 22 September 1939, when it was authorised to act as a strategic photographic reconnaissance unit on behalf of the RAF.

What the unit needed now was a suitable aircraft type, or types, and early in October Wing Commander Winterbotham suggested to the Air Ministry that an establishment of three Blenheims and three Spitfires, suitably converted for the task in hand, might be appropriate. Since Spitfires at that time were like gold dust, the Air Ministry would not agree to providing any, but the Blenheims were delivered.

They were not the aircraft Cotton wanted, but they were all he had, and he set about making a number of modifications designed to improve their performance. These included rubbing down and polishing the airframe, fitting a spinner to the propellers to help cool the engines without having to open the cooling gills (which reduced the maximum speed by as much as 30 mph when extended), deleting the front undercarriage fairing and fitting doors parallel with the underside of the engine nacelles. These refinements added 25 mph to the aircraft's maximum speed. But the Blenheim was totally unsuited to the PR task; during the 'Phoney War' period RAF Bomber Command lost about twenty, most of them from No 139 Squadron at RAF Wyton, while trying to photograph objectives in the Ruhr, and not one photograph of any value was returned. The French, using highly vulnerable Potez 63s, fared even worse.

While the Heston Flight's Blenheims were being modified, Cotton continued to lobby the Air Ministry for Spitfires, and got nowhere at all until his petition reached the desk of Air Chief Marshal Sir Hugh Dowding, the AOC-in-C Fighter Command. Dowding had been impressed by Cotton's work in improving the speed of the Blenheim, and asked for a meeting. He also asked if there was anything he could do for the Heston Flight. Cotton seized his chance, and asked for the loan of a couple of Spitfires. They flew into Heston early the next day, 13 October 1939.

The two Spitfire Mk Is, N3069 and N3071, were immediately stripped of guns, radio and all other equipment considered by Cotton to be superfluous. Gun ports were filled by metal plates and all cracks were blocked with plaster of Paris. Camouflage was obviously going to be extremely important, and Cotton recalled that, in May 1939, he had watched the Maharajah of Jodhpur depart from Heston in his private aircraft; despite good visibility, he had lost sight of it very quickly. The aircraft was painted duck-egg blue, and merged into the sky background. This colour was registered commercially by Cotton under the name Camotint, and the paint – afterwards polished to a hard gloss – was applied to the two Spitfires. It remained the official PR colour scheme until largely replaced by sky blue, although it was retained for low-level sorties.

Once this preparatory work had been completed the two Spitfires were delivered to the Royal Aeronautical Establishment at Farnborough on 20 October for camera installation. The engineer supervising this was Harold Stringer, who had already experimented with camera installations in damaged Spitfire airframes, including that of the prototype, K5054. The Heston Flight's aircraft were fitted with a single F24 5-inch camera in the position in each wing normally occupied by the inboard guns and ammunition boxes. The two cameras operated simultaneously, with a slight overlap for stereoscopic effect. In its new guise the aircraft was designated Spitfire PR.IA, and its top speed was increased from about 360 mph in the standard Mk. I to 390.

On 1 November 1939, again for security reasons, the Heston Flight was renamed No 2 Camouflage Unit. Five days later, a detachment known as the Special Survey Flight and consisting of a single Spitfire (N3071) with Flying Officer Longbottom, was deployed to Seclin, near Lille, and it was from this base, on 18 November, that Longbottom made the first Spitfire PR flight – a sortie over Aachen.

This sortie proved abortive because of bad weather, but it proved that the Spitfire was more than adequate for the task. Longbottom had always felt that the Spitfire was robust enough to carry a large load, and it certainly had the power. Without its service load as a fighter it could carry a considerable amount of extra fuel, oil and oxygen, in addition to the cameras. What was needed now was an extension of its combat radius, and that meant extra fuel tankage. A further 29 gallons took the fuel to 114 gallons, and with this modification – the tank being fitted behind the pilot's seat – the aircraft was known as the Spitfire PR.IB. The first of two PR.IBs was collected from the RAE on 16 January 1940 and flown to Heston; range was now extended to around 750 miles.

On 10 February 1940, the Special Survey Flight was renamed No 212 (PR) Squadron at the request of the Commander of the British Air Forces in France, the parent unit at Heston having meanwhile been renamed the Photographic Development Unit on 17 January.

No 212 Squadron had an establishment of three flights and was equipped with Blenheims and Spit-

fires. By the spring of 1940 the latter had photographed practically the whole of the Ruhr, and shared with the Blenheims the task of locating major units of the German fleet, which for the most part were still in home waters making ready for the coming invasion of Norway. In its first three months of operations the Squadron flew fifty-seven sorties, about equally divided between Heston and the French base. The Squadron's first sortie, in fact, was flown on 10 February 1940, the day it officially came into existence, when Longbottom – now a flight lieutenant – made a four-hour round trip to Wilhelmshaven and Emden.

Air Chief Marshal Sir Neil Wheeler, who flew Spitfires with the PDU/212 Squadron in those early months, describes some of the problems that were encountered.

'Most of our early problems came from the altitude at which we were flying. It has to be remembered that there was not much flying before the war over about twenty thousand feet. (My log book shows thirty times over ten thousand feet in five years before 1939.) Most of our Spitfire sorties took place between 25,000 and 35,000 feet where temperatures were around minus fifty degrees Centigrade. In the early days we had problems with, for example, the vent of the oil tank and some form of heating was required. The same was true of the cameras. Cockpit heating was an obvious necessity. Because we did not appear to be experienced in flying in low temperatures, nobody seemed to think of harnessing the hot air from the coolant radiator until 1942 when, at long last, cockpit heating was provided.

Frankly, I found the extreme cold most uncomfortable. On my feet I wore a pair of ladies' silk stockings, a pair of football stockings, a pair of oiled Scandinavian ski socks and RAF fur-lined boots. On my hands I wore two pairs of RAF silk gloves and some special fur-backed and lined gauntlets which I had to buy for myself. It was essential to retain some fingertip control, particularly for the camera control box. Otherwise, I wore normal uniform (RAF battle-dress had not been invented in 1940) with a thick vest, roll-neck sweater and a thing called a Tropal lining which was stuffed with a form of kapok.

But to me the most serious shortcomings that the lack of high-altitude flying brought were the use of oxygen and the almost total ignorance about condensation trails. Before the war it was mandatory to turn on oxygen at about 10,000 feet on the rare occasions that you went to that great height, but the supply system was primitive. We had a crude, very leaky cloth mask and a form of continuous supply. In other words once you turned it on, you got it whether you were breathing in or out. To say the least, it was most wasteful; and oxygen cylinders are heavy. We had to change things since we were using oxygen for about four or even more hours. We had our own doctor and, with RAE's help and the use of other masks (including a captured German one) we designed a good rubber mask. In November 1940 the oxygen economiser was introduced which worked with a form of bellows and only gave you oxygen when you inhaled. Inevitably we called it 'Puffing Billy'. Even here we had low temperature problems with the fabric used in the construction of the early economisers. Nevertheless, all these things greatly helped our operations.

Until the Battle of Britain I have to admit that I had never heard of a condensation trial. In PRU we had removed the fighter bullet-proof windscreen plus the rear-view mirror on the top. We had fashioned teardrops in the side of the canopy, principally to get a better downward view and in them we fitted small rear-view mirrors. The mirrors were less to see approaching fighters than to prevent one producing a condensation trail over enemy territory – signing one's name in the sky was a certain route to disaster! From Heston we carried out a great deal of research work into the formation of condensation trails, aided by Oxford University, before we established that it was the exhaust and not the propeller that produced the tell-tale trail. Normally one endeavoured to keep just below condensation height, but, on rare occasions, one could pass through the layer and fly above with the advantage that one could see enemy fighters climbing up.

After the evacuation of Dunkirk, it became essential to get photographic cover of the ports from Flushing to Cherbourg on at least a daily basis to monitor preparations for invasion. If we could not get high-level photographs we went in at low level and took obliques. The aircraft generally had an extra thirty gallons behind the pilot, the standard armoured windscreen and the full armament of the fighter version . . . they were camouflaged duck-egg blue, although we did experiment with off-pink.'

The next PRU to be formed, at RAF Oakington on 16 November 1940, was No 3, which had an initial establishment of six Spitfires and two Wellingtons. The first Spitfire, PR.IC X4385, was taken on charge on 23 November, and the second aircraft, X4386, the next day. The first sortie – to Cologne – was flown by Sqn Ldr Ogilvie on 29 November. Interestingly, the Spitfire was fitted with a Zeiss camera taken from a Junkers Ju 88 of 4(F)/121, forced down at Oakington on 19 September with engine trouble.

In June 1941 No 2 PRU was also formed at Heliopolis, Egypt, but it was initially equipped with Hurricanes and a Lockheed Model 12A and did not receive its first Spitfires until a year later. These were PR Mk IVs, not to be confused with the experimental Griffon-engined Mk IV; the PR IV was converted from the Spitfire Mk V, and in service was known as the Mk VD. The conversion involved sealing the wing torsion box forward of the main spar to form integral fuel and oil tanks; no armament was fitted and instead sixty-six-gallon fuel tanks were incor-

Spitfire PR.IV BR419 failed to return from operations in December 1943.

porated, giving the aircraft sufficient radius of action to take it as far as Greece. The total fuel uplift was 215 gallons, giving a range of 1,400–1,500 miles.

The Spitfire PR. VII, which was also a Mk V conversion, was basically an armed version of the PR.IV, having an 'A' type armament of eight machine guns and an extra fuel tank only in the rear fuselage. Inevitably, it was not long before the superior high-altitude performance of the Spitfire Mk IX, with its Merlin 61 engine, led to the development of a photo-reconnaissance version, the PR XI. Paradoxically, the aircraft that was developed from the PR XI, and followed it, was designated Mk

X; it featured a pressurised cockpit and was not a success, only sixteen aircraft being produced. The Spitfire PR. XIII was designed for low-level work; eighteen Mk V airframes were converted and fitted with the Merlin 32 engine. The PR. XIII was the last of the Merlin-engined PR Spitfires.

In 1941 No 1 PRU comprised four Spitfire flights, each with six aircraft; two at Benson, another at Wick in the north of Scotland covering Norway, and a fourth at St Eval in Cornwall covering Brest and western France down to and including the full length of the Franco-Spanish frontier. The flights at Benson were responsible for PR over Germany, the

The Spitfire PR.XI, developed from the Mk IX, proved very successful in the photo-reconnaissance role.

Low Countries and the remainder of France plus northern Italy. Additionally, the flights at Benson and St Eval had one or two standard fighter Spitfires for low-level reconnaissance below cloud, and camouflaged a pinkish or greenish white. Known as 'Dicers', they were dispensed with in 1942.

Such low-level operations were ordered only when very large scale pictures were needed, or when, in an emergency, high level photography was impossible for some reason. They were, however, keenly sought after, for the targets were invariably high priority and exciting, and the missions were usually given to the more experienced pilots. Some of the very high priority sorties involved locating the *Bismarck* and *Tirpitz* in Norwegian fjords, assessing new types of radar, and – later in the war – pinpointing V-1 sites in the Pas de Calais.

In August 1942, following the destruction of Russia-bound convoy PQ 17 by enemy naval and air attack, three Spitfire PR.IVs of No 1 PRU were sent to Vaenga, in North Russia, to keep watch on enemy surface raiders. The detachment, code-named *Orator*, was commanded by Flt Lt E. A. Fairhurst, and the Spitfires carried Soviet markings. The first operation was flown over Alten Fjord, Norway, on 10 September, and the detachment suffered its first casualty on the 27th when Fg Off Walker failed to return from Alten. The detachment returned to the UK in November, and a second

one, code-named *Source*, went to Vaenga in April 1943. This maintained surveillance on the *Tirpitz*, and as a result of the PR activity the German battleship was badly damaged when she was attacked by midget submarines in her anchorage on 22 September.

By the end of 1943, ten specialist PR squadrons had been formed at home and overseas within the framework of the PRUs, which had now grown to a substantial size. Seven of them were equipped with Spitfires. The first were Nos 541 and 542 Squadrons, formed respectively from B and F and A and E Flights of No 1 PRU at Benson; a third, No 543 Squadron, was also formed at Benson in October 1943.

Overseas, No 680 Squadron formed at Matariya, North Africa, on 1 February 1943, and on the same day No 682 Squadron formed at Maison Blanche, Algeria, from No 4 PRU, which had been specially formed in 1942 to support the Allied landings in the western Mediterranean. On 8 February 1943 No 683 Squadron formed from B Flight of No 69 Squadron at Luqa, Malta. In the meantime, No 3 PRU had been deployed to the Far East, where No 681 Squadron was formed from it in January 1943 at Dum Dum, Calcutta. Also in 1943, No 106 Group was established at Benson to control all RAF PR training, operations and photographic interception.

The officer who formed No 4 PRU and took it to North Africa during the Operation *Torch* landings

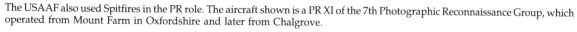

The USAAF also used Spitfires in the PR role. The aircraft shown is a PR XI of the 7th Photographic Reconnaissance Group, which operated from Mount Farm in Oxfordshire and later from Chalgrove.

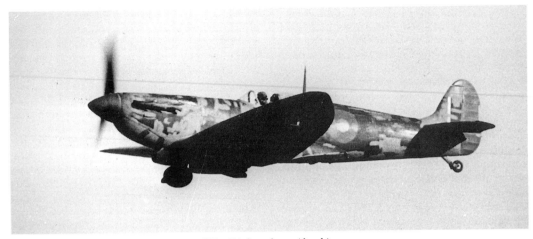

A somewhat sand-blasted Spitfire PR IV of No 680 Squadron, Aboukir.

was Wing Commander (later Air Marshal Sir) Alfred Ball, who gives an interesting insight into the life of a Spitfire pilot in No 1 PRU.

'The day started at 7 am, later in the winter, with a briefing in the Met Office attended by all pilots. It was a very civilised starting hour; this was because photographs could not be taken successfully before 'first photographic light' (shadows, haze etc) and this was about three hours after dawn. Similarly, one aimed to finish photography about three hours before last light. In emergency we operated outside these but the results were never very good and (it) usually had to be done again, with all that that implied.

Prior to the Met briefing, the Flight Commander was given a copy of the daily target list allotted to his Flight. The weather in the target areas, *en route* and at base throughout the day was then carefully studied. Targets and times were then allocated to pilots. Those who were flying went to the Intelligence briefing room to be given details of their targets and information on any other activity taking place in areas through which they might have to pass (this became increasingly important in later years when US aircraft were operating all over Europe in daylight, in 1941 it was not very significant). They then drove to the Flight offices at the aircraft dispersal, marked their maps, calculated their tracks, courses and times, and made out their flight clearances, specifying UK crossing out and in times and places to prevent interception by our own fighters.

One went out to one's aircraft about twenty minutes before take-off and then climbed away, not forgetting to turn on the oxygen (there were several tragic and quite unnecessary fatal accidents as a result of this forgetfulness), aiming to be at operating height by the crossing out point on the coast (e.g. Coltishall, Clacton, Dungeness etc). Then the sortie really began.

Perhaps the most important operational and survival requirement on PR operations throughout the war was the ability of a pilot to keep a really effective look-out for all enemy activity throughout a sortie, and even more important to know how to. It ranked with turning on the oxygen. No matter how good his aircraft, if the enemy saw him first, he was liable to become a dead duck. Unfortunately, seeing before you were seen tended to come with experience, which was why so many PR losses were among relatively newly-arrived pilots, even though they were introduced to operations as gently as possible.

It took only a few minutes to cross the Channel and immediately one started searching the sky for enemy aircraft. The coastal belt was always dangerous for it contained many *Luftwaffe* bases and one expected to see fighters; however, provided one saw them in good time, one could evade them. The same situation obtained on the return flight and one could not afford to relax when crossing out of enemy territory. (We lost some of our best pilots due to this temptation; it was particularly risky coming out of NW Germany with the fighter bases on the Friesian Islands.)

The interception threat, of course, continued all through a sortie, but there were high risk areas, such as the coastal belt and over key industrial cities, particularly if they had just been bombed. Furthermore, having to concentrate on map-reading and navigation *en route* made keeping a continuous and effective look-out difficult, but it was essential. One always had to remember that for a sortie to be successful, one had to bring back interpretable photographs of one's targets, not merely to get back in one piece having successfully evaded enemy fighters, although that had its points! It was, for example, inadvisable to fly in a long straight track to a major target area, such as Hamburg, Stettin or Frankfurt. Irregular feints and dog-legs were much more sensible and pragmatic. Although they complicated navigation and used a little extra fuel, they made interceptions far more difficult for the enemy (it was extraordinary how, if one did so, one often saw nothing *en route* even when, from listening to his radar or from seeing his marker flak, you knew that he was attempting to intercept you). Unplanned dog-legs definitely paid off.

Over major targets, such as the Ruhr and Brest, one was almost invariably shot at, sometimes with remarkable accuracy (one of my chaps was hit at 37,000 feet over Hamburg, and another was shot down at 30,000 over Brest), but on many occasions it tended to be some distance away and low. A PR pilot was particularly vulnerable during long photographic runs when he was concentrating on accuracy and did not see a fighter or flak until too late.

However, there were ways of overcoming this problem. When the *Scharnhorst, Gneisenau* and *Prinz Eugen* were in Brest, a standing patrol of Me 109s, circling up sun over Ushant, used to wait for us coming into Brest every day (only a German mind could plan like that!) The Navy wanted photographs of the ships and port area every day at the same times, first and last light (only a Naval mind could plan like that!) We usually saw the fighters in time and raced in to Brest flat out. We had to get the job done very quickly and so, to avoid having to do two or three photo-runs, we turned the camera time interval down to its minimum and rocked the wings (about a two-second cycle) as we crossed the port, thus covering the whole port area in one run (not the classic style for PIs, but perfectly

satisfactory for confirming the presence of the three ships). Then we were off home, still flat out, with the 109s, hopefully, not yet in range. I was caught only once in twenty-five sorties, but got back to St Eval with the necessary photographs and some rather unnecessary holes.

Another tricky task was large area photography. For example, where maps were out of date or poor, we were sometimes required to cover areas calling for forty minutes or more over target. Inevitably interceptions took place and we lost a number of aircraft. On one occasion, I had to fly eight overlapping runs about twenty-five miles long, some forty to forty-five minutes' photography from 28,000 feet to the northern outskirts of Berlin. Two fighters appeared at about the halfway stage but I managed to lose them as there was some cirrus cloud about and, although they came up again, they seemed to be badly controlled and never got really close. Incidentally, it was their contrails that gave them away in the first place. I completed the task, but the extraordinary thing was that for the next two hours on the way home I saw nothing and had an unusually uneventful trip – I think I must have been badly anoxic or blind or both – but I like to think that there was an Angel on my wing-tip.

In Tunisia at the end of '42, we had a lot of this sort of work to do, mostly front-line mapping for First Army. It was very costly and on one occasion we lost four aircraft in three days from a squadron of nine. The difficulty was the great concentration of Fw 190s and Me 109Gs and standing patrols in the battle area (our own fighters were having a bad time just then, December '42 and January '43). In this case the problem was solved by the replacement of our Mk IV Spitfires by Mk XIs whilst our fighters got Mk IXs.

Let me outline an experience in a Spitfire Mk IV at 24,000 feet (a bad height for the Spitfire but ideal for the Fw 190) near Tunis. I was just completing some forty-five minutes of front line photography when I spotted four Fw 190s some three to four miles away and about 1,000 feet below going in the opposite direction. They turned towards me shortly after I saw them and I opened up to full throttle and dived slightly to gain speed as quickly as possible. Within a very few minutes, however, they were on to me and the first of eight attacks took place. My only chance lay in out-turning them. In the event I was hit by the very first burst of fire – having left my turn (maximum possible) a fraction too late – but although the aircraft was hit in a number of interesting places, the damage was not catastrophic. This one-sided combat went on for five to ten minutes until the Focke-Wulfs broke off, either out of ammunition or short of fuel.

I have touched on interception risks but not on the capabilities of PR Spitfires and enemy fighters – Me 109Es and Fs until mid-1942, then increasingly Gs and Fw 190s. Until the end of 1942 we were still flying the old Mk IVs with RR Merlin 45 engines. We could match the Es in speed and cope with the Fs too, provided we saw them in time for we could out-turn them, but we could not afford to lose much height as they could always outdive us. It was another story with the 109G and the 190s. They were both faster, but the 190's best height was around 24,000 feet and provided we could stay at 30,000 feet, we had a chance at full throttle, but it depended on an early sighting of the enemy fighters, and preferably well before they saw you. The 109G had a better ceiling than the 190 but we could out-turn them both, so an experienced pilot could get away with it so long as he got his time to turn just right, but it was touch and go until we received the Spitfire Mk XI in early 1943.

As a result of these developments, the PR loss rate, which was just about acceptable during the first two years of the war, became quite serious in the last six months of '42 and in early '43, particularly over north-west Germany where experienced pilots only were allowed to operate, and in Tunisia, where there was that unusual concentration of 190s and 109Gs covering Rommel's last stand against Montgomery in North Africa. For the remainder of the war, however, Mk XI (Merlin 60 Series engine) and, later Mk XIX (Griffon engine) Spitfires were able to range freely over Gemany, and indeed world-wide, with acceptable losses, even when they came up against the jet-engined Me 262 and the Me 163 rocket-powered fighter.'

One could write volumes about the single-seat photo-reconnaissance pilots of World War Two. We have already seen something of their exploits in North Africa and Europe; and in the Far East, probably their biggest contribution was in photo-mapping the whole of Burma, the Spitfires of No 681 Squadron operating alongside the Mosquitoes of No 684 and two American PR units. Theirs was a lonely, dangerous, uncomfortable and sometimes excruciatingly painful task. They fulfilled it without complaint, and the contribution they made to the Allied victory was measureless.

Chapter 14
North-West Europe: Invasion and Liberation

FROM THE beginning of 1944, the squadrons of the 2nd Tactical Air Force were giving increasingly frequent demonstrations of their capabilities against targets on the Continent. While the medium bombers of No 2 Group, escorted by Spitfires and Mustangs, continued their attack on the enemy's power industry and communications, the tactical fighter-bombers of Nos 83 and 84 Groups – Spitfires, Typhoons, Mustangs and Mosquitoes – stepped up their operations against the transport system in France and the Low Countries, carrying out attacks on rolling stock and other targets of opportunity. These RAF tactical units, together with the United States Ninth Air Force, formed the Allied Expeditionary Air Force. Its total strength by May 1944 was 5,667 aircraft, of which 3,011 were fighters, medium bombers, light bombers and fighter-bombers.

Some idea of the intensity of these pre-invasion operations, as they affected the Spitfire squadrons, may be gleaned from a couple of extracts taken from the 2nd Tactical Air Force Operations Record for May 1944. For example:

'24 May. Between 14.45 and 18.36 hours, sixteen Tempests and four Spitfires swept and patrolled areas of north-east France and Belgium. Twelve Tempests attacked and damaged a barge sixteen miles south-east of Dunkirk, attacked an army lorry with unobserved results, fired at two factories, strikes being seen in the Antwerp-Brussels area, attacked and stopped a car west of Hirson, attacked a locomotive and twenty trucks between Guise and Rivemone and seven stationary locomotives near Buisyny. The Spitfires attacked a goods train and MT vehicles . . . Between 10.10 and 20.43 hours a total of 170 Spitfires provided escort and support, uneventfully, to Mitchells and Bostons of 2 TAF, attacking airfields and medium gun batteries in northern France. Four Spitfires returned early with technical trouble, and five aircraft suffered mechanical trouble.

Ten Tempests swept the Cambrai area, in conjunction with these operations.

27 May. Between 13.56 and 19.49 hours, two Mosquitoes, forty-two Spitfires and nine Tempests carried out offensive patrols over northern France. Two targets were attacked by twenty-one Spitfires with good results. Five Tempests attacked a staff car south of Rubemare, which crashed into a wall. They also attacked a lorry and left it in flames near Pas. Between 05.02 and 14.00 hours, fourteen Spitfires and two Tempests also carried out weather and shipping reconnaissance patrols off and over the French and Belgian coasts.

28 May. In conjunction with attacks by Bostons and Mitchells of No 2 Group, between 15.15 and 18.55 hours sixty-two Spitfires carried out sweeps over northern France, attacking and destroying a lorry and damaging two goods trains, a large streamlined locomotive, a lorry, three large and two small cars and five railway wagons in a siding. At the same time, nine Tempests patrolled over Cormeille, during which period two Junkers Ju 88/188s were destroyed and two Ju 88/188s damaged, all on the ground.'

The experiences of No 329 Squadron (*Groupe de Chasse GC I/2 Cigognes*), which formed part of the Free French No 145 Wing at Merston, in Sussex, were typical of those of many 2nd TAF Spitfire squadrons during May 1944. Its war diary for the period reads:

'On 2 May, seventy-two Spitfires of No 84 Group, including twelve from No 329 Squadron, escorted a similar number of Mitchell bombers in an attack on Namur Station. The outward trip was uneventful, but on the return a Spitfire of the *Ile-de-France* Group (No 340 Squadron), flown by *Sous-lieutenant* Roeve, collided with that of *Lieutenant-Colonel* Fleurquin and removed part of its right wing. Roeve went down to crash in France, but Fleurquin, accompanied by *Commandant* Martell, managed to reach the English coast, where his engine cut out. He baled out and made a heavy landing near Dover, but rejoined the squadron that same evening.

From 3 to 5 May, poor weather restricted operations to covering some ships off the Isle of Wight, and escorting six Mitchells to the Etretrat area. Cloud cover prevented any observation of results.

On the morning of 7 May, for the first time, the Squadron set out to attack V-1 launching ramps near Abbeville, the Spitfires carrying a 1,000 lb bomb each in place of the forty-five gallon ventral fuel tank. The weather was again poor, and the target was not hit. In the afternoon there was a bomber escort mission to Dunkirk; flak was intense.

The next day another attack was carried out on V-1 sites, this time in the Forest of Crecy. The results were hopeless. At dawn on the 9th the Squadron deployed to Manston for a bomber escort mission to Brussels. Thanks to an Ops Room error, we ended up doing a sweep over Valenciennes and southern Belgium. In the afternoon there was a sweep on the line Etaples-Lille-Amiens. We were alerted that there were bandits near St Pol and went up to 25,000 feet, but never saw them.

On 11 May a general air offensive began against enemy lines of communication in France and Belgium, a direct preparation for the coming invasion. The Squadron made two bombing attacks, one near Malaunay to the north of Rouen, the other in the open countryside. Both were carried out in good conditions, with no flak opposition. The target for the first mission on the 12th was a supply dump near Neufchâtel. The flak was heavy and intense, alerted by a previous attack by No 340 Squadron. Despite this, nine bombs were placed on the target (which was big enough!) A second bombing mission was carried out shortly afterwards on a target near Bethunes. *Sergent-chef* Mazo's aircraft was badly damaged when a gasometer blew up, but he succeeded in reaching base. There were two more bombing missions on the 13th, one at Dieppe, the other at Hornoy.

Group HQ, being far from satisfied with the dive-bombing results achieved by the French squadrons, decided to send them in rotation to the armament practice camp at Llanbedr, in Wales, for further training. Our stint there lasted from 19 to 23 May, and, our results proving satisfactory, we returned to Merston. For the next four days the Squadron participated in reconnaissance and ground attack exercises designed to repel a simulated attack by enemy forces on British soil. On 29 May we resumed dive-bombing operations on the Continent, the objective being the German GHQ installed in a castle near Neufchâtel. On the 30th, we attacked a radar station on the Cap d'Antifer.

On 3 June, the Squadron bombed and strafed targets of opportunity during an armed reconnaissance over France. That evening, black and white 'invasion stripes' were painted on our Spitfires.

Bad weather again prevailed on 4 and 5 June, but on the evening of the 5th we put up one section to patrol the Isle of Wight. Everywhere, our pilots could see ships of all shapes and sizes assembling, particularly landing craft, all ready to set course southwards. At 21.30 the pilots were assembled in the briefing room and told that D-Day was to be at dawn. Detailed charts showed how the operation was to unfold. The mission of the Spitfire squadrons of No 145 Wing was to cover the beach-head and destroy any enemy aircraft they encountered.

This sensational news, although anticipated for some time, provoked great emotions among the pilots. For them, the hope they had nurtured for four long years was about to be realised: the hope that they would be reunited with their families, and stand once more on the soil of France.

At 09.40 on 6 June, after a long wait, the Squadron at last took off with No 145 Wing to cover the beaches in the British sector. Intense flak was encountered to the north of Caen, but the sky was empty of enemy aircraft, which enabled the pilots to observe the massive unfolding of the naval and land operations all along the front, from the Orne to the east coast of the Cotentin Peninsula. All aircraft returned to base by 11.10.

The second mission began at 14.40. Again, the absence of the *Luftwaffe* enabled the pilots to turn their attention to events on the ground, this time more closely. One of the sections shot up some German armour near Lisieux; *Capitaine* Ozanne destroyed a motor-cycle with sidecar. On a third sortie, in the evening, some fuel bowsers were destroyed near Caen.

Spitfire Squadrons in the Order of Battle, Allied Expeditionary Air Force, 5 June 1944.

Group	Wing	Squadrons	Spitfire Mk	Location
Second Tactical Air Force				
83	39 (PR)	400 (RCAF)	XI	Odiham
83	125	132, 453 (RAAF), 602	IX	Ford
83	126	401 (RCAF)		
		411 (RCAF)		
		412 (RCAF)	IX	Tangmere
83	127	403 (RCAF)		
		416 (RCAF)		
		421 (RCAF)	IX	Tangmere
83	144	441 (RCAF)		
		442 (RCAF)		
		443 (RCAF)	IX	Ford
84	35 (PR)	4	XI	Gatwick
84	131	302, 308, 317	IX	Chailey
84	132	66, 331, 332	IX	Bognor
84	134	310, 312, 313	IX	Appledram
84	135	222, 349, 485 (RNZAF)	IX	Selsey
84	145	329, 340, 341	IX	Merston
85	–	56	IX	Newchurch
85	–	91	XIV	West Malling
85	–	124	VII	Bradwell Bay
85	–	322	XIV	Hartfordbridge

(Note: the 85 Group Spitfire squadrons were responsible for the defence of the overseas base during the initial assault phase of Operation *Overlord* and were under the operational control of No 11 Group.)

Air Spotting Pool:	26, 63	V	Lee on Solent	
	808 (FAA)	Seafire III		
	885 (FAA)	Seafire III		
	886 (FAA)	Seafire III		
	897 (FAA)	Seafire III	Lee on Solent	

Group	Wing	Squadrons	Spitfire Mk	Location
Air Defence of Great Britain				
10	1		IX	Predannack
10	41		XII	Bolt Head
10	126		IX	Culmhead
10	131		VII	Culmhead
10	165		IX	Predannack
10	610		XIV	Harrowbeer
10	616		VII	Culmhead

In addition, Spitfires were also used by No 276 (Air-Sea Rescue) Squadron under the control of No 10 Group.

Group	Wing	Squadrons	Spitfire Mk	Location
11	33		IX	Lympne
11	64		V	Deanland
11	74		IX	Lympne
11	80		IX	Detling
11	127		IX	Lympne
11	130		V	Horne
11	229		IX	Detling
11	234		V	Deanland
11	274		IX	Detling
11	303		IX	Northolt
11	345		V	Shoreham
11	350		V	Friston
11	402 (RCAF)		V	Horne
11	501		IX	Friston
11	611		IX	Deanland

In addition, Spitfires were also used by Nos 275, 277 and 278 (Air-Sea Rescue) Squadrons under the control of No 11 Group.

Group	Wing	Squadrons	Spitfire Mk	Location
12	504		IX	Digby
13	118		V	Skaebrae

No 145 Wing flew its fourth and last sortie of the day at 20.00, escorting a glider train on a re-supply mission to the airborne forces that had landed the night before. Although there was nothing glamorous in acting as shepherd dogs over the Channel, the sight over the beach-head was fantastic. Each glider tug turned in front of Caen and released its glider, which landed on the banks of the Orne Canal in a sector still held by the Germans. The gliders had hardly touched down when the troops spilled out, took up their positions and opened fire. Intense light flak rose from the woods and also from boats at anchor on the Orne; some of the glider tugs were hit and set on fire, a glider fell in flames, others crashed on landing, but every ten or twenty seconds one came in to reinforce our men on the ground. One of the canal boats proved particularly offensive so Wing Commander Compton, the Wing Leader, went down with Red and Blue Sections and dealt with it. We spent twenty minutes on patrol, then returned to base.

The Wing flew three low cover missions over the beach-head on 7 June (generally, high cover was entrusted to the Ninth Air Force's P-47 Thunderbolts, low cover to the RAF's Spitfires – *Author*) and on the first one five Ju 88s were encountered north of Caen; one was shot down by Wing Commander Compton. Already, we could see that much destruction had been caused in Caen, with fires visible a long way off. Three sorties were also flown on the 8th, despite poor weather which again prevailed on the 10th, when four missions were flown. We sighted a Focke-Wulf 190 among the clouds, but it was lost to sight almost at once.'

Again, the experience of No 329 Squadron was typical; a succession of beach-head patrols, escort missions and occasional strafing attacks, with very little contact with the *Luftwaffe*. On 10 June, Allied fighters began operating from Normandy for the first time when Spitfires of No 144 (RCAF) Wing deployed from Ford to Ste-Croix-sur-Mer. Eventually, thirty-one temporary forward strips were set up in the British sector and fifty in the American, enabling fighter-bombers to react quickly to

Comforts for the troops. A Spitfire Mk IXE armed with two eighteen-gallon beer barrels *en route* to Normandy, 1944.

requests for assistance from the ground forces.

On 12 June the first V-1 flying bombs fell on British soil, and eleven ADGB fighter squadrons were assigned to deal with the threat, equipped with Typhoons, Tempests, Mustangs, Mosquitoes and Spitfires Mk IX, XII and XIV. The latter, based on a Mk VIII airframe, was the first Griffon-engined Spitfire variant to go into large-scale production, and the first examples were delivered to Nos 322 (Netherlands) and 610 Squadrons in March and April 1944.

In an attempt to deal with the V-1 problem No 11 Group instituted *Diver* patrols, which involved fighters patrolling along three clearly-defined lines: the first between Beachy Head and Dover, the second over the coast between Newhaven and Dover, and the third between Haywards Heath and Ashford. At the same time, nearly 400 anti-aircraft guns and 480 barrage balloons were deployed over the V-1s' approach route to London.

The only fighter with a real chance of catching the V-1s in a straight speed chase was the Hawker Tempest Mk V (in fact, this aircraft destroyed 638 V-1s out of the RAF's total of 1,771). However, much effort was put into increasing the Spitfire's speed; its armour was taken out, as was unnecessary equipment, including some guns, and on many aircraft the paint was stripped and the surfaces polished to give a few extra miles per hour. Although the Mk IX Spitfires were hard put to catch the V-1, the Griffon-engined Mks XII and XIV performed well against it; in No 91 Squadron, fourteen pilots flying the Mk XII

Despite the installation of the Griffon engine and many aerodynamic refinements, the Spitfire XIV retained the classic Spitfire lines.

destroyed five or more flying bombs, including five with scores of over ten. The CO, Squadron Leader Knynaston, destroyed seventeen. Both 41 and 91 Squadrons exchanged their Mk XIIs for LF XIVEs before the V-1 offensive was over, operating this mark alongside Nos 130, 322 (Netherlands), 350 (Belgian), 402 (RCAF) and 601 Squadrons.

From the end of June, pilots were experimenting with a new technique for destroying the flying bombs; sliding their aircraft's wingtip under that of the V-1 until the effect of the airflow caused the latter to tip over, toppling its gyro so that it dived

Spitfire Mk XIV RB146 was a trials aircraft, and among other refinements was fitted with a five-bladed propeller.

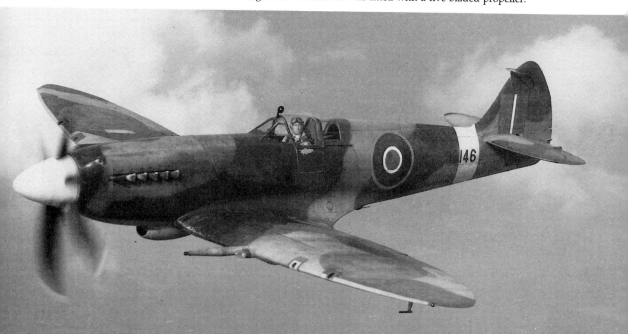

into the ground and exploded short of its target. It was a safer method than gunfire, where the fighter risked being damaged or even destroyed if the V-1's warhead exploded.

The real answer to the threat, of course, was to eliminate the V-1 launching sites, and Spitfire dive-bombers again joined other types in an offensive that saw over 60,000 tons of bombs dropped on them between mid-June and the end of September, when the sites were overrun by the Allied advance. Even then, the flying bomb assault was not over; for some time after that the missiles were air-launched from Heinkel He 111s operating from Holland, but it was the RAF's Mosquito night-fighters that were the principal counterforce against this type of operation.

On the Continent, the round of fighter sweeps, dive-bombing attacks, strafing sorties and bomber escorts continued as the Allied armies strove to break out of Normandy in July. *Luftwaffe* fighters were more in evidence during the month, but in general they were outnumbered and dealt with effectively, and it was the flak that caused the most casualties among the tactical squadrons. The air offensive against the V-1 menace still had maximum priority, as No 329 Squadron's record indicates:

'On 31 July, GC I/2 (No 329 Squadron) flew its longest mission to date in company with the rest of No 145 Wing: an escort for 100 Liberators bombing the entrance to a tunnel at Rilly, near Reims, where the enemy had installed a flying bomb depot. The round trip, to and from Lympne, represented nearly an hour and a half over enemy-occupied territory. Burdened with their auxiliary ninety-gallon fuel tanks, the Spitfires were not easy to fly. There was no flak on the way out, but we were shot at constantly on the way back, luckily without effect.'

Similar operations continued almost on a daily basis throughout August, the Spitfire Wings escorting Liberators, Lancasters and Halifaxes on heavy bombing attacks against V-1 storage depots and fuel dumps. Ground attack operations during this phase were left mainly to the RAF's Typhoons and the USAAF's P-47s, the former performing with notable effect against an enemy armoured counter-attack at Mortain and against the German Seventh Army, trapped at Falaise.

Bomb-carrying Spitfires also carried out a number of attacks on installations at Le Havre and other enemy-held Atlantic ports, and also on concentrations of enemy MTBs which were assembling to attack Allied supply convoys proceeding across the English Channel. These operations continued at intervals until the second week of September, when the tactical Spitfire Wings were deployed to

Spitfire XI of No 41 Squadron with a 500 lb bomb on the fuselage centreline.

new locations to support the advance of the First Canadian and Second British Armies (21st Army Group) following the breakout from Normandy. The squadrons sometimes found themselves in desperately overcrowded conditions; at one point, no fewer than nine squadrons of Spitfires (three Wings) were operating from the airfield at Lille-Vandeville, south of Lille.

On 17 September 1944 the Spitfire squadrons joined other fighter-bomber units of 2nd TAF in the start of an intensive period of operations in support of the British Second Army, which was beginning its armoured dash from the Belgian-Dutch border to Eindhoven and Nijmegen and, ultimately, to Arnhem, the objective being to link up with and relieve the US 101st and 82nd and the British 1st Airborne Divisions which were dropped that day in Operation *Market Garden*. At the same time, eighteen Spitfire squadrons of ADGB provided area cover and escort for the transport serials from the English Coast to the Initial Point (IP) in Holland, and two more acted in the flak suppression role along with Typhoons, Tempests and Mustangs. Immediately prior to this, Spitfires of No 504 Squadron, Manston, had carried out a series of armed reconnaissances along the route with the object of drawing flak to pinpoint enemy batteries.

On 18 September, D plus one, sixteen Spitfire squadrons of ADGB provided cover for the second troop-carrier lift, while three more carried out flak suppression between Schouwen Island and the IP. There was little contact between these squadrons and the *Luftwaffe*, the latter being kept effectively at bay by an outer screen of USAAF P-51 Mustangs, patrolling on an arc between the Scheldt estuary and Wesel. On the following day bad weather severely disrupted air operations, and of the fifteen Spitfire squadrons earmarked to provide escort along the route from southern England to the IP near Gheel, only one was able to complete its mission in full and only sixty-eight Spitfire sorties were flown in total. On the 20th, one Spitfire was lost on a flak suppression sortie out of sixty-five aircraft despatched, and later in the day seventeen Spitfire squadrons flew 173 escort missions for resupply aircraft for no loss.

On D plus four, 21 September – when the Polish Parachute Brigade was dropped in the Arnhem area – bad weather kept most of the Spitfire squadrons on the ground. Only nineteen aircraft took off, their task to escort Short Stirlings on a resupply mission, but they did not rendezvous with the transports until the latter had left Arnhem. The absence of Allied fighter protection resulted in tragedy, for it was on this day that the *Luftwaffe* intervened in strength over Arnhem. Focke-Wulf Fw 190s of *Jagdgeschwader* 2 and 26 broke through the depleted fighter screen and shot down seven out of ten Stirlings of No 190 Squadron, together with eleven other transport air-

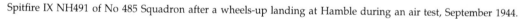

Spitfire IX NH491 of No 485 Squadron after a wheels-up landing at Hamble during an air test, September 1944.

craft. The Spitfires claimed to have damaged three Fw 190s. The Polish paratroop mission, arriving later, was luckier; ADGB fighters flew 118 sorties in support and sighted only a few enemy fighters, which were driven off.

In contrast, resupply missions on 23 September had a massive fighter escort, including fourteen ADGB Spitfire squadrons and four drawn from 2nd TAF. The RAF fighters flew 193 sorties and met with no air opposition, although they lost two aircraft to flak.

From 24 to 26 September, the days that saw the virtual annihilation of the 1st Battalion Airborne Division at Arnhem, RAF resupply missions were flown by one Dakota squadron, No 575, operating from Brussels. Escort was provided by thirty-six Spitfires of 2nd TAF, based in Belgium. Throughout the operation, the Spitfire squadrons had been dogged by bad weather; they had nevertheless performed their task well. The credit for keeping the *Luftwaffe* at arm's length, though, must go to the Mustangs and Thunderbolts of the USAAF, patrolling well beyond the battle area. Without their efforts, the Allied transport aircraft would certainly have suffered insupportable losses.

It was during the Arnhem operation that growing numbers of Messerschmitt Me 262 jets began to make their appearance, operating in the fighter-bomber and reconnaissance roles. Jim Rosser, now a flight lieutenant, was back on operations after a spell as a production test pilot at the Castle Bromwich factory, and was now flying Spitfires with No 66 Squadron from Lille/Wambrechies (B.57). One day in September, he was on patrol at 15,000 feet over Venlo in Holland when he sighted an Me 262 a few thousand feet lower down.

'I don't think anyone had actually managed to shoot down a 262 at that time, and I thought this was my big chance. I went down after him, flat out, but he saw me coming and opened the taps. Smoke trails streamed from his turbines and off he went; I hadn't a hope in hell of catching him, so I gave up and rejoined the formation.

The incident had an interesting sequel. Years after the war, when I was stationed in Germany, I met a colonel in the Federal German *Luftwaffe*. We had a few drinks and got talking, and it turned out that he had flown 262s. We compared dates, places and times, and by one of those extraordinary coincidences it came to light that he had almost certainly been the pilot of 'my' 262. He said that if I

had kept after him, it was on the cards I would have got him. His fuel was very low, and he couldn't have maintained full throttle for more than half a minute. So there it was; I got shot down near Arnhem a few days later, so I never did get another chance to have a crack at a jet.'

In fact, the first Me 262 to fall victim to a Spitfire was shot down on 5 October 1944, when five aircraft of No 411 (RCAF) Squadron trapped one near Nijmegen, and on Christmas Day Flt Lt J. J. Boyle of the same squadron destroyed two which made the mistake of trying to out-manoeuvre the Spitfire. No 411 Squadron, which was part of No 126 Wing, had not equipped with the Spitfire Mk XVIE, which was optimised for ground-attack operations and was basically a Mk IX airframe with clipped wings and an American-built Packard Merlin 266 engine. It was prone to engine-failure, and was not popular with many pilots. The engine con-rods were machine-polished, which 'drew' the surface metal, concealing cracks from standard crack detection tests; under boost, the con-rods broke. Although the three feet or so clipped off the wing gave it a good low-level performance, this refinement did nothing to assist take-off from a grass field or quickly laid strip, especially when the aircraft was carrying two 500 lb bombs and a slipper tank.

Conditions in Holland in the autumn of 1944 were grim, as this photograph of Volkel airfield shows. The aircraft in the background is a Tempest Mk V.

In the autumn of 1944, before bad weather set in, the Spitfire squadrons of 2nd TAF carried out many ground-attack operations, some against positions on the island of Walcheren, where the Germans were holding on tenaciously. In the United Kingdom, a special Wing comprising Nos 229, 453 (RAAF), 602 and 603 Squadrons was formed to attack V-2 rocket launching sites in Holland; these missiles were now falling on London in considerable numbers and were causing great alarm to the British Government, fearful of their effect on the Londoners' morale. The four squadrons were equipped with Spitfire LF XVIEs, armed with either two 250 lb or one 500 lb bomb.

Attacks were made against eleven identified V-2 sites, seven in wooded areas around The Hague, but as it was now winter and the weather bad a high proportion of the sorties had to be abandoned. The heaviest single attack of 1944 was mounted on Christmas Eve, when thirty-three Spitfires of Nos 229, 602 and 453 (RAAF) Squadrons attacked a block of flats near the Haagsche Bosch, thought to be the headquarters of the rocket-firing troops. Considerable damage was done, and the building evacuated.

Attacks against the V-2 sites, though, were generally not very successful, and the most damage was probably done on 22 January 1945 when four squadrons of 2nd TAF Spitfires destroyed the liquid oxygen propellant factory at Ablasserdam. Another liquid oxygen plant, at Loosduinen, was attacked three times in February. But it was the Haagsche Bosch, where the launching sites were concealed, that came in for the most attention, and sometimes a huge explosion told the pilots that their bombs had found a target. On one occasion a V-2 was launched during an attack; one of the pilots took a shot at it as it rose majestically on its column of flame but missed, and so lost his chance to become the first pilot in history to shoot down a ballistic missile.

Not all the V-2s were directed against southern England, as the war diary of No 329 Squadron points out.

'The enemy had not been able to prevent the Allies from occupying Antwerp, but they now attempted to deny them the use of the port by a constant bombardment of the city and its environs with V-1 flying bombs and V-2 rockets. The buildings of the air base at Antwerp (B.70, Antwerp-Deurne, where No 145 Wing arrived on 25 November 1944) and indeed all the buildings in the neighbourhood had taken a severe battering

already from these projectiles . . . the units at Deurne got no rest, day or night, for at any moment the billets and hangars might be shaken by explosions . . .

25 November. The Wing took-off to escort Mitchells to München-Gladbach, leaving B.55 Wevelghem and afterwards landing at Deurne, its new base. The evening was spent in billeting the personnel. Dispersal was a house on the edge of the airfield; it still had its doors and windows and was fairly comfortable. The Officers' Mess was ten minutes' walk away. The NCOs were less comfortably housed in a villa; there was only one shower between two squadrons.

Many V-2s fell in the vicinity during our first day, mostly some distance from the airfield. On the 26th, another escort mission with Mitchells to München-Gladbach; weather fine and cold. Another escort mission in the evening, this time at high level to Appeldoorn. It was so cold that some of the pilots had to be helped from their cockpits on return. Many V-2s fell around the airfield in the course of the day, one blowing all the windows out of the Officers' Mess.

29 November. After two days of bad weather, the Wing took part in attacks on railways near Deventer. In the afternoon, while the pilots were in the briefing room, a V-2 fell on No 341 *Alsace* Squadron's dispersal, destroying twelve Spitfires.'

The weather grew steadily worse in December, with snow, rain and wind combining to halt all air activity except on a few days. At the beginning of the month, the First Canadian Army had succeeded in clearing the whole area west of the Meuse and was now preparing to advance towards the river. In preparation for this offensive, the squadrons of 2nd TAF made dive-bombing sorties, whenever the weather permitted, on the enemy rail network north of the Rhine.

On 10 December, No 145 Wing had its first encounter with Me 262s. Two flights, one each from Nos 329 and 345 Squadrons, took-off to dive-bomb a German HQ on the right bank of the Rhine, near Nijmegen, and the Spitfires were attacked by four of the jets as they approached the target. The 262s made one pass, causing no damage, but they forced the Spitfire pilots to jettison their bombs. The Spitfires were escorted by Tempests, which pursued the Me 262s into the clouds.

Spitfire IX armed with 3-inch rocket projectiles.

On 16 December, taking advantage of snow and fog that kept the Allied air forces on the ground, the Germans launched a major counter-offensive in the Ardennes, achieving complete surprise and initial success. The offensive was accompanied by an increase in V-1 and V-2 attacks on Antwerp, where large concentrations of Allied troops and substantial amounts of equipment were assembled. Several missiles exploded on Antwerp-Deurne on the night of 20/21 December, one destroying some barracks and killing or injuring several pilots and ground crew. The missiles were, in fact, causing far more damage at this stage than was the *Luftwaffe*, which confined itself to sorties by single aircraft – mainly Me 262s – against the Allied airfields whenever there was a break in the weather.

On 23 December the weather cleared at last, and the 2nd TAF Spitfire Wings were tasked with escorting heavy and medium bombers pounding the enemy forces, mainly in the Liége–Verviers–Bastogne sector. On the 29th, pilots of No 331 (Norwegian) Squadron, operating with No 132 Wing from B.79 Woensdrecht, encountered twenty-five Me 109s near Entschede and destroyed twelve for no loss. Earlier in the day, however, the Squadron had lost four Spitfires to flak during an airfield attack sortie in which it knocked out four Fw 190s on the ground.

On 1 January 1945, the *Luftwaffe* launched its last desperate gamble: Operation *Bodenplatte*, a massive attack on Allied airfields in Belgium, Holland and Northern France by about 800 fighter-bombers. The surprise was complete, and about 300 Allied aircraft

– many of them Spitfires – were destroyed on the ground, but this success was wiped out by a comparable German loss made more unfortunate by the fact that some 200 aircraft were shot down by their own flak when they passed through an area that was thick with V-2 launching sites and consequently heavily defended. Among the dead German pilots were fifty-nine experienced fighter leaders. What was conceived as a brilliant operation therefore turned into a disaster from which the *Luftwaffe* never recovered. Nevertheless, the attack badly disrupted the Allied air effort, and it was well into January before 2nd TAF could resume its full scale of operations.

At the end of the month, Field Marshal Montgomery's 21st Army Group launched two offensives, code-named *Veritable* and *Grenade*. Air cover over the battlefield was provided by No 84 Group, with the co-operation of the US XXIX Tactical Air Command, while No 83 Group maintained an interdiction programme beyond the Rhine. Although often frustrated by bad weather, No 83 Group's Spitfires, Mustangs, Typhoons and Tempests penetrated deeply into Germany, seeking out railway traffic north of the Ruhr and road transport. On 22 February, all available fighter-bomber squadrons took part in Operation *Clarion*, in which 9,000 aircraft attacked the transportation system over a quarter of a million square miles of Germany.

Preparations were now under way for the crossing of the Rhine; the task of 2nd TAF's fighter-bombers was again railway interdiction, together with attacks on designated special targets. One of

By the end of the war in Europe, the 2nd TAF Spitfire squadrons were receiving the Mk XVIE, one of which is shown here being armed.

these was a camouflaged village near Zwolle, which concealed a German paratroop depot; on 21 March it was attacked by five Typhoon and three Spitfire squadrons of No 84 Group. Later that day, the same squadrons also attacked the HQ of the German 25th Army at Bussum in Holland.

On 23 March, the day before the Rhine crossing, No 121 Wing (Typhoons) and No 126 Wing (Spitfires: Nos 401, 411 and 412 Squadrons RCAF) attacked anti-aircraft positions that were beyond the range of the British Second Army's artillery. The next day, in support of the crossing, armed reconnaissance and close support sorties were flown by the Spitfires of Nos 131, 132 and 145 Wings, No 84 Group, and the Typhoons of Nos 121 and 124 Wings, No 83 Group. The *Luftwaffe* put in a few appearances, and lost twelve Fw 190s to Spitfires and Tempests.

On 12 April, the Spitfire squadrons of No 125 Wing became the first to cross the Rhine, establish-

ing themselves at Twente. Although German resistance was dwindling, the squadrons of No 83 Group were still called upon to assist the army with bomb and rocket attacks on fortified villages, and interdiction missions continued against airfields from which the *Luftwaffe* was still operating. On 20 April, Spitfires, Mustangs and Typhoons destroyed thirty-nine enemy aircraft for the loss of seven of their own – eighteen of the enemy being Me 109s and Fw 190s surprised in the act of taking-off from the airfield at Hagenau. On 30 April, while supporting the Allied crossing of the Elbe, Spitfires joined other fighters of No 83 Group in a major air battle against formations of Fw 190s and Me 109s, the last the *Luftwaffe* was able to scrape together, and destroyed thirty-seven of them.

The battle was fought in the mid-afternoon. At about the same time, Adolf Hitler killed himself in his Berlin bunker. A week later, Germany signed an unconditional surrender.

Chapter 15
Australia's Spitfires in Action

ON 19 FEBRUARY 1942, following sweeping victories in the Dutch East Indies, the Japanese 1st Carrier Air Fleet launched a devastating attack on the North Australian harbour of Port Darwin. Escorted by thirty-six *Zero* fighters, seventy-one dive bombers and eighty-one torpedo bombers swept down on the port, destroying the American warship USS *Peary*, seven merchant vessels totalling 43,429 tons, and four small harbour vessels.

It was the first of a series of heavy air attacks directed against Darwin and other strategic targets in northern Australia during 1942. Throughout that year, the air defence of that vital area was the responsibility of the 49th Fighter Group, USAAF,

equipped with P-40E Kittyhawks, which was joined after August by Nos 76 and 77 Squadrons RAAF, also equipped with this type.

The P-40, however, was no match for the *Zero*. Neither was the other principal American fighter type in service in the theatre in 1942, the Bell P-39 Airacobra. What the Australians wanted was the Spitfire, and at the request of the Australian government the two Spitfire-equipped RAAF squadrons in the United Kingdom, Nos 452 and 457, were disbanded to reform in Australia as an air defence wing. As no Spitfires were immediately available in Australia, the pilots were temporarily assigned to the Kittyhawk-equipped units at Strauss and Livingstone, with detachments to New Guinea.

The arrival of Spitfire Mk VIIIs in the Pacific Theatre enabled the RAAF to gain the upper hand over Japanese fighters. The examples shown are in Pacific and SEAC theatre markings, the red having been deleted from roundels and fin flashes.

Meanwhile, a third Spitfire unit – No 54 Squadron RAF – had also been made available for service in Australia. In June 1942 this squadron embarked for that destination, only to be deprived *en route* of its crated Spitfire VCs, which were diverted to the Middle East. The personnel eventually arrived at Richmond on 24 August 1942, but the slow delivery of Spitfires meant that it was the middle of January 1943 before all three squadrons – forming No 1 Fighter Wing – and their radar-equipped Mobile Fighter Sector HQ arrived in the Darwin area. No 54 Squadron was based at Darwin, No 452 at Strauss and No 457 at Livingstone.

No 1 Fighter Wing was led by Wing Commander Clive Caldwell, a highly skilled and experienced fighter pilot who had already gained twenty victories in North Africa – five of them on 5 December 1941, when he destroyed five Ju 87 *Stukas* in one sortie. After being posted back to Australia in September 1942, he was at first involved in testing an indigenous fighter type, the Commonwealth Boomerang. He produced a scathing critique on it, reporting back to the authorities that in combat it was likely to prove contrary to its name, since if it met an enemy it would be unlikely to return. (As it turned out, although slow for an interceptor – it had a top speed of only 305 mph – the Boomerang performed surprisingly well in the demanding conditions of air warfare in the south-west Pacific.)

In February 1943 the Japanese re-opened their bombing offensive against northern Australia, and on the 6th of that month Flight Lieutenant R.W. Foster opened the Spitfire's scoreboard in the theatre by shooting down a Mitsubishi Ki 46 *Dinah* reconnaissance aircraft thirty-five miles WNW of Cape van Dieman. It was a good start, because so far the *Dinahs* had been able to operate with virtual impunity, their speed and ceiling making them almost immune to interception by fighters such as the P-40. The arrival of the Spitfire – and the Lockheed P-38F, which was beginning to be deployed by the Americans – now changed that situation.

It remained to be seen how the tropicalised Spitfire Mk VC would perform against the *Zero*. They were confident that whatever performance shortcomings the Spitfire might have when confronted by the Japanese fighter – and at this stage of the war the Allies knew just how well the Mitsubishi A6M performed – they would be levelled out by superior skill and tactics.

This confidence seemed to be justified when, during a raid on Coomalie by sixteen Nakajima B5N *Kate* torpedo-bombers with a fighter escort on 2 March, No 54 Squadron claimed one *Zero* and one *Kate* for no loss, the bomber being destroyed by Wing Commander Caldwell. A second *Zero* was shot down by Squadron Leader A. Thorold-Smith, commanding No 452 Squadron.

No 457 Squadron had its first success on 7 March, when a *Dinah* was intercepted and shot down fifteen miles off Darwin. On 15 March Darwin was subjected to its 53rd air attack, during which twenty-one bombers and twenty-four escorting fighters were intercepted by the whole of the 1st Fighter Wing. In the air battle that developed over the harbour the Spitfires shot down three *Zeros* and four Mitsubishi G4M *Betty* bombers. Three Spitfires and one pilot were lost, the pilot being Squadron Leader Thorold-Smith.

There were no raids on the Darwin area in April 1943, but at 0926 on Sunday, 2 May, an incoming Japanese force was detected by radar while it was still a long way out to sea – forty-nine minutes' flying time from the coast, in fact – and the Wing's thirty-three Spitfires were all airborne within fifteen minutes. The fighters made rendezvous over Hughes and continued their climb, heading for 30,000 feet. The enemy formation, comprising eighteen bombers and twenty-seven fighters, was sighted when the Spitfires were at 23,000 feet. Since the Japanese were still about 4,000 feet higher up, Caldwell knew that to attack them on the climb would have been suicidal, for the nimble *Zeros* would have had all the advantages, so he delayed and continued to climb while the Spitfires got into position above the enemy, with the glare of the sun behind them.

At 10.15 the Japanese flew over Darwin and bombed the harbour area unmolested while the Spitfires were still trying to get into position. After completing their bombing run the enemy altered course and crossed the coast off Point Blaze, losing height gradually as they increased speed. The Spitfires were now at 32,000 feet behind the Japanese formation.

Caldwell's fighters shadowed the Japanese until they were out over the Timor Sea, then he ordered No 54 Squadron to attack the *Zeros* while the other two squadrons took on the bombers. The Spitfires, now with the advantage of height, went into the attack almost vertically at 400 mph and a furious air battle developed as the *Zero* pilots, recovering from their surprise, turned to meet the attackers.

It was now that the Spitfire pilots learned a bitter

lesson. The lightly-built *Zero*, with its high power-to-weight ratio, could out-turn the Spitfire VC with comparative ease. Not only that: it could perform some extraordinary manoeuvres that the pilot of anything but a *Zero* would never dare attempt in the middle of a dog-fight. For example, one experienced Australian pilot was making a shallow diving attack on a *Zero* when the enemy fighter suddenly performed a tight loop that brought it on to the tail of the Australian, who had to break hard to avoid being shot down.

When the battle was over, five *Zeros* had been shot down, but only one bomber; and on the debit side five Spitfires had been lost in combat, two of the pilots being killed, while five more had to make forced landings because of fuel starvation and another three because of engine failure. The Australian popular press was scathing in its criticism.

On 9 May, the airfield at Millingimbi, used as a forward base by Allied bombers for attacks on targets in Dutch New Guinea, was attacked by seven Mitsubishi Ki 21 *Sally* bombers, which caused slight damage. In anticipation of further attacks six Spitfires of No 457 Squadron were detached there for air defence duties, and when nine *Zeros* were seen approaching the airfield the next morning five Spitfires went up to intercept them. They engaged six of the enemy fighters and destroyed two of them, but the other three *Zeros* strafed the field, destroying a Bristol Beaufighter of No 31 Squadron and damaging three more. One Spitfire was lost when, in a

low-level turning combat, it hit the ground at 160 mph and cartwheeled four times. Amazingly, the pilot, Pilot Officer B. Little, escaped from the wreck without serious injury and walked back to base. The third and last attack on Millingimbi took place on 28 May, when six Spitfires took off to intercept eight *Sallys* escorted by five *Zeros* at 20,000 feet over the airfield. Three of the bombers were shot down for the loss of two Spitfires, a third being damaged on landing.

By the end of May 1943 the Spitfires of No 1 Fighter Wing had destroyed twenty-four enemy aircraft for the loss of ten Spitfires in combat. Other Spitfires, though, were lost in forced landings in the bush around Darwin; the Merlin engines were suffering badly from wear and tear, and replacements were almost non-existent. During high-altitude actions the Spitfires' 20mm cannon also experienced problems, the freezing conditions causing malfunction and jamming. Even if only one cannon jammed, the recoil from the other caused the aircraft to yaw so that the aim was spoiled.

The newspapers continued to be critical of the Spitfire in its role of air defence, and the criticism intensified when, on the morning of 17 June, the whole Spitfire Wing was scrambled in a vain attempt to catch a *Dinah* making a reconnaissance over Darwin. The Japanese aircraft, at 28,000 feet, easily got away.

Ignoring the growing storm of criticism about the celebrated Spitfire's apparent lack of success, Cald-

well had continued to refine the Fighter Wing's tactics, confident that the situation was bound to change. It did, on 20 June 1943. That morning, Darwin radar detected enemy aircraft approaching, and within minutes forty-six Spitfires of the three squadrons were airborne, formating over Hughes at 20,000 feet. A short time later, the pilots of Nos 54 and 452 Squadrons, climbing hard, sighted twenty-five Japanese bombers over Bathurst Island, escorted by a similar number of *Zeros*. The enemy, at 28,000 feet, were slightly lower than the two Spitfire squadrons, which immediately launched their attack. No 54 Squadron destroyed seven bombers and a *Zero*, while No 452 shot down three bombers and one fighter.

The enemy formation altered course towards Darwin, where No 457 Squadron pounced on it and shot down a *Betty*. After releasing their bombs the enemy flew across Darwin Harbour, losing another two *Zeros*. Meanwhile, ten more bombers had made a low-level attack on Darwin airfield without opposition, but as they withdrew they were intercepted by No 54 Squadron, which destroyed another bomber.

During the morning's engagements the Fighter Wing lost only two Spitfires, both of No 452 Squadron. Against twelve bombers and four fighters destroyed, it was not a bad balance sheet. For once, the critics were silenced.

Meanwhile, Liberators of the 380th Bombardment Group, US Fifth Air Force, had become established at Fenton and Long, in the Northern Territory, and on 23 June 1943 the B-24s began a series of heavy attacks on Macassar and Kendari, in the Celebes. On the last day of the month, by way of retaliation, twenty-seven *Bettys* escorted by twenty-three *Zeros* attacked Long. Although harassed by the three Spitfire squadrons, the enemy formation pressed on and made a beautiful pattern-bombing attack on Fenton, destroying three Liberators and damaging seven more. Still pursued by the Spitfires, the enemy set course for Timor. The Spitfire pilots continued to press home their attacks until shortage of fuel compelled them to break off. In the course of the running battle the Japanese lost six *Bettys* and three *Zeros*; four Spitfires were written off, three as a result of engine failure.

Throughout this period, Spitfire flights, usually of three aircraft, of No 452 Squadron were deployed to Millingimbie, the small island in the Arafura Sea, and to Drysdale in Western Australia, the object in the latter case being to guard against a possible

enemy carrier strike as the battle for Timor raged.

By July, the Spitfires' engines were so worn-out that when thirty-six aircraft of the Fighter Wing took off to intercept a raid by forty-seven enemy aircraft, only seven managed to engage the Japanese. Nevertheless, the seven that did engage, with superb tactical skill, destroyed seven *Bettys* and two *Zeros*. The rest of the Spitfires either failed to reach altitude or were forced to return early with engine problems. Eight Spitfires were written-off, mostly in forced landings.

On 10 August a section of two Spitfires of No 452 Squadron, operating from Millingimbi, destroyed a Japanese *Rufe* floatplane and damaged another. Ten days later, three Japanese *Dinah* reconnaissance aircraft appeared over Darwin, heralding another raid; the Spitfires shot down all three. The Japanese sent another; it was destroyed by Clive Caldwell, his 28th and last victory.

On 7 September the Japanese tried again, the lone *Dinah* on this occasion being escorted by twenty *Zeros*. Radar detected the enemy formation when it was still 180 miles out to sea and forty-eight Spitfires were scrambled, but the *Zeros* bounced No 54 Squadron and shot down three Spitfires. The other pilots of No 54 Squadron in turn destroyed one *Zero* and damaged two more so badly that it is almost certain that they came down somewhere in the Timor Sea, while four more *Zeros* were shot down by the rest of the Wing as the enemy formation withdrew.

This marked the end of Japanese attempts to penetrate the Darwin area by daylight; they now switched to sporadic night attacks which were to continue, with little effect, until early in 1944. Caldwell's Spitfires had fulfilled their task, albeit with greater losses than had been anticipated, and it was now the turn of the RAAF's Beaufighters to come into their own.

By the summer of 1943, 247 Spitfire VCs had been delivered to Australia, the majority being unloaded in crates at Melbourne, assembled and then flown via Sydney to Darwin. Such was the rate of attrition in No 1 Fighter Wing that no Spitfires were available to form new squadrons before the autumn of 1943, but as Japanese attacks on Darwin petered out No 79 Squadron RAAF was able to form with the type for operations in New Guinea. The older Spitfires of the Darwin Wing were handed over to No 2 OTU at Mildura, New South Wales, and Clive Caldwell was posted there as OC to give student pilots the benefit of his combat experience.

No 79 Squadron began operations in the South-West Pacific Area from a base on Kiriwina Island in the Tobriands late in 1943. At this time the Japanese base at Rabaul was being gradually encircled by Allied airfields, and the enemy forces there were being worn down by attrition, both in the air and on the ground. Within the area of blockade the Spitfires carried out airfield protection duties and escorted medium bombers on raids against Rabaul and enemy barges which were ferrying troops from island to island. The Squadron's first kill was a *Dinah*, which exploded after being hit by cannon fire at a range of about 600 yards.

In March 1944, with Allied forces advancing into the Admiralty Islands, Japanese warship movements – including carriers of the Third Air Fleet and two battleships – presented a potential threat to the coast of Western Australia, and this resulted in a redeployment of air defences. Among the units involved were Nos 452 and 457 Squadrons, which deployed to Perth. The squadrons returned to their normal bases at Strauss and Livingstone on 20 March, and in April all three squadrons of No 1 Fighter Wing, led by Beaufighters of No 31 Squadron, staged through the new Bathurst Island strip and attacked Wetan Island, Tepa Village and Babar Island; all returned safely. Meanwhile, No 79 Squadron, together with the Kittyhawks of Nos 76 and 77

Squadrons, had moved its Spitfires forward to Los Negros Island in the Admiralty Group; there they flew ground strafing missions in support of the US invasion forces. Led by Wing Commander Gordon Steege, the Spitfires of No 79 Squadron were the first to fly north across the Equator.

In April 1944 the Australian Spitfire squadrons began to re-equip with the Mk VIII, which, with its uprated Merlin 61 engine, gave them a definite measure of superiority over their Japanese opponents. On 9 May, Nos 54 and 457 Squadrons were deployed to Exmouth Gulf, together with Beauforts of No 14 Squadron and PBY Catalinas of the US Navy, to provide air cover for the replenishment of the aircraft carriers HMS *Illustrious* and USS *Saratoga*, the battleships HMS *Queen Elizabeth* and the French Navy's *Richelieu*, together with their destroyer screens. This operation took place on 15 May, and on the 17th the warships departed to carry out a strike on Surabaya, Java.

On 12 June Spitfires of No 452 Squadron shot down a *Dinah*, but this was a rare success; because of weakening enemy strength in the air, the North-West Area Spitfire squadrons now had little to do except carry out training. The only combat in July 1944 came on the 20th, when Spitfires of No 54 Squadron shot down another *Dinah* over Drysdale Mission.

The Spitfire Mk V floatplane conversion, three of which were produced, was intended for service in the Pacific and also the Mediterranean. None saw operational service in either theatre, but all three were sent to Aboukir for trials in 1943.

By this time, two more Spitfire squadrons, Nos 548 and 549, had arrived in the area to become established at Livingstone and Strauss respectively. These were both RAF units and their personnel had actually arrived at Lawnton, Queensland, in December 1943, but it was April 1944 before they got their first Spitfires. On completion of training they left for Townsville, in the north, but five precious Spitfires were written off in bad weather *en route*. One pilot came down in a swamp and spent all night paddling his way out of it; it was only when he was picked up that he learned the swamp was infested with crocodiles.

The two new squadrons carried out only two operations before the Japanese surrender over a year later. The first was a sweep over Selaroe Island, 300 miles north of Darwin, on 3 September 1944, and the second an attack on the airstrip at Cape Chater, Timor.

The air defence of Darwin was now an all-RAF concern, Nos 548 and 549 Squadrons joining No 54, which was now based at Truscott. Their arrival permitted the release of Nos 452 and 457 Squadrons, which were now assigned to the First Tactical Air Force, RAAF. Formerly known as No 10 Operational Group, this formation was not confined to a definite area, but could deploy rapidly to wherever it was needed. The primary task of the Spitfires was to provide escort for the ground-attack Beaufighters of Nos 30 and 31 Squadrons, alongside which the Spitfires were based at Morotai in the Moluccas.

No 452 Squadron was in fact the first to be deployed there, in December 1944, and on Christmas Eve an enemy bomber was shot down over the airfield by Flying Officer J.A. Pretty. The main function of the First Tactical Air Force, based far to the rear of the main area of operations of the SWPA forces in the Philippines, was, in conjunction with the US Thirteenth Air Force, to maintain a constant assault against Japanese targets which had been bypassed by the main Allied advance; on 13 January 1945 No 452 Squadron strafed targets in the Halmahera area of the Moluccas, and lost one Spitfire to flak. In the main, Kittyhawks and Spitfires were used over Halmahera, while Beaufighters attacked targets in the Celebes, Ceram and Ambon.

No 457 Squadron arrived at Morotai on 8 February 1945, followed by No 79 Squadron in the middle of the month, so that a three-squadron Spitfire Wing was now operational there.

In April 1945 the 1st Australian Corps was ordered to occupy Tarakan Island, Borneo, which had rich oilfields and excellent anchorages. The island's airfields would also provide substantial support facilities for future operations. The air garrison at Tarakan was to comprise the Kittyhawks of No 78 Wing (Nos 75, 78 and 80 Squadrons) with the Spitfires of No 452 Squadron attached for the operation, which was to be completed by 1 May. Softening-up air strikes began twenty days before the invasion, which met with only light opposition.

No 457 Squadron, meanwhile, was attached to the

three Kittyhawk squadrons (Nos 76, 77 and 82) of No 81 Wing for the impending invasion of Labuan, which commanded the entrance to Brunei Bay. Australian troops landed on the island on 10 June 1945 and quickly secured the airstrip, the Spitfires of No 457 Squadron flying in (and losing two aircraft in landing accidents) on the 17th. On 20 June, two Spitfires shot down a *Dinah* fifty-five miles east of Labuan.

Following these operations, the two Spitfire squadrons returned to Morotai, where they came under a new command known as 11 Group. This consisted of Nos 79, 452 and 457 Squadrons and No 120 (Netherlands East Indies) Squadron, a Kittyhawk unit. In July, No 452 Squadron lost a Spitfire which crashed during a strafing run at Simalumong, and two more during attacks on Tawao. On the night of 24/25 July, the Squadron shot down an unidentified enemy aircraft which was bombing Balikpapan. All three Spitfire squadrons undertook strafing attacks during the closing weeks of the war, the policy being to drive the Japanese into the jungle where they were then attacked by Dyak irregulars.

Hostilities ended on 15 August 1945. Shortly afterwards the Australian Spitfire squadrons disbanded, some of their aircraft being assigned to training units; the Kittyhawk squadrons re-equipped with the P-51 Mustang, some of which served as part of the Allied Occupation Forces in Japan and later had a distinguished combat role in Korea. The RAF Spitfire squadrons in Australia disposed of their aircraft in September 1945 and their personnel embarked for the United Kingdom in the following month. Only No 54 Squadron was destined to reform as a fighter unit in the post-war years.

Chapter 16
Spitfires in the Burma Campaign, 1943–45

URING THE long retreat through Burma to the Indian frontier before the relentless Japanese advances of 1942, it was the Hawker Hurricane and the Curtiss P-40, the latter flown by the American Volunteer Group, which had borne the brunt of the enemy's air onslaught. More than a year later, the Hurricane was still the RAF's principal fighter and ground attack aircraft in the theatre, and had proved its worth time and again in the close support role. In the air superiority role, however, the Hurricane was no match for its main opponent, the Nakajima Ki 43 *Hayabusa*, known as *Oscar* to the Allies; nor did it have the necessary performance to catch the enemy's troublesome *Dinah* reconnaissance aircraft, which were going about their business virtually as they pleased.

It therefore came as a considerable relief when, in September 1943, the first Spitfires – Mk VCs – arrived in the theatre and were issued to three Hurricane squadrons, Nos 136, 607 and 615. The last two were quickly deployed to Chittagong, and within a month the Spitfires had shot down four *Dinahs*, greatly reducing the enemy's photographic intelligence of the Allied positions on the Arakan front. On 31 December, No 136 Squadron, operating from Ramu, scored a major success when its pilots destroyed twelve Japanese bombers and fighters of a force that was attempting to attack shipping off the Arakan coast.

By this time two more Spitfire squadrons had arrived in India, having been redeployed from Italy. These were Nos 81 and 152 Squadrons, both equipped with Mk VIIIs. In January 1944, No 136 Squadron also equipped with the Mk VIII, Nos 607 and 615 following suit in March and June respectively. The second squadron to equip with the Mk VIII, in fact, in January 1944, was No 155, which up to that time had been operating ageing Curtiss Mohawk IV fighters; the third was No 67 Squadron, which exchanged its Hurricane IICs for Spitfires in February 1944. Nos 67 and 155 Squadrons, which formed No 293 Wing of Eastern Air Com-

mand, South-East Asia together with the Beaufighter night-fighters of No 176 Squadron, were responsible for the air defence of the Calcutta area.

On 1 January 1944, therefore, with No 67 Squadron yet to convert, there were six Spitfire squadrons on Eastern Air Command's Order of Battle. Nos 136 and 607 Squadrons (No 165 Wing) were at Ramu, both still with Spitfire VCs; No 615 Squadron, also with VCs, was at Dohazari with No 166 Wing; Nos 152 and 155 Squadrons (No 293 Wing) were respectively at Baigachi and Alipore, with Spitfire VIIIs; and No 81 Squadron, also with Mk VIIIs, was at Tulihal, covering the Imphal sector.

In November 1943, all Allied forces in the China–Burma–India Theatre had come under the control of the newly-formed South-East Asia Command (SEAC), and in the weeks that followed major preparations went ahead for a major Allied campaign in the Arakan, which was due to begin on 4 February 1944. As a preliminary, the Allied Air Commander, South-East Asia – Air Chief Marshal Sir Richard Peirse – set about achieving complete air superiority over western Burma with the aid of his new Spitfire squadrons, and in January the RAF fighter pilots claimed twenty-four enemy aircraft for the loss of seven Spitfires in air combat. In addition to the *Oscar*, the RAF pilots were encountering increasing numbers of the Mitsubishi A6M3 Model 32 fighter, an improved clipped-wing version of the *Zero* known to the Allies as *Hamp*. These aircraft served with the *Oscars* in mixed air units, notably the 21st, 33rd, 50th and 64th Air Regiments of the Japanese Army Air Force.

In the first week of February 1944, all was poised to launch the Second Arakan Campaign when the Japanese launched a major and unexpected offensive of their own. Their plan was to split the British Fourteenth Army in two, destroy each half in succession and then drive on into India. This scheme failed for two main reasons: first, because the Japanese committed a tactical blunder in relying upon the Allies to do what they, the Japanese, wished

Landing trouble again: Spitfire PR XI PL961 of No 681 Squadron at Peshawar, India.

them to do, and secondly, because they had ignored the fact that the Allies now had overwhelming air superiority. Instead of falling back in disorder, as the Japanese had confidently anticipated, the Fourteenth Army dug in and fought where it stood, relying on the Allied air forces for tactical support and supply.

The transport squadrons did not fail the troops on the ground. As each Fourteenth Army formation was cut off by the Japanese assault it was passed to the air supply list; soon, three divisions (5, 7 and 81) were all on the receiving end of air drops and getting exactly what they wanted. While Hurricanes and Vultee Vengeance dive-bombers of the RAF and Indian Air Force carried out ground-attack missions, the Spitfires flew top cover, dealing effectively with any Japanese aircraft that appeared. The Spitfire pilots claimed twelve enemy aircraft destroyed during February 1944, with six probably destroyed and fifty-six damaged. These figures are revealing; they show that the Japanese were not staying to fight, as they had done in January when the Spitfire was still a relatively unknown quantity to them. Spitfire combat losses during the month were seven aircraft.

Phase One of the Japanese plan to invade India ended in failure, but this did not deter the enemy from launching Phase Two. On 8 March 1944, three Japanese divisions, supported by armour, attacked across the Kabaw valley and reached Tiddim, cutting the important supply route to Imphal and Kohima, bases which lay forty miles inside Indian territory and were of great defensive importance. On 4 April the Japanese opened their attack on Kohima, and one of the bloodiest battles of the war ensued. As far as air operations were concerned, Kohima was a battle fought by the ground-attack aircraft; in sixteen days, four Hurricane fighter-bomber squa-

drons flew 2,200 sorties against the Japanese 31st Division, while four Vultee Vengeance squadrons struck at the enemy's supply dumps and base camps. The isolated Kohima garrison was completely supplied by air; even their water was dropped by parachute. The garrison was eventually relieved on 20 April 1944, although the area was not cleared until mid-May by XXXIII Corps, which then swung south towards Imphal.

The responsibility for the air defence of Imphal was in the hands of No 221 Group under Air Commodore S.F. Vincent, which used six airstrips within the perimeter. The same Spitfire squadrons that had taken part in the Second Arakan Campaign now took it in turns to operate from within the besieged area, their primary task being to provide cover for the transport aircraft bringing in essential supplies. The official RAF history describes the situation.

'As soon as the decision to stay and fight had been taken, Vincent called his airmen together in the large bamboo canteen at Imphal and explained the situation. Their temper and spirit rose with every word he uttered. Orders were given that every man should carry arms; emergency radio networks were set up to take the place of the ordinary telephone system should it break down; the ground crews and other administrative services on the airfields were formed into self-supporting 'boxes', of which the garrison was required to hold out until overrun. Retreat from them, as from Imphal, was not even considered. At night, until the decision to remove most of the fighters to other airfields outside the plain was taken, pilots and ground crews guarded their own aircraft and lived in foxholes nearby. One Spitfire box looked like a honeycomb. Each section of pilots, armourers, fitters, riggers, electricians, wireless technicians and maintenance crews was responsible for its own dugout and all were arranged to guard the perimeter. Pilots, armed, stayed by their aircraft. Such defensive positions, 'pimples', to give them their local name, spread like a rash over the fair plain of Imphal. A very strict blackout and absolute silence were maintained from dusk to dawn. Then, with the bright light of day, the fighters and fighter-bombers took-off to fly and fight, for now more than ever it was essential to hold the mastery of the air.'

The siege of Imphal lasted for eighty days, and during that time the Japanese Army Air Force managed to shoot down only two Dakotas and one Wellington on supply duties, so effective were the Spitfires. The idea was to keep three Spitfire squadrons available at Imphal at any one time, with a fourth in immediate support, and the scheme worked well. In general, the Spitfire pilots took advantage of the Mk VIII's superior performance at altitude to position themselves above enemy fighters, attack at speed out of the sun, then climb away hard out of range. The Japanese *Oscars* – the only fighter type encountered at Imphal – were more manoeuvrable than the Spitfire, had greater endurance, and were generally present in greater numbers, so the Spitfire pilots avoided turning combats whenever possible.

In March 1944 the Spitfires of Nos 81 and 136 Squadrons, doing their stint at Imphal, destroyed ten *Oscars* and two *Dinahs*, claiming three *Oscars* probably destroyed and five damaged. No 81 Squadron lost six Spitfires, two in a strafing attack on the ground. No 81 Squadron shot down three more *Oscars* and a *Dinah* in April and, together with No 615 Squadron, which had flown into the perimeter, claimed five *Oscars* probably destroyed. A further twenty-three aircraft were claimed to have been damaged. Only two Spitfires were shot down during the month, and one damaged.

The air defence task in May was shared between Nos 81 and 607 Squadrons; No 607 claimed eight *Oscars*, and between them the two squadrons shared eight more probably destroyed and twenty-nine damaged for the loss of eight Spitfires, three of which were written-off when a Dakota transport crashed into them on landing.

In June there was a marked decrease in enemy air activity, only six enemy fighters being destroyed by Nos 607 and 615 Squadrons, the latter having replaced No 81 Squadron. Only one Spitfire was lost in air combat, although three of No 615 Squadron's aircraft were destroyed in a storm. During the month, the Spitfires flew a number of ground attack sorties against enemy transport in the Imphal area.

By the end of June 1944 the siege of Imphal was over. The Japanese had been decisively defeated on the Imphal Plain and the Allies now turned to the offensive, the beginning of a great rout which was virtually to end in Rangoon.

On 1 July 1944, the position of the Spitfire-equipped squadrons in the Battle Order of Air Command, South-East Asia, was as follows. All squadrons were equipped with the Spitfire Mk VIII.

Group	Wing	Squadron	Location	Remarks
222	—	17	Vavuniya, Ceylon	Conv. March 1944
		273	Ratmalana, Ceylon	Conv. March 1944
—	293	67	Baigachi	HQ Eastern Air Command
		155	Baigachi	
—	171	681 (PR)	Alipore	Spitfire XI
221	168	81	Kumbhirgram	
221	170	607	Imphal Main	
221	170	615	Palel	
224	165	152	Palel	
224	166	136	Chittagong	

In November 1944, Nos 17 and 273 Squadrons were also transferred to the Burma Front. By the end of the year, Nos 1, 2, 3 and 8 Squadrons of the Indian Air Force were operational with the Spitfire Mk VIII; they were followed, in May and June, by Nos 4, 6, 7, 9 and 10 Squadrons.

In parallel with the Fourteenth Army's offensive in central Burma, another by XV Corps in the Arakan was also gaining momentum. A major breakthrough was made on 2 January 1945, when Hurricane pilots of No 20 Squadron, patrolling over Akyab, reported some inhabitants signalling that the enemy had moved out. The island was subsequently occupied without opposition and turned into a secure base for further operations along the coast. Spitfires were flown in for air defence, and on 3 January these shot down five out of six *Oscars* that attempted to attack the Allied amphibious force engaged in landing personnel and stores.

Of the Spitfire squadrons that fought at Arakan and Imphal, two – Nos 81 and 136 – were withdrawn to Ceylon in July and August 1944. No 81 Squadron remained there until disbandment in June 1945, but No 136 deployed to the Cocos Islands in March and, after the Japanese surrender in September, went to Kuala Lumpur in Malaya. It remained there until May 1946, when it moved to Bombay and assumed the identity of No 152 Squadron.

Of the other squadrons, No 615 went to Calcutta for air defence duties in August 1944, returning to Burma in February 1945 to operate in the tactical role with Nos 67, 152, 155, 607 and the Spitfire-equipped

Spitfire VIIIs of No 136 Squadron in the Cocos Islands, 1945.

Indian Air Force squadrons. In May Rangoon was captured, and in the north Mandalay had also fallen. The slaughter of the hemmed-in Japanese on the Mandalay Plain now began, the fighter-bombers of No 221 Group inflicting terrible casualties on the disorganized enemy columns. By the second week in May, Japanese resistance in central Burma had been effectively smashed.

The Fourteenth Army's rapid advance towards Rangoon had by-passed strong pockets of Japanese, and much bitter fighting remained before these were eliminated. The casualties suffered by the enemy in this last phase of the campaign were appalling; on 21 July, for example, the Japanese tried to cross the Sittang River with up to 18,000 men and were attacked by every available squadron of No 221 Group, despite low cloud and heavy rain. Spitfires carrying one 500 lb bomb joined Thunderbolts – which had now replaced most of the Hurricanes – carrying three; in nine days the RAF flew over 3,000 sorties and killed 10,000 enemy troops.

It was the end in Burma, and the Spitfire squadrons that had fought so valiantly in the campaign, often battling against atrocious weather conditions as well as the enemy, were split up or disbanded. Nos 17 and 273 re-equipped with Spitfire XIVEs and departed for Malaya and Thailand respectively; No 17 Squadron eventually went to Japan to form part of the Allied Occupation Force, temporarily disbanding in 1948, while No 273 moved from Bangkok to French Indo-China, disbanding at Saigon in January 1946.

Nos 607 and 615 Squadrons disbanded in July 1945, later to reform in the Royal Auxiliary Air Force in the United Kingdom, and No 67 Squadron disbanded in August, to reform five years later in Germany with Vampire jet fighters. No 152 Squadron left for Singapore in September 1945 and later received Tempest F.2s.

For No 155 Squadron, there was to be further action. In February 1946 it took its Spitfires to Sumatra to provide tactical support for SEAC forces in action against Indonesian rebels, disbanding in July.

Scenes at Kai Tak, Hong Kong, after the Japanese surrender in 1945.

Spitfire Mk XIVs were replacing the Mk VIII in SEAC at the time of the Japanese surrender.

Spitfire XIV RM958 was assigned to the Indian Air Force in February 1945.

A Spitfire taxies past parked Mosquitoes at Seletar, Singapore, after the war's end.

Chapter 17
Seafires in the Far East

I N OCTOBER 1943, the escort carrier HMS *Battler* arrived in the Indian Ocean to form the nucleus of an anti-submarine group which, during the early months of 1944, began hunter-killer operations against German and Japanese submarines which were preying on shipping in the area from their base at Penang. *Battler*'s air group consisted of a single squadron, No 834, which included a flight of Fairey Swordfish, one of Grumman Wildcats and one of Supermarine Seafire IIs.

Although the British aircraft carriers that operated subsequently in Far Eastern waters were equipped mainly with American aircraft, the Seafire was also to make its mark in this theatre of war. Later in the year, the trade protection group in the Indian Ocean was strengthened with the arrival of the escort carriers *Shah*, *Begum*, *Ameer* and *Atheling*; the latter carried two fighter squadrons, No 890 with Wildcats and No 889 with Seafires.

In January 1944 the carriers penetrated into the Bay of Bengal and approached Akyab Island. The Japanese were alerted and a force of bombers escorted by *Zeros* went out to attack the warships, which were about 100 miles off the Burmese coast. One of the fighter pilots was Lt Kuroe of the Japanese Army Air Force.

'I led the second wave of eight *Zero* fighters and eight light bombers. The first wave had found no Allied fighter escort, so when I arrived over an hour later I expected no fighter opposition. I was greatly surprised, therefore, to find the enemy fleet covered by Seafires. We attacked the ships, but none of our bombs hit the target; then the Seafires struck back at us, and five of our bombers and two fighters were shot down.

It was then I did something stupid. Instead of staying with the other fighters and bombers I went chasing off after a Seafire. He took evasive action and I followed him all the time. I chased him for more than thirteen minutes, but then discovered that another Seafire was also chasing me. He got me in a bad position and attacked. Afterwards, I found thirty bullet holes in my

Seafire Mk III seen in South-East Asia Command markings.

aircraft. My fuel tank was hit, my undercarriage damaged, and I was unable to alter the pitch of my propeller. It was my turn to run now, and I made for an emergency landing strip. I landed all right, but the business with the Seafire gave me a nasty fright.'

At the end of the year the escort carrier force on trade protection duties in the Indian Ocean was reduced to three ships, *Empress, Ameer* and *Shah,* none of which carried Seafires. In March 1945, however, the 21st Carrier Group – comprising the *Stalker, Attacker, Emperor, Hunter* and *Khedive* – also began operations in the Bay of Bengal, bringing with them ten fighter squadrons, three of which were equipped with Seafires. These were No 807 (HMS *Hunter*), 809 (HMS *Stalker*) and 879 (HMS *Attacker*). Between 30 April and 2 May 1945, the Seafires and Hellcats flew 180 combat air patrol sorties during Operation *Dracula,* the Allied amphibious landings in the Rangoon area; there were no air combats, and the Fleet Air Arm fighters strafed Japanese positions near the beach-head. This was followed on 5 and 6 May by attacks on enemy shipping among the islands off the long southern coast of Burma and on airfields in the Tenasserim area. Avengers and Hellcats from the *Shah* and *Empress* also hit enemy airfields in the NicobaR and Andaman Islands as a diversion, following up these strikes by an attack on Japanese positions around Tavoy on 7 May. Only two Hellcats were lost to enemy action, but six Seafires – which had been operating in the fleet defence role – were written-off in landing accidents.

During June and July the escort carriers were involved in mopping-up operations against crumbling Japanese resistance in the Andamans. Several strikes were also made on airfields and rolling stock in Sumatra and southern Burma. Many enemy convoys in southern Thailand were also attacked, the Hellcats and Corsairs proving very effecting in blocking the tortuous roads with their strafing

The Seafire Mk XV was the Royal Navy's equivalent of the RAF's Griffon-engined Mk XII Spitfire. Deliveries began in 1945.

attacks. Once again, because of their lack of combat radius, the Seafires were restricted to the role of air defence.

Their chance came on 27 July 1945, when seven Japanese aircraft came in low over the sea towards the ships of the 21st Carrier Squadron in the Bay of Bengal. Three were shot down by CAP Seafires, two more were hit by AA fire and blew up, and another slammed into the side of the minesweeper *Vestal*, which exploded and sank. The seventh aircraft narrowly missed the carrier *Ameer*, which received slight damage in the explosion. It was the 21st Carrier Squadron's first and only experience of a *Kamikaze* suicide attack.

Seafires also served with the British Pacific Fleet, which had sailed from Trincomalee, Ceylon, for Sydney in January 1945, striking *en route* at the Japanese oil refineries at Palembang, in southern Sumatra. With it went two Seafire squadrons, Nos 887 and 894, both on board the fleet carrier HMS *Indefatigable*.

After assembling at Sydney under the command of Rear-Admiral Sir Philip Vian, the fleet reached

Ulithi Atoll in the Caroline Islands on 19 March 1945, where – designated Task Force 57 – it formed part of the American Fifth Fleet. As well as the carriers *Illustrious*, *Indomitable*, *Indefatigable* and *Victorious*, TF 57 included a powerful screening force of battleships, cruisers and destroyers.

On 23 March the British warships sailed to take part in Operation *Iceberg*, the landing on Okinawa. Task Force 57's mission was to strike at six enemy airfields in the Sakishima Gunto island group, which lay to the south-west of Okinawa and the other Ryukyu Islands. It was an important task, for these airfields – which were used as staging posts between Formosa and Okinawa – could be put out of action, the Japanese would be unable to fly in reinforcements and Okinawa would be isolated.

On 26 March TF 57 reached its flying-off position about 100 miles south of Sakishima Gunto and the first strike of forty Grumman Avengers was launched. While these attacked airfield installations with 500 lb bombs, Fairey Fireflies of No 1770 Squadron (HMS *Indefatigable*) attacked flak positions with rocket projectiles. The offensive contin-

A Royal Navy Seafire Mk XV

ued for two days, and in between the main Avenger strikes – of which there were eight – small formations of bomb-carrying Corsairs and Hellcats were sent in to keep the enemy in a state of nerves. However, the strikes did comparatively little damage to the airfields themselves; the runways were made of crushed coral and were easily repaired during lulls in the bombing. Few enemy aircraft were caught and destroyed on the ground, but twenty-eight were shot down by Corsairs and Hellcats in the target area for the loss of nineteen Fleet Air Arm aircraft. Once again, the Seafire squadrons were restricted to Fleet CAP during these operations.

On 28 March the Task Force withdrew for replenishment at sea, the operation being prolonged by unexpected bad weather, but the carriers were back on station by the 31st and ready to renew their attacks. On 1 April Japanese aircraft appeared over the fleet in strength, and on that day the Seafires made their first combat claims in the Pacific. Sub-Lieutenant R. Reynolds of No 894 Squadron, who

had already destroyed two Blohm und Voss Bv 138 flying boats over the Atlantic, destroyed three *Zeros* and so became the Royal Navy's only Seafire 'ace'. The Seafires, Hellcats and Corsairs, together with the formidable AA barrage put up by the fleet, accounted for most of the enemy aircraft, but one broke through and crashed at the base of *Indefatigable*'s island. Flying operations were suspended for only forty-five minutes while the wreckage was pushed over the side, thanks to the armoured deck that was a feature of the British fleet carriers.

During the third series of operations against Sakishima, on 6 April the *Kamikazes* attacked again. This time, a burning *Zero* made a desperate attempt to hit the *Illustrious*, but only succeeded in striking the carrier's island with its wingtip before plummeting into the sea. During this attack, the Corsairs of No 1830 Squadron (HMS *Illustrious*) and the Hellcats of No 1844 (HMS *Indomitable*) accounted for five Aichi D4Y *Judys* and one Nakajima P1Y *Frances*.

American Intelligence had indicated that many of

The next step was the Seafire Mk XVII, one of which is seen about to land on the carrier HMS *Illustrious* after the war. It began operations with No 883 Squadron in September 1945, just too late for war service.

the *Kamikaze* attacks were being launched from Formosa, and Admiral Spruance, commanding the US Fifth Fleet, asked Task Force 57 to mount a series of strikes on airfields in the northern part of the island. The first attack was carried out in poor weather on 11 April by forty-eight Avengers and forty Corsairs. While the Avengers bombed the port of Kiirun, the fighters strafed airfields in the vicinity. The attacks continued on the 12th, when they were contested by Japanese fighters. The Hellcats of No 1844 Squadron shot down four *Oscars*, a *Zero* and a Kawasaki Ki 61 *Tony*, while the Corsairs of Nos 1834 and 1836 Squadrons claimed an *Oscar*, a *Zero* and a *Dinah*. The Fireflies of No 1770 Squadron were particularly lucky; they encountered a formation of five Mitsubishi Ki 51 *Sonia* bombers heading for Okinawa and shot down four of them. A *Kamikaze* attack later in the day brought a kill for a Seafire of No 887 Squadron; three more enemy aircraft were destroyed and six damaged.

After this operation, HMS *Illustrious* was withdrawn from the task force, suffering from an accumulation of mechanical troubles that were the accumulation of four years of combat operations. She was replaced by HMS *Formidable*, with one squadron of Avengers and two of Corsairs. The newcomer immediately went into action with the task force during another series of strikes against Sakishima between 16 and 20 April. By this time the fleet had spent over a month at sea on operations; the carriers required replacement aircraft and aircrew and the tankers and supply ships of the Fleet Train badly needed replenishment. On the night of 20 April the fleet sailed for Leyte in the Philippines, where it stayed until 1 May.

When Task Force 57 returned to operations on 4 May the target was once again the enemy airfields on Sakishima. While Avengers attacked Ishigaki, the 14-inch guns of the battleships *King George V* and *Howe* pounded the airfields and installations on the neighbouring island of Miyako. At 11.00, shortly before the first strike returned to the carriers, TF 57 was attacked by a formation of twenty *Kamikazes*. Almost every FAA fighter squadron was involved in breaking up the attack; the Corsairs of Nos 1834 and 1836 Squadrons (HMS *Victorious*) shot down a Nakajima C6N *Myrt*, a *Judy* and two *Zeros*, the Seafires of Nos 887 and 894 Squadrons claimed a *Val* and four *Zeros* between them, while the Hellcats of Nos 1839 and 1844 Squadrons destroyed a Nakajima B6N *Jill* and two *Zeros*. Only two *Zeros*

penetrated the fighter screen and the AA barrage; the first struck the *Indomitable* aft, slid across the flight deck and went over the side, and the second hit the *Formidable*. The damage was quickly patched up and the carrier was fully operational again by the end of the day. Eleven aircraft were destroyed by the *Kamikaze* on the *Formidable*'s deck; fortunately, most of her aircraft were airborne. Together with the *Victorious*, she survived another *Kamikaze* attack on 9 May, although twenty-two aircraft were destroyed.

The strikes against targets on Sakishima Gunto continued until 25 May, by which time Okinawa was in American hands. HMS *Formidable* had left the area for Sydney three days earlier, following an accidental hangar fire in which thirty of her aircraft were destroyed.

In two months at sea, the aircraft of Task Force 57 had flown 5,335 sorties, dropped 1,000 tons of bombs and fired 1,000 rockets. Nearly 200 enemy aircraft had been destroyed, ninety-eight of them in air combat; most of these victories had been achieved by the Corsairs and Hellcats, either over enemy territory or while flying on the outer CAP screen. The Seafire's role in air combat had been very much a secondary one, its lack of combat radius having restricted it to operations in close proximity to the task force. On the relatively few occasions when it did engage the enemy, however, it had performed well.

The Fleet Air Arm's losses had been far from light; seventy-three aircraft had been destroyed in the *Kamikaze* attacks and the *Formidable*'s hangar fire, another sixty-one – many of them Seafires – had been written off in accidents, and twenty-six had been shot down by enemy flak and fighters. Eighty-five personnel had been killed, including forty-one aircrew.

Towards the end of June the fleet carrier HMS *Implacable* joined the British Pacific Fleet at Manus Anchorage, in the Admiralty Islands. The carrier had arrived in the Pacific three weeks earlier, and on 10 June she had carried out a series of strikes against the badly-battered Japanese base at Truk, in the Carolines. Now, fully worked up to operational standards, she replaced the *Indomitable*, which departed for a refit.

Implacable brought with her two more squadrons of Seafire Mk IIIs, Nos 801 and 880. Also, among her stores, she carried American auxiliary fuel tanks which had been 'liberated' from a USAAF depot in New Guinea in exchange for several cases of

The ultimate Seafire was the Mk 47, which corresponded to the RAF's Spitfire Mk 24. In 1950 Seafire 47s from HMS *Triumph* took part in operations in Korea.

Scotch. With these slung under their bellies, the Seafires were able to extend their combat radius by fifty per cent.

There was to be little opportunity, however, for the Seafire pilots to enjoy their new-found freedom of action. The Seafires participated in strikes against enemy shipping at the end of July, but then operations were delayed for nine days because of bad weather and the dropping of the atomic bombs on Hiroshima and Nagasaki.

At dawn on 15 August 1945, the Avengers of No 820 Squadron were intercepted by *Zeros* during an attack on targets in the Tokyo area. The Japanese fighters were immediately overwhelmed by the Seafires of Nos 887 and 894 Squadrons, which shot down eight of the enemy for no loss.

Two hours later, all offensive operations against the Japanese home islands were suspended.

Deck-landings with the Seafire remained a risky business, as these post-war photographs show. The aircraft are Mk XVs.

Chapter 18
Spitfires in the Malayan Emergency, 1948–51

ALTHOUGH THE Royal Air Force and associated Commonwealth units concentrated their efforts in support of the Security Forces' activities against the Communist terrorists who sought to establish control of the Malay Peninsula for a decade or more after 1948, their primary role remained the air defence of Malaya, the colony of Singapore, North Borneo and Sarawak.

Air operations in support of the ground forces during Operation *Firedog*, as the anti-terrorist campaign was known, came under the overall control of the Commander-in-Chief, Air Command Far East (which was redesignated the Far East Air Force on 1 June 1949), operational control being exercised by the Air Officer Commanding, Malaya.

The onset of the Emergency soon revealed that the RAF was badly placed to mount major anti-terrorist operations, both from the point of view of offensive support and air supply. From a front-line strength of seventy squadrons, with 1,324 operational aircraft, which Air Command South-East Asia had possessed in mid-1945, Air Command East's strength had shrunk to eleven squadrons with just over 100 aircraft by the middle of 1948. These limited resources were concentrated entirely on Singapore Island, the mainland base of Kuala Lumpur having closed down, and so the prospect of setting up a mobile air task force on the Malayan Peninsula posed considerable problems.

At the beginning of the Emergency the resources available to HQ ACFE for undertaking offensive operations were very slender, amounting to the equivalent of only three and a half squadrons with twenty-nine aircraft between them. At Sembawang, Nos 28 and 60 Squadrons had sixteen Spitfire FR 18s and PR 19s, while No 84 Squadron at Tengah was equipped with eight Bristol Beaufighters and No 209 Squadron at Seletar had four Short Sunderland flying boats.

On 3 July 1948 three Spitfires of No 60 Squadron flew north to Kuala Lumpur to form the nucleus of an air strike task force, and were joined shortly afterwards by the remaining aircraft of the squadron together with one photo-reconnaissance PR 19 of No 28 Squadron. On 6 July, two Spitfires of No 60 Squadron armed with cannon and rocket projectiles attacked and virtually destroyed a terrorist camp near Ayer Karah in Perak. The next strike was flown on 15 July, against a group of huts located in mountainous country near Bentong in Pahang, and on the following day another strike was mounted against a hut near Telok Anson in central Perak which was surrounded by swamp and was not easily accessible from the ground. This attack was very successful, ten terrorists being killed.

On 28 July, No 60 Squadron's Spitfires carried out a further air strike in support of a road convoy of the Malay Regiment at Sungei Yu, which had run into an ambush while on its way to relieve a police post at Gua Musang, captured by terrorists. Although strike aircraft were kept at a readiness state of four hours during this early period of operations, their reaction time was in fact considerably less, and the speed of the response from Kuala Lumpur was greatly appreciated by the ground forces. The success of the early strikes emphasized the value of fighter-bomber support, and demands for offensive support operations increased sharply in August 1948. The majority of these were carried out in support of *Shawforce*, a Malay/Gurkha force operating in Pulai valley of northern Perak.

The Spitfires, however, were showing their age, and when faulty wiring in one of them caused the accidental release of a rocket on the ground, killing a civilian in the village of Salak South, a complete embargo was placed on the carriage of bombs and rockets by these aircraft. The gap was filled by the detachment of two Beaufighters of No 84 Squadron from Tengah to Kuala Lumpur. With its powerful armament of four 20mm cannon, six .303 machine-guns, eight RPs or two 250 lb or 500 lb bombs, each Beaufighter was the offensive equivalent of two Spitfires.

The number of air strikes requested by the Security Forces declined in the closing months of 1948, mainly because there was little contact with terrorist forces. The reason for this was that the CT were splitting into smaller groups and withdrawing into secure areas in the jungle, having failed in their bid to establish supremacy in southern Kelantan. The Spitfires of No 60 Squadron returned to Sembawang for a few weeks, but moved up to Kuala Lumpur again after drastic government measures, including plans for resettlement and deportation, led to an increased flow of information about terrorist locations and a corresponding increase in air-strike activity. Twenty strikes were carried out in December 1948, the Spitfires using cannon only, bringing the total since the start of the campaign to eighty-four.

Up to this point, air strikes had usually been called in after ground forces were in position to ambush terrorists fleeing from the target area. Early in 1949 there was a change in tactics whereby troop movements preceding an air strike were disguised, so that the associated air strikes might achieve the maximum element of surprise. On 28 February 1949, using these modified tactics, four Beaufighters and eight Spitfires (the latter now cleared to carry 20 lb fragmentation bombs) carried out a very successful attack on a target near Mengkuang in south Pahang, killing at least fifteen terrorists. Another very successful series of six strikes was flown over a twelve-day period in April 1949, the target lying in the Kuala Langat Forest Reserve area of southern Selangor. Forty-five terrorists were eliminated in these attacks.

In May 1949 the Spitfires of No 28 Squadron moved from Sembawang to a new location at Hong Kong, but their loss was offset by the arrival of No 33 Squadron, with Hawker Tempest F.2 aircraft, at Seletar on 8 August. A week later, the strength of No 60 Squadron was increased from eight to seventeen Spitfires. By the first week in September, the air strike force available for operations in Malaya comprised seventeen Spitfires, sixteen Tempests, eight Beaufighters and ten Sunderlands. On 6 December, No 45 Squadron exchanged its elderly Beaufighters for Bristol Brigand light bombers, aircraft that were to be dogged by technical troubles throughout their service in Malaya. (No 45 Squadron had begun arriving in Singapore in August 1948, replacing No 84 Squadron, which moved to the Middle East.)

In the closing months of 1949, information from surrendered terrorists led to an increase in the number of CT targets available for selection, and

for a time the demands made upon the air-strike force outstripped its capability. The biggest strike so far, against a target near Gemas in Negri Sembilan, was carried out on 21 October and involved some sixty-two sorties by Spitfires, Beaufighters, Tempests and Sunderlands of the RAF and by Fireflies and Seafires of Nos 827 and 800 Squadrons of the Fleet Air Arm, which had arrived in the theatre on the aircraft carrier HMS *Triumph*. During the last two months of 1949, sixty-two strikes, involving 388 sorties, were flown against targets in western and central Malaya. Joint strikes by the RAF and RN continued into the early weeks of 1950.

The fourteen Spitfire FR 18s of No 60 Squadron, the last in first-line service with the RAF, were withdrawn in December 1950 and January 1951, having carried out 1,800 operational sorties against the terrorists. The squadron re-equipped with the de Havilland Vampire FB 5, and was out of the line until the end of April 1951 for training in its primary role of air defence.

Three of No 60 Squadron's FR Spitfires were transferred to No 81 Squadron at Seletar on 21 November 1950, bringing its total strength to nine Mosquitoes, five Spitfires and an Avro Anson. Throughout the Emergency almost the whole of the photographic reconnaissance (PR) commitment was fulfilled by No 81 Squadron, which in June 1948 was at Tengah with its nine Mosquito PR 34s and, at that time, two Spitfire FR 18s. When the Emergency began, the two Spitfires were based at Kuala Lumpur, and in June 1949 they were joined by a third aircraft which had been converted to the PR role. In March 1950 these three aircraft were transferred to No 60 Squadron to form a PR flight, while No 81 Squadron acquired two Spitfire PR 19s a little later in the year. Normally, the PR Spitfires of No 60 Squadron were limited to operations within 150 miles of Tengah, and all other reconnaissance missions were flown by the Mosquitoes of No 81 Squadron at Seletar, but urgent tasks that the aircraft were unable to fulfil in their own operational areas were passed on to the other squadron. The Spitfire pilots of No 60 Squadron would be briefed at Tengah but would land at Seletar for de-briefing, except where they flew missions in northern Malaya from the advanced base at Kuala Lumpur.

The five PR Spitfires of No 81 Squadron (the three transferred back from No 60 Squadron in November 1950, plus the two PR 19s) continued in service until the end of 1953, when they were replaced by five Gloster Meteor PR 10s. The Mosquitoes were not

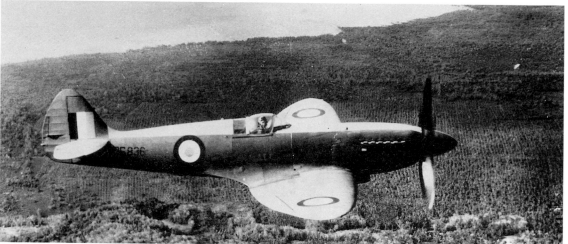

The last Spitfire sorties of the Malayan emergency were flown by the Spitfire PR.19s of No 81 Squadron. The PR.19 was the last of the PR Spitfires, and was based on a late-production Mk XIV airframe.

withdrawn from service until the end of 1955.

The first operational sortie carried out by No 81 Squadron in Malaya in fact took place before the Emergency was declared. On 21 April 1948, a PR Spitfire took off from Taiping in support of a police sweep (Operation *Haystack*) in the Sungei Perak valley, but the sortie was aborted because of bad weather. Regular tactical PR operations began in July 1948, with the detachment of two Spitfires at Kuala Lumpur. There was no real co-operation or systematic planning at this stage; in fact, for the first two or three months of the campaign all tactical PR requirements were met by one Spitfire and one pilot of No 81 Squadron, who once flew for fifty-six days in succession and carried out sixty sorties, of which forty were successful. During the first eighteen

months of the campaign the Spitfires flew a monthly average of twenty to thirty sorties; these were sufficient to meet the demands of the Security Forces, leaving the Mosquitoes free to continue their task of surveying the 51,000 square miles of Malayan territory so that new and revised maps could be completed as quickly as possible.

Operations by Spitfires in Malayan skies might have gone on somewhat longer than they actually did, had plans to integrate the type into the Malayan Auxiliary Air Force (MAAF) come to fruition. Established in mid-1950, the MAAF was to have had four fighter squadrons, based at Penang, Singapore and Kuala Lumpur. Three squadrons had been formed by December 1951, the idea being that personnel would train on Tiger Moths and Harvards and then on surplus Spitfires before progressing to Vampires. The objective, prior to the receipt of jet fighters, was that each squadron would be established with eight Spitfire FR 18s, plus two Harvards for training.

Progress in flying training, however, proved to be very slow, and in the summer of 1951 the Singapore Squadron – the first to be formed – had only three pilots who were ready for conversion to Spitfires. In the other squadrons, no progress at all was being made towards Spitfire conversion. Three Spitfires were in fact delivered to the Singapore Squadron at the end of 1952, but they were withdrawn early in the following year, by which time it had become apparent that none of the MAAF pilots under training would be ready to fly Vampires by the target date of 1954, and so the policy of providing auxiliary air defence squadrons was abandoned. It was agreed that the MAAF would eventually be replaced by a regular Malayan Air Force, and that in the interim the MAAF's light aircraft would be used for short-range liaison and visual reconnaissance.

Chapter 19
Spitfires in Hong Kong

IMMEDIATELY AFTER the Japanese surrender, the British government placed high priority on the rapid re-occupation of the colony of Hong Kong and the re-establishment of a civilian administration. It was considered important that the Japanese surrender in Hong Kong should be accepted by a British officer, and that the RAF element of the forces sent there should be operating British (rather than American) aircraft.

Rear-Admiral C.H.J. Harcourt, Flag Officer 11th Aircraft Carrier Squadron of the British Pacific Fleet, was the nearest British commander, being based at Luzon in the Philippines. He reached Hong Kong on 29 August 1945 with a task group headed by the aircraft carrier HMS *Indomitable*, and the colony was re-occupied on 1 September.

Twelve days later the first convoy sailed into Hong Kong, carrying 3 Royal Marine Commando Brigade. It was accompanied by the carrier HMS *Smiter*; on board were the Spitfire XIVs of No 132 Squadron, which earlier in the year had assembled at Vavuniya in Ceylon in readiness to support the planned invasion of Malaya. *Smiter* was one of the Royal Navy's smaller carriers, and the squadron pilots were not entirely happy about flying off. The Spitfires could not be catapult launched, but they managed to take-off successfully with half full fuel tanks, no ammunition and with the carrier steaming at full speed into a stiff breeze. Within a few minutes the whole squadron had landed safely at Kai Tak

No 132 Squadron was principally involved in anti-piracy patrols during its short tenure in Hong Kong; it disbanded on 15 April 1946, after which patrol work was undertaken by a detachment of Sunderland flying boats. Then, in the summer of 1949, civil war in China and the upsurge of communist-inspired nationalist movements in the Far

Last of the Spitfires: in these superb air-to-air shots, a Mk 24 is flanked by a Mk 21 and Mk 22. The Spitfire Mk 21 was the first of the Griffon-engined Spitfires to feature a new wing shape, although the Spitfire ellipse is still discernible.

East brought an urgent need for air reinforcements, and in May 1949 the Spitfire FR 18s of No 28 Squadron deployed to Kai Tak from Malaya.

In parallel with this move, No 80 Squadron (Sqn Ldr Tremlett, DFC), which had converted to Spitfire F.24s from Tempest IIs in 1948, was deployed to the Far East from 2nd TAF in Germany. The aircraft were flown from Gutersloh to Renfrew via Eindhoven and Manston, where they were joined by the aircraft (Tempest IIs) and personnel of No 33 Squadron, also bound for the Far East.

The two squadrons embarked in the carrier HMS *Ocean* and sailed for Singapore, where No 33 Squadron disembarked, destined for operations in Malaya. *Ocean* continued on to Hong Kong, where the aircraft and personnel of No 80 Squadron were transferred by lighter to Kai Tak, to join No 28 Squadron in forming a new fighter Wing under Wing Commander Nel, DSO.

No 80 Squadron now comprised a backbone of experienced ex-Germany pilots plus eight replacements with no experience of flying Spitfire 24s. From its arrival early in August 1949 until the end of September, the Squadron underwent an intensive programme of continuation training, local area familiarisation and conversion flying for the new

pilots. For the latter it was hard work, for the F.24 was not an easy aircraft to fly, utterly lacking the docility that characterized earlier marks of Spitfire. With its increased weight, high speed wing, far more power, and lengthened under-carriage legs, the aircraft had a strong tendency to swing on take-off, often with interesting results. The surrounding terrain was also hazardous, with rugged mountain ridges flanking long, narrow, convoluted valleys, inlets, and a large plain bisected by the border between the colony and China. The weather, too, was often unpredictable and violent; the early training programme was interrupted by a typhoon that caused extensive damage and loss of life, and one pilot was killed on his first flight.

Despite all the problems, however, No 80 Squadron was declared operational at the beginning of September 1949, and assumed its tactical role. This was ground attack and interception by day at low and high level, the FR 18s of No 28 Squadron covering medium-level interceptions. Additional tasks included Navy and Army co-operation, which mostly involved anti-aircraft affiliation, and anti-piracy patrols in coastal waters. Squadron training comprised low-level and dive-bombing, air-to-ground rocket and cannon firing at the Kai Tak

Spitfire Mk 24s of No 80 Squadron, Hong Kong.

Wing's range in Silversands, eight miles from the airfield, battle and precision flying, mock attacks, practice interceptions from sea level to 35,000 feet (10,670 m), Wing exercises with British and American carrier-based aircraft, Army manoeuvres, fighter affiliation, low flying, aerobatics and instrument flying.

A high level of skill was necessary, for in late 1949 Kai Tak was the third busiest airfield in the world.

Apart from the military presence, it was the junction for the major world airlines and for Chinese internal flights. It was open from dawn to dusk, night flying being considered too dangerous. Traffic patterns for the two 1,500-yard (1,370 m) runways were complicated by the presence of the steep peaks that encroached within the normal circuit to a height of 2,000 ft (610 m) from the north-west to the east, and the need for visual approaches in bad weather. With

runway 13 in use, civil aircraft made direct approaches with doglegs to avoid the foothills, and the fighters joined a right-hand circuit with the usual low break. On all take-offs, an immediate right turn was needed to avoid the hills above the fishing village. On runway 31, a normal left-hand circuit was flown by all aircraft, with the turn on finals being made close to the threshold to avoid the hills; to avoid a long backtrack, the Spitfires took off downwind whenever conditions allowed. As runway 07 ended one mile from the base of a 1,000 ft (305 m) high peak, take-offs and overshoots on this runway were forbidden, and landings banned on its reciprocal runway 25. It is no exaggeration to say that the pilots of the two Kai Tak Spitfire squadrons were probably the most experienced in the RAF at crosswind/downwind departures and landings.

Tactical requirements took little account of the dangers of flying in the lee of mountains, and each pilot averaged at least ten hours a month flying at very low altitude in close or battle formation up and down the twisting valleys, learning how to judge the effects of turbulence. Constant practice made them expert at attacking targets at the base of cliffs, on hill flanks, and in the steep-sided valleys. With its great manoeuvrability and power, the Spitfire 24 was an

ideal aircraft for these conditions, and there were no losses or damage during these operations. Some damage was, however, sustained from flying debris during ground-attack training, the Spitfire being prone to radiator damage.

As the Chinese civil war approached the Canton area, the Wing was brought to readiness to counter any violation of the border. Dawn-to-dusk patrols and long range reconnaissance sorties were also flown, and cockpit readiness sections maintained at the end of the runway. With GCI assistance, many airliners, a lost Chinese Nationalist Air Force B-25 and a C-46 carrying refugees to Taiwan, were intercepted and identified. During this busy period each squadron was flying a daily average of forty to fifty sorties, and some aircraft sustained damage in landing or take-off accidents; two pilots were also killed when their Spitfires crashed into the sea for reasons that were never established. There were no border violations, but the communists sited 40mm anti-aircraft batteries on the outer islands of the Lema group and occasionally opened fire on aircraft that came close to the frontier.

On 7 March 1950 No 80 Squadron deployed to Sek Kong, a strip newly laid down by the Royal Engineers, and the personnel spent a few uncomforta-

Fine air-to-air view of Spitfire PK312, the first of the F.Mk. 22s.

ble weeks there before returning to Kai Tak on 28 April. The Sek Kong strip comprised rolled earth covered with long strips of tarred felt; these proved entirely unsatisfactory, lifting off the ground in snakelike undulations under the battering of the Spitfires' slipstream.

Weapons training continued, and both squadrons now added rocket-firing at a towed splash target to their curriculum. The Spitfire 24 was equipped with four pairs of zero-length RP rocket rails, and bomb carriers under the wings and fuselage. A typical load would be four 60 lb (27 kg) rockets, two 250 lb (113 kg) bombs, and 175 rounds per cannon. Thirty-degree dives from 3,000 feet (915 m) were standard for air-to-ground strafing and RP firing, 60 degree dives from 8,000 feet (2,440 m) with release at 3,000 feet (915 m) for dive bombing. The Mk 24 was a good gunnery platform, and its fine control response permitted a good steady run in turbulent conditions, but during pullout from a dive the pilot could black out completely, recovering as the aircraft climbed. Low-level bombing was complicated by the target disappearing under the long nose before the release point was reached, and for the same reason large angle deflection shooting was a matter of guess-work. If one cannon failed, the asymmetric recoil yawed the aircraft, and the shoot had to stop.

The Spitfire 24 had a ceiling in excess of 40,000 feet, and flying at this altitude was practised. As one pilot put it, the experience was well worth the effort,

although it was a test of lung capacity and endurance. The normal tankage of 120 gallons (545 ltr) gave an endurance of sixty to seventy-five minutes, and with rear fuselage tanks filled for a total of 186 gallons (846 ltr) this was increased to up to two hours. Maximum range with a ninety gallon (409 ltr) drop tank was 970 miles (1,560 km) and the endurance over four and a half hours. Long trips were not popular; quite apart from the discomfort of sitting on a lumpy dinghy pack, sweat soaked through a pilot's overall and Mae West to the parachute harness in the heat and humidity of summer.

The Spitfire 24's highly efficient flying controls gave outstanding response over the whole speed range. Once a pilot had grown accustomed to the increased engine noise and relative roughness, and had mastered the sensitive feel, it became an exhilarating aircraft to fly. With the combination of small airframe and high power, it could be put through a full aerobatic sequence in a limited airspace, the big, tabbed ailerons enabling slow rolls and hesitation rolls to be performed with precision. Loops were possible from level flight at 200 knots, but needed constant change of rudder trim to counteract torque effect with the varying speed.

Ample warning of stall onset was given by airframe buffeting, and aileron snatching as the stall became fully developed; with the throttle closed, and full up elevator held on, the nose and one wing would drop, but with power on the aircraft would

The later marks of Spitfire served well into the post-war era, like this LF.XVIE bearing the four-letter Flying Training Command code for the Central Gunnery School.

hold a stalled altitude with slow loss of height. High speed stalls were heralded by buffeting and juddering, with no natural tendency to enter a spin. Spinning in either direction was normal, with no tendency to wind up or porpoise, and recovery was immediate. Inverted spinning was not practised, but required only the standard recovery action. The aircraft was easy to fly in the circuit, but had to be handled with care on landing, and needed a threshold speed of ninety knots. The landing roll in zero wind and high ambient temperature was 500–600 yards (460–550 m).

Compared with contemporary jet fighters, the Spitfire 24 came out well ahead in all respects except level flight at medium altitudes. With a limiting Mach number 0.15 higher than that of the Meteor, Vampire or F-80, an ability to out-turn all comers, and the ability to operate from 1,200 yard (1,097 m) strips with a full service load, it was an amazingly efficient piston-engined aircraft. In fact, when the Korean War broke out in the summer of 1950, No 80 Squadron's pilots expected to be deployed to the combat zone, to share operations with the F-51 Mustangs of the USAF and RAAF. All that happened, however, was that recognition stripes were painted on the Spitfires, the pilots issued with sidearms, and patrols reinstated. At this time the Squadron re-deployed briefly to Sek Kong, the airstrip having been relaid with pierced steel planking (PSP). A makeshift GCA was also set up there by the Kai Tak radio section, which obtained a Sunderland ASV set and fitted it on a Bedford truck with a home-made scanner.

The dawn patrol produced problems, for take-off was at dawn minus thirty minutes. In the absence of runway lighting, two hurricane lamps were hung from poles on either side of the end of the runway.

With engine running and producing long orange flames from the exhaust stubs, the aircraft lined up. Take-off was started on instruments, and because of the exhaust glare was sometimes completed without the lamps being seen at all. Landing on the narrow strip in the early morning, into a low sun, was complicated by the flashing of the propeller blades; often, the first indication the pilot had that he was safely down was the clanking of the PSP under his aircraft.

Pilots of the two squadrons were forbidden to volunteer for duty in Korea, but some took extended leave and turned up there anyway via Japan, hoping to 'have a go' with an obliging Mustang unit. It is not recorded whether any of them succeeded.

By early 1951 Sek Kong had been tarmac-surfaced and endowed with Nissen huts, and in March No 28 Squadron moved there after exchanging its Spitfire FR 18s for Vampire FB 5s.

On Battle of Britain Sunday, 1951, No 80 Squadron flew low in salute over the Hong Kong War Memorial; it was the last time that a Spitfire squadron performed this tribute. Three months later, in December, the Squadron began re-equipping with de Havilland Hornets. Eight of its Spitfire 24s were assigned to the Hong Kong Auxiliary Air Force; their serial numbers were PK687, PK719, PK720, VN308, VN313, VN318, VN482 and VN485. It was VN485 which made the last sortie by a Spitfire 24 when, in the hands of Flight Lieutenant Adrian Rowe-Evans, who was then Bursar at Hong Kong University, it took part in the Queen's Birthday Flypast on 21 April 1955. By this time the Hong Kong AAF had only four Spitfires: two F.24s (VN318 and VN485) and two PR 19s, PS854 and PS852, both ex-81 Squadron aircraft. All four were grounded after the Birthday Flypast.

Spitfire F.21 of No 602 Squadron, RAF Reserve Command. The Squadron re-equipped with Vampires in August 1953.

Spitfire F.22 of No 608 Squadron, RAF Reserve Command, Thornaby, 1948.

Chapter 20
Israel's Spitfires

ON 15 MAY 1948 – the day the State of Israel came into being – two Spitfire LF Mk IXs of the Royal Egyptian Air Force attacked Dov airfield in Tel Aviv. One was hit by ground fire and its pilot made a belly landing on the beach at Hertzlia. Although badly damaged, the aircraft was salvaged and, with the use of spare parts left behind by the Royal Air Force, was made airworthy again. It was the Israeli Air Force's first Spitfire.

Surrounded by hostile Arab neighbours who made no secret of the fact that they planned to destroy the infant State of Israel as soon as Britain's mandate on Palestine came to an end and British forces withdrew, the Israeli government launched a desperate search for arms, with combat aircraft high on the priority list. The main air threat came from the Egyptians, whose assets included a mixed bag of forty Spitfire Mk IXs and Fiat G.55s, fifteen Harvards, five Hawker Furies and twenty-five Dakotas, all converted to carry small bomb loads.

In March 1948, the embryo Israeli government began negotiations with the Czechoslovak Defence Ministry for the purchase of a small number of surplus fighter aircraft. The aircraft involved were Avia S.199s (designated Avia C.210s for export) and they had an interesting history. During the Second World War, several versions of the Messerschmitt Me 109 had been built by the Avia factory in Czechoslovakia, and when the Germans withdrew in 1944 the Czechs found themselves with enough component parts and complete facilities to build 500 of the fighters. In 1945, production of the Me 109G-14 continued at Avia's Prague-Cakovice factory, and the aircraft entered service with the post-war Czech Air Force as the S.99. Later versions were powered by the Junkers Jumo 211F engine instead of the usual Daimler-Benz, supplies of which were soon exhausted, and the Jumo-powered aircraft were designated S.199.

Few aircraft in history can have been as universally hated by its pilots as the S.199, whose handling qualities varied from poor to downright vicious. The accident rate was frightful; the aircraft had a tendency to swing violently and without warning on take-off and landing, and many Czech pilots were killed when their S.199s lurched off the runway and burst into flames. The aircraft was known as the *Mezec* (Mule).

To the Israeli Air Force, the S.199 was a godsend. Twenty-five were purchased, taken to pieces and airlifted to Israel; all arrived except one, destroyed when the C-46 transport that was bringing it to Israel crashed, and entered service between May and July 1948. It was not long before they registered their first combat success. One morning during the second week of June, two Egyptian Dakotas escorted by four Spitfires approached Tel Aviv on a bombing mission. They were intercepted by an S.199 flown by Modi Alon, a twenty-seven-year-old ex-RAF flight lieutenant, who shot down both Dakotas and drove off the Spitfire escort. Three days later Alon destroyed a Spitfire, but was mortally wounded in combat with another and died later in hospital.

Until the arrival of the S.199s, the Egyptian Spitfires had been able to roam over Israel unmolested. On 22 May, a lone Spitfire appeared soon after dawn over Ramat David airfield, and, after circling several times, dropped two 250 lb bombs and made a couple of strafing runs, destroying two aircraft on the ground. The problem was that the aircraft were

An early Spitfire LF.IX of the Israeli Air Force, serial 2010.

not Israeli; they were RAF Spitfire FR.18s, for at that time Ramat David was still occupied by Nos 32 and 208 Squadrons. Two hours later the airfield was again attacked by Spitfires, which destroyed a Dakota on the ground and damaged seven more aircraft. This time, the RAF was on the alert and four FR.18s were airborne; they shot down two of the three Spitfires involved in the attack and the third was brought down by AA fire. The next day, the Egyptian authorities apologised to Britain for the 'regrettable navigational error' made by their pilots.

In June 1948, following intense fighting on the ground that ended, albeit briefly, with a ceasefire imposed by the United Nations on the 11th, Israeli representatives in Prague concluded negotiations for the purchase of fifty Spitfire Mk IXs which the Czech Air Force was in the process of phasing out. Czechoslovakia was now firmly under communist control, and her armed forces were re-equipping with Soviet material.

It was decided to transfer the Spitfires to Israel by air by fitting them with external long-range wing fuel tanks taken from S.199s in addition to the belly tank; this increased the Spitfire's range to over 1,400 miles, just enough to permit a flight from Kunovice to Podgorica, on the Adriatic coast of Yugoslavia, and from there to Israel. The transfer operation, known as *Velveta I*, began on 24 September 1948, when six aircraft set out from Czechoslovakia. Only three reached Israel; one was damaged on landing at Podgorica and two more made emergency landings on the Greek island of Rhodes because of fuel transfer problems. One of these was eventually released and arrived at its destination, but the other was damaged under somewhat mysterious circumstances while at Rhodes.

Israeli Spitfire Mk IXs of No 101 Squadron running-up at Hatzor in the Negev, during the War of Independence.

Ten more Spitfires were shipped to Israel by surface transport, and eighteen were made ready for Operation *Velveta II*, the second air transfer. Six of these left Czechoslovakia on 18 December 1948 and twelve more set out the next day, but one crashed *en route* and seven were unable to continue from Podgorica because of technical problems. Two of these were dismantled and flown to Israel in C-46s, and the others completed their journey by sea.

By the time the former Czech Spitfires reached Israel, the Israelis had assembled a second aircraft from parts left behind by the RAF, and this aircraft, together with the ex-Egyptian machine shot down on 15 May, formed the nucleus of No 101 Squadron. By the beginning of October 1948 the squadron had five Spitfires on strength, but only four were airworthy. During the month, these aircraft flew numerous ground attack sorties and bomber escort missions in support of Israeli ground forces which were once again involved in heavy fighting, the tenuous ceasefire having broken down in July.

On 21 October 1948, John Doyle – a former RCAF pilot and one of the volunteers, not all of them Jewish, from half a dozen countries who had volunteered to fly and fight for Israel – shot down an Egyptian Air Force Spitfire over the Negev and damaged two more, so scoring the first air combat victory by an IAF Spitfire. By the end of December No 101 Squadron had fourteen Spitfires on strength, and on the 28th of that month Jack Doyle scored the IAF's second Spitfire victory, shooting down a Fiat G.55 over Faluja and damaging a second. On the last day of December, Israeli Spitfires attacked the Egyptian airfield at Bir-Hama, destroying two Fiat G.55s on the ground and a third in air combat, the volunteer pilot being Danny Wilson.

The Israeli forces had now launched Operation *Horev*, the final offensive that was designed not only to drive the last Egyptian forces from the soil of Israel, but also to deal the Egyptian Army such a blow that it would be incapable of undertaking any aggressive action for some time to come.

During this operation – and for some time prior to its execution – Royal Air Force units in the Suez Canal Zone were placed on full alert. Between mid-November 1948 and 7 January 1949, when *Horev* was completed, some twenty reconnaissance sorties were flown over Egyptian-held territory by the Mosquito PR 34s of No 13 Squadron, Kabrit, and to a lesser extent by the Spitfire FR.18s of No 208 Squadron from Fayid. During the height of the fighting in December and early January, some of the Mosquito missions were escorted by Hawker Tempests of No 324 Wing; this followed the loss, on 20 November, of a Mosquito which was shot down south of Tel Aviv by Israeli Spitfires of No 101 Squadron.

Such operations assumed greater urgency on 30 December 1948, when Israeli forces crossed into the Sinai Peninsula and presented a potential threat to the Canal Zone. Britain, fearful for the security of her interests in the Zone, invoked a twelve-year-old Anglo Egyptian friendship treaty and sent an ultimatum to Israel, demanding the withdrawal of all Israeli forces from Egyptian territory. Faced with the threat of possible British military intervention, the Israelis called off a planned attack on El Arish and instead launched an assault on Rafah, beginning on 3 January 1949, with the object of eliminating Egyptian forces in the Gaza Strip. Three days later the Egyptian government announced that it was willing to enter into armistice negotiations, and on 7 January 1949 the fighting came to an end on Israel's southern frontier.

On that day an extraordinary incident occurred which precipitated a serious crisis with Britain and came close to ruining Israel's bargaining position. Early in the morning a Mosquito PR 34 of No 13 Squadron carried out a medium-level reconnaissance mission over Sinai, close to the Israeli border. The Mosquito was escorted by four Tempests of No 213 Squadron. All five aircraft returned to base without incident.

Later, a second recce sortie was flown by four Spitfire FR.18s of No 208 Squadron. Flying in two pairs, one at 500 feet and the other 1,000 feet above and astern, the Spitfires followed the Ismailia–Beer-

sheba road and then turned north to survey the road leading from El Auja to Rafah, which they followed as far as the frontier. There remains some doubt about whether the Spitfires actually crossed into sovereign Israeli territory, but the Israeli AA opened fire and one of the Spitfires was hit, its pilot baling out. The three remaining Spitfires, circling overhead, were immediately attacked by two Spitfires of No 101 Squadron. All three RAF aircraft were shot down; two pilots baled out and were picked up by Israeli troops, to be handed over later, but the third pilot was killed.

When the Spitfires became overdue, a flight of four Tempests of No 213 Squadron was sent out to search for them. This time there was no doubt that the RAF aircraft infringed Israeli air space. As they extended the route taken by No 208 Squadron's aircraft, they were attacked by Israeli Spitfires; the Tempest pilots returned fire and disengaged, but not before one had been shot down. It crashed four miles inside Israeli territory, killing its pilot.

When the Israeli War of Independence ended in July 1949, the IAF had twenty-one Spitfires on charge, with twenty-six more being assembled after arriving by sea from Czechoslovakia. No 101 Squadron, in addition to its operational role, was also responsible for conversion and training; it was now based at Ramat David, having moved from Hatzor earlier in the year.

The Israeli Air Force ultimately had fifty-six ex-Czech Spitfires on strength. In 1950 a second squadron, No 105, was established, and in the following year a contract was signed with the Italian government for the purchase of thirty more Mk IXs, although they were not delivered until 1953. At the beginning of that year No 101 Squadron converted to P-51D Mustangs, turning over its Spitfires to a newly-formed unit, No 107 Squadron. The latter had a short life, disbanding in March 1954; all the surviving Spitfires were now centralised in No 105 Squadron. In 1955 thirty refurbished aircraft were sold to Burma, and in February 1956 the remaining Spitfires were withdrawn from use when No 105 Squadron also disbanded.

So the combat career of the Supermarine Spitfire was at an end. And there is no escaping the irony that, in one of its last battles, Spitfire fought Spitfire.

Spitfire LF.IXE owned and flown by Ezer Weizman. Serial number is 2057. At the time of writing, Ezer Weizman was President of Israel.

Appendix
Spitfires in Foreign Service

I N ADDITION to its service with the RAF, Commonwealth air forces and the USAAF, the Spitfire served as first-line equipment with the air arms of nineteen foreign countries, including Israel. Brief details are as follows.

Belgium In October 1946, when the Belgian-manned Spitfire squadrons that had formed part of 2nd TAF passed to the control of the Belgian government, they retained fifty-one Spitfire Mk IXs and twenty-five Mk XVIs, the latter on loan pending delivery of the first batch of Mk XIVs ordered from Britain under Western Union agreements. Belgium received 132 Mk XIV Spitfires, delivered between 1948 and 1951.

Burma In 1951 the Union of Burma Air Force took delivery of twenty de-navalized Seafire Mk XVs, refurbished by Airwork Ltd at Gatwick.

Czechoslovakia In 1945, seventy-three Spitfire LF IXs were ferried to Prague to form the fighter equipment of the reconstituted Czech Air Force. Two years later, when Czechoslovakia came under communist domination, the Czech AF began to re-equip with Soviet types and the Spitfires were retired. Many of them, as related in the main text, found their way to Israel.

Denmark The Royal Danish Air Force took delivery of forty-one Mk IX Spitfires and one Mk XI in 1947–8, the aircraft equipping three *Eskadrille*. The Spitfires were gradually phased out between 1949 and 1955, as the RDAF's tactical fighter squadrons re-equipped with Gloster Meteors and F-84 Thunderjets.

Egypt The Royal Egyptian Air Force received thirty-seven Spitfire Mk IXs between August and September 1946, and some of these saw combat in the Arab–Israeli war of 1948–9 – the only conflict in

Converted Seafire XV UB403 (formerly SR642) of the Union of Burma Air Force, one of twenty such aircraft delivered.

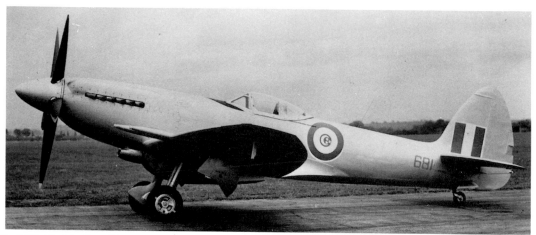

Spitfire F.Mk.22 of the Royal Egyptian Air Force, one of a batch of twenty supplied in 1950. The Syrian Air Force also received ten F.22s.

which Spitfire fought Spitfire. Twenty refurbished Spitfire F.22s were also sold to Egypt in 1950; these had been replaced by de Havilland Vampire FB.5s and relegated to the training role by the beginning of 1955.

Eire   Twelve de-navalized and refurbished Seafire Mk IIIs were delivered to the Irish Air Corps in 1947. In effect, these aircraft were delivered to Spitfire VC standard. The IAC also received six Spitfire Mk IXs, all of them trainers.

France   Between October 1945 and March 1946, 172 Spitfire Mk IXs were delivered to the *Armée de l'Air* from surplus RAF stocks, many being immediately assigned to North Africa and French Indo-China. At

the same time, France took delivery of seventy Mk Vs, these being used mainly for training. The French Naval Air Arm (*Aéronavale*) also received a number of Seafires, Mks III and XV, in 1948.

Greece   When Greece was liberated at the end of the Second World War, the operational component of the Royal Hellenic Air Force comprised only Nos 335 and 336 Squadrons, equipped with Spitfire Vs. A third Spitfire squadron, No 337, was formed shortly afterwards, and in 1947 the Spitfire Vs were replaced by Mk IXs. Deliveries of seventy-four Mk IXs were completed in 1949, and were followed by the delivery of fifty-five Mk XVIs, the latter remaining in service until 1955. Greece also received one PR Spitfire Mk XI.

The last two Spitfire Mk IX two-seat trainer conversions, 162 and 163, delivered to the Irish Air Corps. There were twenty Mk IX trainer conversions in all.

Three of the Spitfire Mk IX trainer conversions went to the Royal Netherlands Air Force. They are seen here at Eastleigh prior to their delivery flight to Valkenburg on 23 March 1948.

Holland   Late in 1946 the Royal Netherlands Air Force took delivery of fifty-five Mk IX Spitfires, all from surplus RAF stocks. The R. Neth. AF also received a small number of Mk XVIs.

Israel   See main text.

Italy   In 1947 Italy was limited by treaty to an air force consisting of not more than 200 fighters. At the time the Italian Air Force had about 110 Spitfire Mk IXs, and thirty of these were subsequently supplied to Israel in 1950–51.

Norway   In 1947 Norway, whose 2nd TAF Spitfire squadrons had made a significant contribution in north-west Europe during the Second World War, purchased an initial batch of thirty Spitfire Mk IXs

for service with Nos 331 and 332 Squadrons, and further acquisitions brought the total to forty-seven. Both squadrons re-equipped with the Republic F-84G Thunderjet in 1952–3.

Portugal   The Portuguese Air Force was an early overseas customer for the Spitfire, fifteen Mk IAs being delivered in August 1943 together with some Hawker Hurricanes and Westland Lysanders. This initial purchase was followed by fifty Spitfire VBs, most of which were also delivered in 1943. The Spitfire Vs remained in first-line service until 1952, when they were replaced by Republic P-47D Thunderbolts.

Sweden   Although both Britain and Germany made attempts to sell combat aircraft to Sweden during

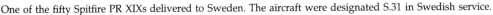

One of the fifty Spitfire PR XIXs delivered to Sweden. The aircraft were designated S.31 in Swedish service.

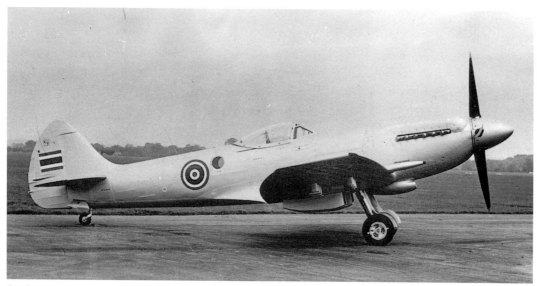

Spitfire FR. XIV of the Royal Thai Air Force. Thirty reconditioned aircraft were delivered, beginning in 1948.

the Second World War – and at one point the British even offered to donate 200 Spitfires if the Swedes would halt the supply of ball bearings to Germany – the Swedish government maintained its policy of neutrality, equipping the small Swedish Air Arm with indigenous types or with aircraft purchased from the USA before that country placed an embargo on the sale of arms overseas in 1940. In 1948, however, with the perceived threat from the Soviet Union becoming increasingly apparent, Sweden took steps to modernize her armed forces, and between then and 1955 bought 50 PR XIX Spitfires from RAF surplus stocks. Designated S.31s, the Spitfires were used for reconnaissance flights over the Baltic and the Gulf of Bothnia. The Spitfires were all operated by one unit, F11 at Nyköping.

Syria   Ten Spitfire F.22s were delivered to Syria in 1950, drawn from surplus RAF stocks and refurbished by Airwork Ltd. They remained in first-line service until 1953, when they were replaced by Gloster Meteor F.8s.

Thailand   From 1948 the Royal Thai Air Force took delivery of thirty reconditioned Spitfire FR. Mk. XIVs, the latter replacing a miscellany of elderly types (including Japanese) left over from the Second World War. The Spitfires were replaced by Grumman F8F Bearcats in the mid-1950s.

Turkey   This country was a major recipient of Spitfires during the Second World War, taking delivery of fifty-six Mk VBs and 185 Mk IXs from 1943 onwards. The aircraft were sold to Turkey at nominal prices, the British government realising the need to keep her in a state of neutrality following the failure of attempts to persuade her to join the Allied cause. Not to be outdone, the Germans also supplied the Turkish Air Force with a number of Focke-Wulf Fw 190A-5s, the two types operating side by side until they were replaced by P-47D Thunderbolts in the late 1940s.

USSR   The first Spitfire operations from Russian territory took place in September 1942, when a pair of PR. Mk IVs of No 1 PRU deployed to North Russia to give PR support for two squadrons of Handley Page Hampden torpedo bombers of RAF Coastal Command, also deployed there for offensive operations against enemy shipping. The Hampdens were later handed over to the Russians, as were the Spitfires. On 4 October the Soviet Ambassador in London presented a request for the urgent delivery of Spitfires to relieve the critical pressure on the Stalingrad front; this was approved by Winston Churchill and, early in 1943, 137 Spitfire Mk VBs drawn from Middle East stocks, plus fifty in spares, were handed over to the Russians at Basrah in Iraq. These aircraft, armed with two cannon and two machine-guns, were deployed with units of the 220th and 268th Fighter

Odd couple: a Spitfire Mk VB of the Turkish Air Force formates with a Focke-Wulf Fw 190A-5.

Spitfire Mk IX in Soviet Air Force markings. In all, out of a total of 1,332 Spitfires delivered to Russia, 1,188 were Mk IXs. All except a handful of PR aircraft arrived by way of Iraq.

Divisions in time to take part in the major Russian counter-attack that led to the encirclement and destruction of the German Sixth Army at Stalingrad; a few were assigned to the Moscow Air Defence Region, where they had some successes against German reconnaissance aircraft.

In addition to the Mk Vs, the Russians also took delivery of 1,188 Spitfire Mk IXs before the end of the war, plus five PR Mk IXs and two PR Mk XIs. They fought on every front, but their main area of operations was in the north, where they performed sterling service in the air defence of Leningrad and in the air battles over Karelia. Sadly, and purely for political reasons, none of the official Soviet Air Force

historians documenting the Second World War made mention of the Spitfire, or for that matter the role of any other Allied aircraft (with the possible exception of the Bell Airacobra) serving on the Eastern Front. It is known that some Spitfires were still serving in the late 1940s, mainly with various trials units; at least two were allocated to catapult launching trials with the Soviet Navy.

Yugoslavia Although the sole Yugoslav Spitfire squadron, No 352, disbanded at Prkos in June 1945, the Spitfire Mk VCs continued to fly for some time afterwards, the then Yugoslavian leader, Marshal Tito, being anxious to retain the nucleus of an air arm. The pro-Soviet marshal sought to build up a post-war air force using Russian types such as the Yakovlev Yak-3 fighter, which he acquired; but from 1948 Yugoslavia again turned to the West for its military equipment.

Index